D0425041

SPORTS AND THE COURTS

Dr. Herb Appenzeller

*Athletic Director and
Professor of Education
Guilford College
Greensboro, North Carolina*

Thomas Appenzeller, MEd

*Candidate for MS Degree in
Sports Studies
University of Massachusetts
Amherst, Massachusetts*

THE MICHIE COMPANY
Law Publishers
CHARLOTTESVILLE, VIRGINIA

To
Elizabeth Eure Little
"Miss Essie"
Mother-in-law — Grandmother
Extraordinary

ACKNOWLEDGEMENTS

This book became a reality because people cared and shared their information and expertise in an unselfish way. Our deep appreciation goes to all of them who made *Sports and the Courts* possible.

We especially thank:

.... Dr. James Gifford, Duke University, for his untiring support in our behalf. His suggestions in every phase of the book improved it and his friendship made the endeavor worthwhile.

.... Dr. James C. Brewer, for valuable suggestions and contributions to the medical aspects in the book.

.... Dr. Robert McMillan, who spent countless days encouraging, discussing and contributing to the chapter on the team physician.

.... C. Thomas Ross, attorney with Craige, Brawley, Liipfert and Ross for his contribution to the Introductory Chapter and his legal advice on other sections of the book.

.... Bynum Hunter and Donald Cowan, attorneys with the law firm of Smith, Moore, Smith, Schell and Hunter, for their interest and continued cooperation in providing material and ideas for the book.

.... John Haworth, President of the North Carolina Bar Association, for the many hours spent in discussing the legal issues in the book.

.... Sheila Kendall and Leona Patterson for typing preliminary parts of the book.

.... Becky Dye, who typed the preliminary and final copies of the manuscript in such a wonderful spirit of cooperation and friendship.

.... Paul Cook, of the Michie Company, who has been the man behind the scene for the series of books and helped make them a reality.

.... Linvel Hendren, for his creativity in designing the book.

.... To the members of our family who gave so generously of their time with a genuine spirit of love and inspiration.

Herb and Thomas Appenzeller

PREFACE

The Roman poet Martial described a dilemma when he wrote to a friend: *"Nec tecum possum vivere nec sine te"* (I can't live with you and I can't live without you). His unusual statement describes the situation that confronts the participants in sports in today's society. While outspoken critics of sports litigation deplore an unprecedented number of sports-related lawsuits, others applaud it as a way to improve sports. Opponents of litigation believe it actually threatens to destroy the existence of sports; proponents insist that the courts are the sole vehicle able to control such abuses of sports as violence and negligence.

There are a number of historians who see a dangerous parallel between the fall of the Roman Empire and the direction the United States is taking. They believe that Rome left more than its legal genius as a legacy for all to follow. These historians urge Americans to heed the lessons exemplified by the Romans in the sports arena. Arnold Beisser, writing in *The Madness in Sports,* decries the fact that: "While Romans cheered their games and gladiators, their empire was crumbling." He warns his readers that:

> The lessons of ancient Rome should be sufficient justification for a close examination of America's athletic interest and motivation. There are many parallels between our sports and those of the declining years of the Roman Empire. A single Coliseum may have served Roman spectators; today, thousands of stadiums and their satellite television sets serve almost everyone in the United States.

Sports and the Courts endeavors to convey to the reader not only the legal implications of sports issues

vii

but a portrait of the conditions of modern society as sports litigation reveals it. It presents a selection of recent court cases dealing with a variety of sports-related issues that are brought before the bar for judicial remedy. The reader then may take an informed position on the proper role of the courts in relation to sports.

Since only a few thousand athletes compete in professional sports whereas millions participate in amateur sports, the majority of the book is devoted to cases at the amateur level. Occasionally litigation involving professional sports is discussed where legal principles are involved that affect all levels of sports participation.

Sports and the Courts completes a series of four books devoted to the legal aspects of physical education and sports. The previous books are: *From the Gym to the Jury* (1970), *Athletics and the Law* (1975), and *Physical Education and the Law* (1978).

We have attempted to present the material from our background as participants, coaches, and administrators in a style that is easy to understand, interesting, but legally sound.

Herb Appenzeller
Thomas Appenzeller

TABLE OF CONTENTS

Chapter   Page

CHAPTER 1

Introduction

Those who defend sports and their enormous budgets will have to justify them as never before and many hallowed preconceptions will be challenged.[1]

Today's sports participants are often as familiar with a court of law as they are with the sports "court." Athletes, coaches, administrators, officials, physicians, equipment manufacturers, operators of sports facilities, and even unsuspecting sports fans share a common bond — the risk of sports litigation.

Richard T. Ball, an Arizona attorney who is a special counsel on products liability, warns that the very existence of sports is threatened when he predicts:

> Litigation arising out of athletic injuries is accelerating out of control and, if the tide is not turned quickly, the institution will crumble and fall.[2]

Sports litigation now goes beyond the traditional arenas of contract disputes and allegation of negligence.

A high school football player in Charlotte, North Carolina was found to be overage by the State Athletic Association's regulations. This violation threatened to eliminate his team from the state playoffs. He took his case to court to get a restraining order which would enable him and his team to participate in the playoffs.

---

1. JAMES A. MICHENER, SPORTS IN AMERICA, Random House, N.Y., 1976.
2. RICHARD T. BALL, *Litigation: Will It Destroy Athletics?*, THE FIRST AIDER, Vol. 48, No. 1, Sept. 1978.

A judge in Asheville ruled against the athlete, opening the way for an Asheville team to replace the Charlotte team in post-season play. But a Charlotte judge ruled in favor of the plaintiff and a playoff game thus was made necessary between the Asheville and Charlotte teams. This delayed the football season an additional week.[3]

Coach Lou Holtz of the University of Arkansas dismissed three starters for breaking team rules. The players hired a lawyer to try to get themselves reinstated in time to play against Oklahoma in the Orange Bowl. The judge refused to issue such an order and the players did not participate in the post-season Bowl game.[4]

The parents of Bob Vorhies, an outstanding freshman football player at Virginia Tech, demanded a grand jury investigation when their son died after he completed punishment drills. Vorhies was punished for "clowning around" in the athletic dormitory after a game against Wake Forest. The drills consisted of "10-50 yard dashes, 10-100 yard dashes (with each dash having to be completed in 30 seconds); two 100 yard bear crawls, 50 sit-ups, 50 push-ups, and four other 100 yard drills." One of the coaches called the drills routine. The investigation concluded that it could not attribute the boy's death to the drills.[5]

The parents of a player dismissed from the Colorado University football team sought $45,000 in damages, claiming that the coach called the boy's mother "girl" and allegedly brushed against her legs on his way out of his office. A Boulder District Court jury dismissed

3. Greensboro Daily News, Apr. 12, 1975.
4. Greensboro Daily News, Dec. 30, 1977.
5. Roanoke Times and World News, Nov. 23, 1977.

the charge against the coach ruling that the coach did not "intentionally inflict emotional distress on the parents." [6]

Jim Stanley, fired with two years remaining on his contract at Oklahoma State University, threatened to go to court to force the University to honor his contract. He refused to be reassigned to another position, arguing that his contract specified the duties of head football coach.[7] The Board of Regents agreed to pay him $74,000 on his contract and hired a new coach.[8]

Not only are the number and type of cases involving sports increasing, but sympathetic juries continue to award astronomical amounts of money in damages to sports participants. Million dollar awards are increasingly common; million dollar suits are routine. Some recent cases typify the amount of money plaintiffs are seeking in court.

Six University of Maryland athletes sued the Washington Star and three of its reporters for a staggering $36 million. The athletes claimed that two articles featuring their pictures and academic record at the University held them up to "public scorn, ridicule, and contempt." The court considered them to be public figures and as such gave the newspaper the right to publish the stories. It dismissed the case against the paper.[9]

A high school football player sued his physician and high school coaches for $7.6 million for an injury he claimed he sustained at a pre-season football camp. The judge dismissed the suit after another physician

---

6. Las Vegas Review Journal, Jan. 27, 1978.
7. Greensboro Daily News, Nov. 23, 1977.
8. Greensboro Daily News, Dec. 16, 1978.
9. Greensboro Daily News, Dec. 17, 1978.

testified that the condition was not due to an injury but a defect found in young blacks.[10]

A man in Washington, D.C. was paralyzed when he was injured while diving into a swimming pool. He contended that the diving board was too flexible for safe use and that there was not enough water in the pool. He was awarded $7 million, but it was later reduced to $4.6 million.[11]

The list of million dollar cases goes on. It has been said that:

> Many of today's cases would have been laughed out of court at one time. But behind the growing rush to litigate is an array of far-reaching changes in the United States society that are no laughing matter.[12]

With the diversity of sports-related court cases and the huge amounts of awards, a subsequent problem faces the schools. Many schools report that the price of insurance is increasing to a point that it is becoming prohibitive.

Cliff Allen, the supervisor of insurance for Los Angeles City Schools, complains that his city schools paid $750,000 in general liability insurance in 1976 for coverage of $50 million, including a $250,000 deductible fee. He predicts that the premiums for the same coverage will rise even more this year although the deductible fee will increase to $500,000. To compound the problem, Allen reports that his school district alone processes over 600 claims a year and that this has

---

10. The Times, Thomasville, North Carolina, Oct. 26, 1978.
11. *Why Everybody Is Suing,* U.S. NEWS AND WORLD REPORT, Dec. 4, 1978.
12. *Id.*

caused insurance companies to avoid insuring his district.[13]

The insurance industry reports a loss of $2.5 billion in miscellaneous liability suits, including product liability, as litigation against sports manufacturers increasingly results in enormous judgments. Because of these awards, product liability insurance has skyrocketed. One firm paid $10,000 in 1975 for insurance and one year later paid $80,000. A sporting goods manufacturer secured $1 million of coverage for $17,000 in 1972, but paid $297,000 in 1976. Many are unable to get any coverage at all.[14]

Such problems with insurance costs due to increased litigation resulted in Los Angeles State University dropping football. Athletic Director, John Herman, remarked that "the expenses of insurance, plus overall inflation have caused the school to drop football after 26 years." [15]

On the other hand, insurance companies wonder how long they can pay $116 in claims for every $100 they receive in premiums. They point out that product-liability suits numbered 50,000 in 1960, 500,000 in 1970 and reached an all-time high of one million with an average award of $338,000 in 1975.[16]

It is obvious that expensive lawsuits will, in all probability, change the nature of sports as we know them. With so many lawsuits in sports, involving so many different groups, it is important for all sports administrators to know what to do and what to expect if a lawsuit develops.

---

13. Sentinel, Winston-Salem, North Carolina, July 21, 1977.
14. Greensboro Daily News, Dec. 10, 1976.
15. Multi-Association Action Committee For Product Liability, Vol. 1, No. 1, Jan. 1978.
16. *Supra* note 13.

What to Do if Involved in a Lawsuit [17]

The question must arise, "What do I do when something happens that may lead to a lawsuit?"

The answer is simple — call your insurance carrier and your lawyer, in that order. This will permit a prompt investigation of the entire case when all events are still fresh in everyone's mind, so that the actual facts may be accurately preserved for presentation later, perhaps years later. It will also protect you against taking any action that could prejudice your position at a later date.

Be sure to keep detailed notes on everything that you know or can remember about what happened, including names and addresses of all potential witnesses, even those people who say they don't know anything. Many times, under skillful questioning, they know much more than they think.

Be reluctant to discuss any aspect of the case without the advice of your attorney, particularly to the news media. This should not imply that you are trying to "cover up" or "hide" anything, but merely that any public statement should be delayed until all the facts are known. Many times statements are made at or about the time of an incident which later turn out not to be the true facts at all after an investigation has been completed.

Trials resulting from lawsuits are actually relatively simple mechanisms to understand, but are difficult and expensive to use. Your chances of being involved in litigation are greatly reduced if you conduct your

----

17. C. Thomas Ross, who contributes two sections to this introduction, is a partner in a Winston-Salem, North Carolina law firm specializing in litigation. He brings to the law profession a background in sports.

activities as carefully as possible, use safe, well-maintained equipment and disclose as much as possible to participants and parents.

Many people do not realize that anyone can file a lawsuit against anybody for just about anything, but before a recovery can be obtained liability must be proven. Before liability can be established in a typical case, a breach of duty or violation of a right must be proved by the allegedly aggrieved party. This proof comes in almost all cases at the trial of the lawsuit, anywhere from six months to five years after the lawsuit is started. Fortunately, in some respects, many legitimate lawsuits are settled before trial or even before a lawsuit is filed.

What to Expect at a Trial [18]

All jurisdictions, both Federal and state, have rules which govern the procedures that must be followed in every civil lawsuit. These are commonly called Rules of Civil Procedure. They are very specific and sometimes can be very technical. However, these rules are extremely valuable and helpful in charting the course that a lawsuit will follow.

Many things happen in that six-month to five-year period. In order to file a lawsuit, a pleading, usually called a complaint, has to be filed. This document does nothing more than set forth the facts which the aggrieved party alleges gave rise to his or her injury. In all cases the party being sued, usually called the defendant, must get notice of the lawsuit and have an opportunity to respond and rebut the allegations. This

18. *Id.*

responsive pleading is usually called an answer. If the defendant for any reason feels the plaintiff may be liable to him, he must also incorporate into the answer something which is very logically called a counterclaim. Sometimes it may be necessary to add additional parties so that all those people or institutions who may be liable are within the jurisdiction of the court.

Once the initial pleadings are filed and everyone is "in court," there follows a prescribed period of time, usually at least four months but sometimes longer depending on the complexity of the case, called the discovery period.

The purpose of the discovery period is for all the parties to "discover" as many facts as possible about the lawsuit, such as exactly how an injury occurred, who the witnesses were, how much damage has been sustained and similar matters of a factual nature. This can be accomplished through depositions, where the party to be questioned is physically present with attorneys for all parties. The attorneys ask questions which are answered by the witness and everything said is taken down verbatim by a court reporter and transcribed and added to the record in the court file. These documents can be used at the trial to refresh the witness' recollection or to attack the witness' credibility in the event the answers have changed.

After discovery has been completed, the trial lawyers are then confronted with several alternative courses of action. If it appears that the facts are not in dispute and the outcome of the case depends solely on which law is to be applied, then the lawyer may file a motion for summary judgment. This permits the judge to make final decision on the outcome of the case without a trial and a jury. In order for the judge to grant summary judgment, there must be no dispute over any genuine issue of a material fact.

If there is a genuine dispute over material facts, then summary judgment would be improper and a trial will be necessary. Prior to the actual beginning of a trial, the lawyers have the most important portion of their work to do — careful, detailed preparation for every contingency that could occur at the trial. It will be necessary to carefully review all the facts again, talk in detail to all witnesses and potential witnesses, complete the legal research necessary to permit the drafting of a trial brief to state the client's legal position as favorably as possible and to assist the judge in getting a grasp on the case as quickly and easily as possible.

Once all the preparation is complete, you are prepared to begin the trial of the case, the ultimate point towards which the filing of the suit has been leading.

Generally speaking, a trial has several distinct parts. A jury must be selected and many trial lawyers consider this to be one of the most important aspects of the trial. After a jury of twelve presumably disinterested and impartial jurors has been selected, the lawyers present opening statements to the jury, in which they tell the jury what they will attempt to prove or disprove. After opening statements, the plaintiff then presents his or her case. If the plaintiff cannot offer sufficient evidence to establish a *prima facie* case, then the defendant(s) must present evidence to prove they are not liable, damages are not as large as they are claimed to be. After all the evidence has been presented, the judge still has the option of granting a directed verdict if it appears one party clearly is entitled to a verdict. If a directed verdict is not granted, the case then "goes to the jury." The lawyers make their closing arguments as to why their client should win and how much in damages should be awarded, if any. After the closing arguments, the judge then instructs the jury on the law to be applied to the facts as they were presented during the trial. The jury is solely responsible for finding the facts of the case and they must apply the law to those facts as the law is explained by the judge. The jury then retires to reach their verdict and report it to the court. The verdict of the jury is then reduced to a judgment, which is but an order of the court directing disposition of the case.

Obviously, the losing party in any trial has an automatic right to appeal the judgment to an appellate court, who will review the record of errors of law or abuse of discretion. Appellate decisions are written and reported and then become binding as a portion of the body of law of a jurisdiction.

It seems appropriate, therefore, that the sports administrator develop a close relationship with a legal counselor to prevent potential legal problems and thereby conduct the sports program in a safe and efficient manner.

In the following chapters sports-related cases will be reviewed. These chapters discuss the participant, administrator, coach, official, spectator, team physician and athletic trainer. They will also consider issues involving sports facilities and sports equipment.

At the end of each chapter is a brief section entitled "In My Opinion" in which we have attempted to use our personal experience and background to tell things as we see them.

CHAPTER 2
Injuries to Athletes

*The mere act of putting on a uniform and entering
the sports arena should not serve as a
license to engage in behavior which
would constitute a crime if
committed elsewhere.*[1]

Several thousand spectators witnessed a brutal brawl
during an ice hockey game that shocked not only the
fans but even the players, who traditionally are
accustomed to rough play.

David Forbes of the Boston Bruins and Henry
Boucha of the Minnesota North Stars were returning to
their respective team benches after spending time in the
penalty box. Forbes reportedly attacked Boucha from
the rear with his hockey stick and inflicted severe
injuries. During the trial, the following description of
the incident was presented:

> The butt end of Forbes' hockey stick struck
> Boucha just above the right eye. The force of
> the blow caused Boucha to drop to the ice,
> stunned and bleeding profusely. Forbes then
> dropped his stick and pounced upon the helpless
> Boucha. He punched him in the back of the head
> with his clenched fist, then grabbed the back of
> Boucha's head by the hair and proceeded to
> pound his head into the ice until Forbes was
> restrained by another North Star player.[2]

---

1. Flakne and Caplan, *Sports Violence and the Prosecution*,
   TRIAL Vol. 13, No. 1, Jan. 1977.
2. *Id.*

After 17 grueling hours of deliberation the Minnesota court was unable to reach a unanimous decision and declared the case a mistrial. Several jurors explained that a retrial was not necessary because the highly publicized trial had served to warn sports people everywhere that intentional and deliberate acts to injure participants would no longer be tolerated. They also reasoned that another trial would end up deadlocked again.

Forbes stated in a Philadelphia newspaper that:

> I'm disillusioned with the whole system. I just don't see, no matter how wrong the act is, how anything that happens in an athletic contest can be criminal.[3]

Gary Flakne, a Minnesota County attorney who prosecuted Forbes, and Allan Caplan, an assistant county attorney, took issue with Forbes by insisting that:

> If a participant in a sporting event were allowed to feel immune from criminal sanction merely by virtue of his being a participant, the spirit of maiming and serious bodily injury, which at present occurs all too frequently in a sport such as hockey, may well become the order of the day.[4]

Consider one more case involving professional athletics and its accompanying violence.

Denver defensive back Dale Hackbart was watching another player intercept a pass when he was hit by Booby Clark of the Cincinnati Bengals from behind with

---

3. Philadelphia Inquirer, Pa., July 18, 1977.
4. *Supra* note 1.

a forearm.[5] Hackbart sued the Bengals, claiming that the blow that injured him constituted reckless conduct.

The issue raised during the trial by the Colorado court was what a reasonably prudent professional football player should be expected to do under the circumstances when confronting an opposing player in this type of incident. The defendants relied on the traditional doctrine of assumption of risk to negate Hackbart's contention. The Colorado court made several comments that are worthy of consideration by any sports participant, particularly those who compete in collision sports such as football. It declared that Hackbart had assumed the risk of injury by playing football and reasoned that even if his opponent had violated a duty he owed the plaintiff, there could be no verdict in favor of the injured player because:

> [T]he level of violence and frequency of emotional outbursts in NFL football games are such that [the injured player] must have recognized and accepted the risk that he would be injured by such an act as that committed [by the opposing player.] [6]

The court then described the action of the coaches in the league to arouse their players to a state of "controlled rage." It felt that players obeyed rules to avoid penalties rather than to prevent injuries to their opponents. The court then made a comment that, if true, sets a standard that could cause countless injuries on all levels of sports, by asserting that:

> The character of NFL competition negates any notion that playing conduct can be

---

5. Hackbart v. Cincinnati Bengals, Inc., 435 F. Supp. 352 (D.C. Colo. 1977).
6. *Id.*

circumscribed by any standard of reasonableness.[7]

Similar concerns can be raised concerning amateur sports. Susan Graves, writing in *Family Health,* questions how safe school sports are today and then answers her own question by blaming the "win-at-all cost mentality" that characterizes American sports and the example set by professionals. She concluded that the over emphasis on winning is the cause of many sports-related problems.[8]

Sports litigation can involve participants in any sport. Cases on record arise from football, soccer, basketball, softball, baseball, ice hockey, bowling, skiing, tennis, golf, track and fishing. As a rule, plaintiffs charge negligent conduct for the injuries they sustain.

The basic elements of negligence are:

(1) A duty, which is an obligation recognized by the law, requiring actor to conform to a certain standard of conduct, for the protection of others against unreasonable risks.

(2) Breach of duty, a failure to conform to the standard required.

(3) Proximate or legal cause, a reasonably close causal connection between the conduct and the resulting injury.

(4) Damage, actual loss resulting to the interests of another.[9]

The key to liability is the presence of negligence.

---

7. *Supra* note 5.
8. Graves, *School Sports . . . How Safe Are They,* FAMILY HEALTH, Vol. VIII No. 3, Mar. 1976.
9. WILLIAM L. PROSSER, JOHN W. WADE AND VICTOR E. SCHWARTZ, TORTS, CASES AND MATERIALS, 6th ed., Foundation Press, 1976.

Defenses Against Negligence in Sports Litigation

The best defense against a claim of negligence is to prove that one of the four elements of negligence is not present. Other defenses that can result in a "no-liability" verdict for the defendant include assumption of risk, contributory negligence, comparative negligence, and an Act of God.

Assumption of risk occurs when a person assumes the responsibility for his own safety. In *Teachers and Torts,* Ruth and Kern Alexander explain the rationale behind the theory of assumption of risk by pointing out that:

> The theory here is that the plaintiff in some manner consents to relieve the defendant of his duty or obligation of conduct. In other words, the plaintiff by expressed or implied agreement assumes the risk of danger and thereby relieves the defendant of responsibility. The defendant is simply not under any legal duty to protect the plaintiff. The plaintiff with knowledge of the danger voluntarily enters into a relationship with the defendants, and by doing so agrees to take his own chances.[10]

The Alexanders add that:

> Essential to the doctrine of assumption of risk is that the plaintiff have knowledge of the risks; if he is ignorant of the conditions and dangers, he does not assume the risk. If he does not take reasonable precautions to determine the hazards involved, then he has not assumed the risk but he may be contributorily negligent.[11]

---

10. RUTH ALEXANDER AND KERN ALEXANDER, TEACHERS AND TORTS, Maxwell Publishing Co., Middletown, Ky.
11. *Id.*

Contributory negligence prevents a person from recovering damages if he is at fault to even the slightest degree in causing his own injury. A court will consider what standard of conduct is appropriate for someone of the person's age, physical capabilities, sex and training before it makes a decision as to fault.

Pamela Brackman was struck in the face by a bat thrown by another student in a softball game in Tennessee and required extensive dental surgery as a result of the accident.[12] She sued her teacher for negligent conduct which she claimed resulted in her injury. At the time of the incident, Pamela, the captain of her softball team, was catching behind the bat without a catcher's mask. The players had been given their choice of positions to play. The decision to wear a catcher's mask was also left up to the player and, in this case, Pamela decided not to wear one.

The Court of Appeals of Tennessee found that Pamela had passed her fourteenth birthday and therefore could be held guilty of contributory negligence for the injury. It reversed the lower court's decision in favor of the girl and ruled that the teacher was in no way guilty of negligence.

Comparative negligence means that the fault for a given circumstance should be prorated. George Peters, a products liability attorney in California, comments that most states are concerned that an injured party cannot recover damages because the party was negligent to some degree. Peters predicts that many state legislatures will follow the example of California and pass legislation permitting the use of the

---

12. Brackman v. Adrian, 472 S.W.2d 735 (Tenn. App. 1971).

comparative negligence concept.[13] Some states, such as California and Virginia, now permit an individual who is partially at fault to receive compensation on a prorated basis.

Peters illustrates this with the case at Occidental College in California. A student was injured when he stepped on a loose basketball and crashed into an unpadded gymnasium wall during "free play," or intramurals. The court found the college 75 percent at fault and the student 25 percent negligent. Under comparative negligence legislation, the student, while negligent, still collected $15,000 in damages for his injury, where he would have received $60,000 had he not been at all negligent.

An *Act of God,* sometimes referred to as an Act of Nature, is something that occurs which is beyond the ability of a coach or other authority to control. If golfers were on a golf course on a clear, sunny day and a violent bolt of lightning suddenly struck one of them, the injury could be attributed to an unforeseen and unexpected Act of God or Nature.

Liability of One Participant for Injury to Another

The following cases illustrate the defenses in this category when they are litigated in court.

Ronnie Gaspard was hit on the head by a baseball bat that slipped from the hands of another boy during a game at school.[14] The defendant was the insurance company which represented the father of the boy who let the bat slip from his hands. The defendant argued

---

13. George Peters, lecture delivered at the Second National Conference on Sports Safety, Chicago, Ill., Oct. 1976.
14. Gaspard v. Grain Dealers Mut. Ins. Co., 131 So. 2d 831 (La. App. 1961).

that Gaspard assumed the risk of injury when he voluntarily agreed to play baseball that day.

During the trial, testimony was furnished that revealed that Gaspard was familiar with the fundamentals of baseball and that he knew that it was a common occurrence for a bat to slip out of a batter's hands. On the day of the accident it was extremely hot and humid and the players hands were sweaty. The defendant tried to wipe his hands on his pants, but still the bat flew out of his hands.

The trial judge commented on the defendant's conduct when he said:

> What more could he [defendant] have done, other than refrain from batting entirely? To impose liability under such circumstances would, in my opinion, render the participation of the children of this State in almost any game or sport a practical impossibility, and become a constant nightmare to parents throughout the State.[15]

The court favored the defendant.

When people go on family picnics and outings, they often engage in informal sports. Such was the occasion in California when a man was injured in a softball game during a family outing.[16]

A group of children and adults had gone to a "makeshift" field to play softball after lunch. The plaintiff was an adult who was playing second base. He took a throw from an outfielder and attempted to tag the base runner (defendant) out. The defendant

---

15. *Id.*
16. Travernier v. Maes, 51 Cal. Rptr. 575 (Cal. App. 1966).

attempted to slide safely into second base and, in so doing, broke the plaintiff's ankle.

Both parties involved in the accident were well versed in the fundamentals and rules of the game. The defendant testified that:

> [H]e had no particular type of slide in mind; that he had no intention of sliding into the plaintiff and knocking him down; that he was not attempting to break up a double play; and that he was trying to evade plaintiff and reach second base . . . .

The jury was advised to determine its verdict by considering the alleged negligence of the defendant or the assumption of risk by the plaintiff. The court then described assumption of risk as follows:

> It should be noted that in order to bar recovery, assumption of risk must be voluntary. To be voluntary these two factors must be present, both of them: first, the person in question, namely the plaintiff here, must have knowledge of the danger involved and an appreciation of the magnitude of that danger, and second, he must have had freedom of choice.

The trial court favored the defendant and the plaintiff appealed the decision.

The District Court of Appeal then made reference to *Restatement of Torts* by Prosser, and observed that:

> One who enters into a sport, game or contest may be taken to consent to physical contacts, consistent with the understood rules of the game.

Prosser went on to conclude that:

> players, coaches, managers, referees, and others who, in one way or another, voluntarily

participate must accept the risks to which their
rules expose them.[17]

The court affirmed the decision of the lower court by
ruling that the plaintiff had assumed the risks of the
game of softball and that the defendant was not guilty
of negligent conduct.

A highly publicized New York case got the attention
of people involved in sports everywhere because of the
nature of the lawsuit and the amount of damages
awarded by the courts.

Ray Passantino participated in baseball from the age
of eight until his unfortunate and tragic accident during
his junior year in high school.[18] Passantino was on third
base when his coach signalled for the squeeze play
which required him to break for home plate as soon as
the opposing pitcher committed himself. The batter was
instructed to bunt the ball so the runner could score
easily when the ball was thrown to first base.

Passantino broke for home and was 30 feet from
home plate when the batter missed the ball. The catcher
blocked the plate and waited for the base runner.
Instead of retreating back to third base Passantino
continued to run and tried to use his head as a
"battering ram" to run over the catcher. Both went
down and only the catcher got up. Passantino was
completely paralyzed and is now a permanent
quadriplegic.

The injured plaintiff sued the City Board of Education
and his baseball coach for negligence. He admitted, at

---

17. WILLIAM L. PROSSER, RESTATEMENT OF TORTS 2d ed., at 103.
18. Passantino v. Board of Educ. of City of New York, 383
    N.Y.S.2d 639 (N.Y. Sup. Ct. 1976), rev'd, 395 N.Y.S.2d 628
    (N.Y. App. Div. 1976).

the trial, that his coach taught him the fundamentals of baseball including the techniques of base running and sliding. Passantino contended, however, that his coach praised him after a previous game for running over an opposing catcher. He insisted that this praise motivated him to run over the catcher in this instance and was responsible for his crippling injury.

The Supreme Court, Queens County heard the testimony and awarded Passantino $1.8 million in damages. The Appellate Division of the Supreme Court considered the award excessive and reduced it to $1 million.

Justice Cohalan objected to the verdict and voted in a powerful dissent to dismiss the case and reverse the previous decisions. Stating that he sympathized with Passantino but felt that the boy was to blame for his actions, Cohalan declared:

> [F]or one unfortunate moment, [he] permitted his aggressiveness to overcome his common sense. As a result he is condemned, as a quadriplegic, to a life of complete helplessness, unable even to care for his most personal needs.[19]

Cohalan emphasized that unlike physical education, which is generally a required activity, sports are voluntary. Therefore, he asserted, the plaintiff assumed the risk of the sport when he volunteered for baseball and was responsible for the injury he sustained. In response to Passantino's inference that he tried to run over the catcher to gain the favor of the coach, Cohalan compared these remarks to some made by Stephen

---

19. Passantino v. Board of Educ. of City of New York, 395 N.Y.S.2d 628 (N.Y. App. Div. 1976).

Douglas in his famous debates with Abraham Lincoln which:

> ... Lincoln demolished by saying that they were "as thin as the homeopathic soup that was made by boiling the shadow of a pigeon that had starved to death." [20]

Cohalan surmised that Passantino was also guilty of contributory negligence in addition to assuming the risk since he knew the danger involved in his actions. The justice concluded his vigorous dissent by charging that Passantino was "solely and wholly" responsible for the disastrous accident and contrary to his attorney's plea that he was an "infant in the eyes of the law," he was "16 years old and an accomplished athlete; and that he was playing with his peers in size, strength and age."

Cohalan's powerful dissent was later affirmed by the action of the court that reversed the previous decisions and dismissed the charges against the School Board and the coach.[21]

New Era of Tort Law in Sports Litigation

After reviewing the cases above, one begins to believe that any sports-related injury comes under the protection of the doctrines of assumption of risk and contributory negligence. A new trend has developed in *tort* law that has far-reaching implications for sports participants. This new trend challenges the idea that a participant has little recourse when injured as long as the injury took place in a sports-related accident. The courts can now point to a very important case in Illinois to express its opposition to violence in sports.

----

20. *Supra* note 19.
21. *Supra* note 19.

Julian Nabozny, a goalkeeper in Winnetka, Illinois, was kicked in the head by an opponent in a soccer game.[22] Witnesses testified that Nabozny was kneeling in a non-contact area when he was kicked in the head by the opponent, who could have avoided the accident.

The trial court routinely followed the precedent set by earlier cases and ruled that the defendant was not guilty of negligent conduct since Nabozny had assumed the risks inherent to soccer. The Illinois Appellate Court took a bold step by reversing the trial court's ruling and sent it back to them for reconsideration by emphatically declaring that:

> The law should not place unreasonable burdens on the free and vigorous participation in sports by our youth. *However, we also believe that organized athletic competition does not exist in a vacuum. Rather some of the restraints of civilization must accompany every athlete onto the playing field.* (Emphasis added.)

The court added that:

> A reckless disregard for the safety of other players cannot be excused . . . it is our opinion that a player is liable for injury in tort action if his conduct is such that it is either deliberate, willful, or with a reckless disregard for the safety of the other players so as to cause injury to that player.

This important case later was settled out of court for a reported $65,000 by the insurance company of the parents of the boy who inflicted the injury on the plaintiff.

---

22. Nabozny v. Barnhill, 334 N.E.2d 258 (Ill. App. 1975).

Several judicial decisions prior to Nabozny indicate that other courts were thinking along the same lines about the various defenses used in sports-injury cases.

Jerome Bourque attempted to complete a double play by tagging second base and then stepping away from the base to avoid the baserunner.[23] The baserunner ran five feet away from second base so that he could collide with the second baseman and prevent a double play. As he ran into the plaintiff the baserunner raised his forearm and hit Bourque under the chin. He sustained a fractured jaw and "his chin required plastic surgery; seven teeth were broken and had to be crowned, and one tooth was replaced by a bridge." As a result of his rough play, the defendant was immediately ejected from the game.

Witnesses reported that the baserunner never slowed down but deliberately ran over the unsuspecting plaintiff. The defendant readily admitted that he ran toward the plaintiff but contended that he stood straight up so that he could block the infielder's view of first base. He claimed that the plaintiff failed to get out of his way.

The Court of Appeals of Louisiana made several pertinent observations during the trial and declared that Bourque was injured because the defendant failed to play the game in the proper manner. It agreed that Bourque assumed the normal risk of injury at second base from sliding and the possibility of being spiked, but argued that he did not assume the risk of an opponent going out of his way to deliberately injure him. The court supported the theory that a sports participant does assume risks that are obvious and foreseeable, but

---

23. Bourque v. Duplechin, 331 So. 2d 40 (La. App. 1976).

does not when a participant is hurt by opponents acting in an unsportsmanlike or reckless way. It therefore ruled that the defendant was guilty of negligence.

An unusual aspect developed in this case when the defendant's insurance carrier objected to paying damages because their client was found guilty of negligence. The insurance company contended that his coverage did not extend to cover an intentional tort where an obvious injury could result. The court disagreed with the insurance company and ordered it to pay the injured plaintiff $12,000 for his pain and suffering and $1,496 for special damages. The court based its judgment on the fact that the defendant was merely trying to break up a double play and did not try to deliberately injure the plaintiff.

One justice did voice an objection because he thought that the defendant, who was over 60 pounds heavier than the plaintiff, did commit an intentional act by planning to break the play up with "unpermitted contact." He believed that the insurance policy did exclude coverage for such an intentional act.

Albert Hawayek was fishing in Lake Pontchartrain with his brother-in-law, William Simmons.[24] The two fishermen were sitting in a motor boat when Simmons attempted to overhand cast. His three-pronged hooks hit something which turned out to be his brother-in-law's cheek and eye. When sued, Simmons denied any negligence on his part, arguing that his brother-in-law had assumed all risks of injury when he went fishing.

The lower court awarded Hawayek $154.65 for his medical bills and the Court of Appeals of Louisiana

---

24. Hawayek v. Simmons, 91 So. 2d 49 (La. App. 1956).

reviewed the decision. It took into consideration the doctrine of *res ipsa loquitur* (a Latin phrase that means the act speaks for itself), which applied in this case since the plaintiff was unaware of what actually happened when he was injured.

The court quoted from a Louisiana case in which the doctrine was involved. In that instance the Supreme Court of Louisiana commented on the doctrine by saying:

> In cases where the plaintiff cannot be expected to have any information as to the causes of the accident, whereas the defendant, on the contrary, must be assumed to be fully informed on the subject, and where the accident is of the kind which ordinarily does not occur when due care has been exercised, the rule of evidence is that the accident speaks for itself — res ipsa loquitur — that is to say, — that a presumption of negligence arises from the fact itself of the accident.

The court then added:

> In such cases, the plaintiff not only need not allege the particular acts of omission or commission from which the accident has resulted, but need not even prove them. The accident itself makes out a prima facie case, and the burden is on the defendant to show absence of negligence.[25]

The theory behind the *res ipsa loquitur* doctrine is that a person's rights when injured must be protected when the cause of the accident is unknown. Since

---

25. Lykiardopoulo v. New Orleans & C. R., Light & Power Co., 53 So. 575 (La. 1910).

Hawayek was not looking in Simmons' direction when he was casting, he could not know what caused the accident and subsequent injury to his eye.

The court ruled that Simmons was guilty of negligence because:

> [i]t seems to us that when a fisherman makes an overhead-forward cast, his lure would not be expected to take a lateral and horizontal tangent and strike another person in the boat but for some fault or negligence on the part of the one who makes the cast.

Since Hawayek's injury resulted in his missing his final examinations at Tulane University, the court awarded him an additional $1500.

Golf

It has become an almost universally accepted fact that any injury that occurs on a golf course is automatically covered by the doctrine of assumption of risk. While this doctrine is a reliable defense, it is not a panacea for guaranteed protection in golf-related injury cases. It has been reported that in lawsuits involving spectators or others in the area of golf courses the opportunity for recovery has been unusually successful.[26]

A Nebraska court awarded a golfer $8500 in a unique case in which two golfers in separate foursomes were found to be negligent for their actions against another golfer.[27] The plaintiff was searching for his ball in the rough, when a member of his group waved the trailing foursome through. The plaintiff reported that he was

---

26. 82 A.L.R. 2d 1184.
27. Schmidt v. Orton, 207 N.W.2d 390 (Neb. 1973).

unaware that his partner had allowed the group behind to play through. One of the players in the trailing group tried to hit in a hurry so the group could move on quickly and neglected to warn the members of the foursome ahead that he was hitting his ball. He struck the plaintiff in the eye and severely injured it.

The court not only found the defendant who hit the ball guilty of negligence, but also included the golfer who waved the foursome through.

It summed up its opinion, which was unusual to say the least, by asserting that:

> He must give adequate and timely notice to persons who appear to be unaware of his intention to hit the ball when he knows . . . that such persons are so close to the intended flight of the ball that danger to them might reasonably be anticipated.

Although there are a multitude of golf cases involving caddies, golf carts, property adjoining the golf course and other golf-related injuries, one final case is worthy of special consideration because of the defendant's age.

Jay Shlansky had taken golf lessons for over two years and knew the rules of golf. He was playing with his parents and another adult when he became involved in a situation that led to a lawsuit.[28] Shlansky hit a tee shot that struck a player who had just holed out and was crossing a bridge toward the next tee.

The court held the 11-year-old boy liable for the injury because he was playing an adult's game on an adult's course. It reasoned that he owed the golfer he hit the

---

28. Neumann v. Shlansky, 312 N.Y.S.2d 951 (N.Y. Sup. Ct., App. Term 1970).

same duty of care required of adults which was to act as a prudent person. The court supported its ruling by quoting from Prosser's *Restatement of Torts*:

An exception to the rule stated in this section may arise where the child engages in an activity which is normally undertaken only by adults, and for which adult qualifications are required.[29]

It continued to quote from Prosser, who states:

As in the case of one entering upon a professional activity which requires special skill, he may be held to the standard of adult skill, knowledge, and competence, and no allowance may be made for his immaturity.[30]

It is obvious from the cases in this chapter that while defenses of assumption of risk and contributory negligence may still be reliable, the courts may have entered into a new era of tort law that will not guarantee a defendant blanket protection just because a player participated in a sports activity.

IN MY OPINION

Quintillian, a Roman poet, once said that education is not what you are able to remember, but the things you can't forget.

I still remember the words of a highly successful college football coach before a nationally important intersectional game. He offered money as a bonus for touchdowns, blocked kicks, intercepted passes and last — the most important, to put an opponent out of the game. The objective was accomplished, the game won,

---

29. WILLIAM L. PROSSER, RESTATEMENT OF TORTS, § 283 A., Comment C.
30. *Id.*

the designated opponent carried off the field, and as promised, the money was paid.

During a bitter rivalry in college baseball, a player on the visiting team broke up a double play ball by standing straight up as he ran into second base. The coach of the home team threatened to bench the short stop permanently if he failed in the future to hit the runner "between the eyes." The objective was accomplished the next inning, as the runner was hit in the head, and carried off the field unconscious.

Professional athletics? No, just collegiate football and baseball. These two examples may not be typical or even common occurrences, but I still can't forget them and don't like what they represent in sports.

Through the years, the general attitude of most people seems to be that any sports-related injury is just one of those things. The general consensus is that anyone who takes part in sports automatically assumes the risk of injury even if the injury is the result of a deliberate foul or the breaking of a rule.

This is why the decision in the *Hackbart* case troubles me. Can anyone really believe that a court of law actually said that *there is no reasonable standard of care or conduct in a professional sport such as football?* If this decision is upheld by the Appellate Court, no professional athlete in collision sports will be safe from the threat of serious injury inflicted in a deliberate and willful manner. It could set sports back 50 years by sanctioning violence. After all, the courts will undoubtedly rule, the athlete assumes all risks especially when no standard of care is provided.

The *Passantino* case was one of the most frightening ones to come out of the courts in years. The tragedy of the injury to the young athlete is deplorable, but if the

$1 million dollar verdict had been allowed to stand against the coach and school district, no one would be able to coach with any assurance that his every decision would not be challenged ultimately in court. Such decisions could drive many coaches from the profession.

In this chapter we noted several instances where the courts have decided that deliberate acts of violence will not be tolerated. The *Nabozny* decision may herald a new era of tort law as the Illinois court said, in effect, enough is enough! Its ruling signifies the court's attempt to halt indiscriminate acts of violence in sports and provide participants with healthy competition.

An attorney told me recently that a friend of mine was being sued for hitting a spectator at a Pro-Am with his tee shot. The attorney assured me that my friend was safe since anyone that steps on a golf course assumes the risks of the sport. I replied that I just could not accept that and promised to do some research in the area. I found, to my surprise, that there is probably more litigation regarding injuries and liability in golf than any other sport on record. In addition, I learned that while the court has been fairly consistent in ruling that the assumption of risk doctrine is still reliable as a defense against negligence, it will not guarantee automatic success in litigation.

Courts have ruled that while all the people associated with golf assume the *normal* risks of the sport, they do not assume the risks of negligent conduct. This applies potentially to all sports, and this attitude perhaps makes the *Nabozny* case important to litigation of future incidents of violence in sports.

The threat of spiraling lawsuits seems a nemesis to many people, but if the threat of court action keeps violence out of sports and creates a safe and healthy environment for the participants, it serves a useful purpose.

I want to emphasize these words of the Illinois court in the *Nabozny* case:

> Organized athletic competition does not exist in a vacuum. Rather some of the restraints of civilization must accompany every athlete onto the playing field.

CHAPTER 3

The Handicapped Athlete

Now the physically and mentally handicapped are emerging as one of the country's newest and most aggressive political action groups.[1]

Handicapped people in the United States are making tremendous progress in their efforts to overcome discrimination. Steven Roberts, writing for the *New York Times News Service,* describes the growing movement for equal treatment by the handicapped when he notes:

> First came black power and brown power and red power. Then came the women's movement, the white ethnics, the gays and the elderly. Now the physically and mentally handicapped are emerging as one of the country's newest and most aggressive political action groups.[2]

The Department of Health, Education and Welfare received 377 claims of discrimination against the handicapped in the first four months of 1978. This represents more claims than for race and sex discrimination combined.[3]

The handicapped are beginning to make rapid gains in sports. John Ross, a blind state champion in wrestling, earned his varsity letter at the University of Minnesota. He published the first braille sports magazine, *Feeling*

---

1. Greensboro Daily News, June 25, 1978.
2. *Id.*
3. *Supra* note 1.

Sports.[4] P. J. Mallory and Company have developed a softball with a three ounce sound-emitting device that enables visually handicapped persons to play softball.[5]

New Jersey is one of the most advanced states in recognizing the importance of sports for the handicapped by offering them vigorous programs of physical education on a state-wide basis.[6] Educators in New Jersey believe that all blind children need to be involved in every aspect of school life including physical education and competitive sports. A physical education consultant for the visually handicapped spends his time visiting over one hundred schools a year within the state. The buddy system has been used to help avoid injuries and reduce the burden on the teacher in the physical education class.[7]

The results of participation in sports by New Jersey handicapped athletes are often impressive. Eugene Darnell, who is totally blind and has only one leg, won two varsity letters in wrestling. Gary Carvaho, who is legally blind, broke the long jump record at Roselle Catholic High School and Robert Donoher, who also is legally blind, played football and basketball in the Cook A-A 12 and 13-year-old league and was named to the All-Star team.[8]

---

4. *Vivid Sports Coverage — For Visually Handicapped,* THE PHYSICIAN AND SPORTSMEDICINE, Vol. 3, No. 1, Jan. 1975.
5. *A Sound Idea,* THE PHYSICIAN AND SPORTSMEDICINE, Vol. 3, No. 1, Jan. 1975.
6. Charles E. Buell and Angelo Mortagnini, Jr., *Blind Children Integrated into Physical Education Classes in New Jersey Schools,* UP DATE, Feb. 1976.
7. *Id.*
8. *Supra* note 6.

The highly publicized case of *Mills v. D.C. Board of Education* [9] became an important case in the field of special education since the decision guarantees the right of all handicapped children to an education supported by public funds. It also provides various procedural safeguards to insure the implementation of that right. The decision in *Mills* gives judicial support to the principle that a handicapped person has a right to lead as normal a life as possible.

The Department of Health, Education and Welfare gave new emphasis to the handicapped's opportunity to participate in athletics and physical education when it mandated that federally assisted programs may not prohibit such participation. The regulation is referred to in the Rehabilitation Act of 1973, 29 U.S.C.A. 794 and provides:

> No otherwise qualified handicapped individual ... shall, solely by reason of his handicap, be excluded from the participation in, be denied the benefits of, or be subjected to discrimination under any program or activity receiving Federal financial assistance. [10]

The Act, 29 U.S.C.A. 706 defines the handicapped as follows:

> Any person who (a) has a physical or mental impairment which substantially limits one or more of such person's major life activities, (b) has a record of such an impairment, or (c) is regarded as having such an impairment. [11]

---

9. *Do Handicapped Children Have a Legal Right to Minimal Adequate Education?*, JOURNAL OF LAW AND EDUCATION, Vol. 3, Apr. 1974.
10. Federal Register, Dept. of Health, Education and Welfare, Part IV, May, 1977.
11. *Id.*

The Act prohibits discrimination in sports as specified by PL 94-142 section 84.47 of 504 by mandating:

> In providing physical education courses and athletics and similar programs and activities to any of its students, a recipient to which this subpart applies may not discriminate on the basis of handicap. A recipient that offers physical education courses or that operates or sponsors intercollegiate, club, or intramural athletics shall provide to qualified handicapped students an equal opportunity for participation in these activities.[12]

The law as stated above protects the right of the handicapped in sports as never before and signals the beginning of a new era for them in sports.

The Physically Impaired Athlete

Several years ago the American Medical Association strongly advised school officials to exclude athletes with certain disqualifying conditions from participation in sports. The conditions included such things as inadequately controlled diabetes, jaundice, absence of one eye, active tuberculosis, enlarged liver, one kidney, renal disease and a variety of other conditions.[13] (See Appendix A for the AMA Guidelines).

Many athletes with these physical conditions insist that they are not handicapped and when they are denied participation in sports activities they often institute lawsuits. In most suits they argue that school

12. *Supra* note 10.
13. *Disqualifying Conditions for Sports Participation,* MEDICAL EVALUATION OF THE ATHLETE — A GUIDE (Reprinted with the permission of the American Medical Association, Chicago, Ill. 1977.)

authorities cannot deny a handicapped person participation in sports. They contend that they are protected by the equal protection clause of the Fourteenth Amendment of the Federal Constitution.

One of the notable cases took place in New York in 1973. Joseph Spitaleri was a young athlete despite a handicap he sustained when he was six years old.[14] Spitaleri received a serious injury that resulted in almost complete loss of vision in one eye. Despite the impaired vision, he competed and was outstanding in all sports, including football.

Spitaleri was disqualified for competition in football at the high school level by the school physician. The physician referred to the criteria set by the American Medical Association, which recommends prohibition from contact sports when the athlete is without a vital organ such as a kidney or an eye.

The boy's father argued that the denial of the right to play football was damaging to the psychological well-being of his son. He pleaded with the school authorities to permit Joseph to play, and promised to waive all responsibilities by assuming all the risks involved.

The case went before the New York Commission of Education who supported the judgment of the physician. A court also upheld the decision by stating that the verdict to disqualify the athlete was not a capricious or arbitrary act, but one intended to protect the boy's welfare.

The only cases recently decided by court actions involve athletes that lack one vital paired organ. Several cases illustrate the litigation that has taken place lately.

---

14. Spitaleri v. Nyquist, 345 N.Y.S.2d 878 (N.Y. Sup. Ct. 1973).

A. Impaired Vision

Mike Borden, a two-time high school MVP tried out for the junior varsity basketball team at Ohio University.[15] He made the team one day, was examined by the school physician the next, and dismissed the following day because he had only one eye.

Borden's dismissal aroused the Ohio campus, the state of Ohio and gained him national attention and support. Borden declared that people had encouraged him all his life because he had only one eye and now it was being held against him. Borden maintained that he was not materially handicapped since he had been blind in one eye from the time he was three years of age, yet had been successful both in school and in sports. He remarked:

> I didn't know what it was like to have two eyes — that would be a dream — but I know I can compete with anyone.[16]

The American Civil Liberties Union offered to file a lawsuit in Borden's behalf using Title 29 of the United States Code (Sec. 794) that avows:

> No otherwise qualified handicapped individual in the United States, as defined in Section 706(6) of this title, shall, solely by reason of his handicap, be excluded from the participation in, be denied the benefits of, or be subjected to discrimination under any program or activity receiving Federal financial assistance.[17]

Borden immediately sought and received an injunction from the court enabling him to rejoin the

---

15. The Post, Athens, Ohio, Nov. 1975.
16. *Id.*
17. *Supra* note 15.

team. The university complied with the court order and reinstated Borden. In his first game he scored 22 points and pulled down 8 rebounds.

The following year, although the court order was no longer in effect, the university officials refused to pursue the issue any further. Legal Affairs Officer John Burns stated that:

> It's still spiritually intact. It would be silly to go to court each year.[18]

Burns explained that the University was not opposed to Borden at all but felt that it had to support the American Medical Association's recommendations because the danger of injury and the risk of blindness to Borden was too great. Borden was, therefore, allowed to participate on the Ohio University basketball team.

Kinney Redding and Keith Evans, both outstanding collegiate athletes at Missouri Western State College, were told by the team physician that they could not play football because each one was blind in the left eye.[19] Both athletes were highly regarded football prospects and it was reported that Redding was on the prospect list of professional teams in the NFL.

Both players were granted permission to play for Missouri Western as soon as each signed a waiver releasing the college from liability. The federal judge who granted them the injunction thought that failure to play would cause serious damage to them and that it would represent a violation of their constitutional rights.

---

18. The Columbus Dispatch, Ohio, Dec. 7, 1977.
19. Evans and Redding v. Looney, No. 77-6052-CV-SJ, U.S. District Court for the (W.D. of Mo., Sept. 2, 1977).

In New York two students, each having one eye, were refused permission to take part in contact sports by the court. The court reasoned that the danger of the injury to their eyes was just too great a risk to take.[20]

The New York Legislature was attempting to correct situations similar to the *Spitaleri* case in which the boy was denied the right to participate in sports because of impaired vision. The reason for the legislation, known as Senate Bill 1440 was explained in the following manner:

> Because the State Education Department has tied together the medical and legal issues, a student who has a disqualifying condition cannot expect to receive permission to play a contact sport, regardless of the fact that objectively he might be medically capable. In addition, such decisions are insulated by the procedure for appealing administrative determinations; this procedure does not afford to a petitioner the review of the merits of conflicting opinions. The concern of both the court and Commissioner is with the possible arbitraries of a determination. If a school physician's decision has some basis in reason, it will be upheld. The conflicting opinion from a private physician is not reviewed or considered even though it might be more reasonable.[21]

One student, Margaret Kampmeier, appealed the decision since the New York Legislature had passed legislation known as the "Spitaleri Bill" or S. 1440, which was directed at school districts that prohibit

---

20. Kampmeier v. Harris, 403 N.Y.S.2d 638 (N.Y. Sup. Ct. 1978), *rev'd*, 411 N.Y.S.2d 744 (N.Y. App. Div. 1978).

21. *Id.*

athletes from sports because of physical impairments. The bill provides:

> Upon the verified petition of a parent/guardian and affidavits of two licensed physicians, the court would weigh the merits of the conflicting opinion of the school physician and the private physicians. A determination could be made as to which of the two opinions would be in the best interests of the student.[22]

The bill extends protection for the school district and the physicians by implying:

> Concommitantly, this determination would release the physicians and school district from liability for the student's participation in a sport since the court would be necessarily dictating what is reasonable and prudent under the circumstances.[23]

Margaret Kampmeier had been classified by the school physician as handicapped and denied the opportunity to compete in contact sports. Later, she was also prevented from engaging in physical education and intramural activities that involved contact sports.

The Supreme Court of New York, County of Monroe, recognized that the plaintiff had followed the requirements of the *Spitaleri* law by furnishing the court with affidavits from two physicians, a pediatrician and a specialist in ophthalmology. Both physicians expressed the opinion that she could participate in school sports and that they believed the sports program would be "reasonably safe" for her.

---

22. *Supra* note 20.
23. *Supra* note 20.

The court was confused by the wording of the *Spitaleri* law and remarked:

> The court is puzzled, at the need for the reasonably safe requirement since it is difficult to imagine a situation in which participation could possibly not be reasonably safe, and yet somehow be in any student's best interest.

The court conceded that the girl could protect her eye with special safety glasses, and meet the reasonably safe requirement, but it questioned the "best interest" test. The reason for its dilemma was a particular statement in the law which specified that:

> No school district shall be held liable for any injury sustained by a student participating pursuant to an order granted under this section.

The Supreme Court of New York, County of Monroe, contended that the statute, so written, insulated the school district in advance:

> From liability for injuries bearing no connection whatever with the student's handicap, and ever for gross negligence.

This kind of immunity troubled the court, and the fact that the parents of the plaintiff might not be able to secure insurance to protect their daughter in the event an injury occurred also dismayed the court. For these reasons the court could not favor participation, since the conditions did not seem to fulfill the "best interest" test. It therefore ruled that it was not in the best interest of the girl to participate in contact sports.

The court did serve warning to the school district, however, that:

> Pending any legally valid identification, evaluation, or classification of the petitioner as

physically handicapped and in need of special education or related services, respondents are enjoined from excluding the petitioner, solely on account of her visual handicap, from participation in contact sports otherwise available under respondents' physical education program.[24]

Margaret Kampmeier's case went to the Supreme Court of New York, Appellate Division, Fourth Department, where it was ruled that the court should not consider the "statutory immunity from liability" as a factor in her situation.[25] It felt that she was athletically inclined and that it was in her best interest to participate in sports. In addition, it surmised, it would be reasonably safe for her to participate as long as she used her protective eyeglasses.

It, therefore, reversed the previous decision and granted Margaret permission to participate in the junior high school sports program.

In another situation, similar to that of Margaret Kampmeier, the New York Supreme Court, Albany County, permitted a high school freshman to participate in sports despite impaired vision.

Kim Swiderski had defective vision in her right eye since birth. The impairment was attributed to a "congenital cataract and an undeveloped optic nerve." [26]

Her mother sought a court order which would allow her to participate in athletics at Albany High School. Kim's mother furnished two affidavits from licensed

---

24. *Supra* note 20.
25. Kampmeier v. Harris, 411 N.Y.S.2d 744 (N.Y. App. Div. 1978).
26. Swiderski v. Board of Educ. — City School Dist. of Albany, 408 N.Y.S.2d 744 (N.Y. Sup. Ct. 1978).

physicians to support her claim that it was in her daughter's best interest to participate in sports. The school district opposed the motion and relied on the statement of the school physician arguing that an injury to Kim's eye could cause the school district to be found liable.

The Supreme Court, Special Term, Albany County, decided that Kim's best interest would be satisfied by participation in sports. It ruled, therefore, that she be allowed to engage in sports as long as she used protective eye shields as recommended by her doctor. The court then provided that the school district would not be held liable for injury to the girl under Section 4409 of the Education Law.

B. Single Kidney

The parents of a boy, referred to as "P.N.," who had one kidney, sued the Board of Education in Elizabeth, New Jersey because it refused to allow their son to play on the high school soccer team.[27] During his senior year "P.N." had been examined, prior to the start of the soccer season, and the medical inspector had informed the superintendent of schools that he had discussed the boy's medical history and condition with three urologists. The three urologists agreed that "P.N." could participate in noncontact sports but not in contact sports because of his condition. The medical inspector, therefore, recommended to the superintendent that "P.N." be excluded from football, wrestling and soccer, despite the fact that "P.N." had competed in football

---

27. "P.N." by his parents v. Board of Educ. of the City of Elizabeth, Union County (Decision of the New Jersey Commission of Education, 1975).

and wrestling during his sophomore year. "P.N.'s" parents insisted that the medical inspector's disqualification of their son was discriminatory. They demanded to know why he had reversed his decision after he had allowed "P.N." to play the previous years. In his junior year he won first place honors in a United States Marine physical fitness program and also played on the soccer team.

One significant influence was the refusal of the school's insurance carrier to honor any claim in the event his remaining kidney was injured. This letter, apparently, influenced the superintendent's decision to support the opinion of the school's medical inspector.

The New Jersey Commissioner of Education reviewed all the facts in the controversy and ruled:

> The interests of the pupil, his parents and the community at large are best served by permitting the Board to exercise its legal discretion in adhering to the advice of its own medical inspector, absent a clear showing that the medical inspector's determination was arbitrary or discriminatory. Petitioner has failed to make such a clear showing.

Warren Grundsman was refused permission to play junior high school basketball in New Jersey.[28] The school physician used the AMA's guidelines to justify his decision since Grundsman had only one kidney. The boy's parents would not accept the physician's recommendation and got their family doctor's approval for Warren to play. They also agreed to sign a waiver. The Tom's River School Board voted 8-1 to override the

---

28. THE PHYSICIAN AND SPORTSMEDICINE, Vol. 3, No. 6, June 1975.

school physician and granted the boy permission to participate in basketball.

C. Impaired Hearing.

John Colombo had a marked hearing loss of 50 percent in his left ear and a total loss of hearing in his right ear.[29] The hearing loss had existed since birth and he used a hearing aid in his left ear. The doctor who examined him reported that Colombo could hear normal conversation if he was facing the person who was talking, but little else. For this reason the doctor discouraged participation in sports such as football, lacrosse or soccer. The doctor described the boy's hearing defect as one that:

> leaves him with a permanent auditory blind right side that causes him to be vulnerable to the risk of bodily injury when compared to students with a full sensory perception.

The New York State Department based its decision to deny Colombo participation in contact sports on the recommendations of the AMA regarding disqualifying physical conditions. His parents pursued the issue by pointing out that the school physician was not aware of certain relevant facts when he refused to permit their son to play. These included:

1. Both parents gave their son approval to play;
2. The boy was an exceptional and talented athlete;
3. The boy had competed successfully in sports without an injury;

---

29. Colombo v. Sewanhaka Central High School, Dist. No. 2, 383 N.Y.S.2d 518 (N.Y. Sup. Ct. 1976).

4. The boy had played football with nonschool groups;

5. The ruling not to allow him to participate caused him psychological damage and resulted in a lack of interest in school because he felt inferior to his classmates.

The boy's father explained that the family lacked the finances to send John to college and hoped, instead, that he would win an athletic scholarship if allowed to play. The father promised to assume all risk of injury to his son, including total deafness.

The Assistant Director of Admissions at Gallaudet College, a school for the deaf, testified in behalf of the plaintiff. He reported that between 1200 and 1800 deaf athletes competed in the Deaf Olympics, and of that number 700 took part in contact sports. He noted that 59 schools sponsored contact sports for the deaf and that Gallaudet competed against regular college opponents. In all of this competition, he knew of no injury attributed to a hearing disability.

Dr. Donald Kasprzak, Chairman of the Committee on the Medical Aspects of Sports, commented that he saw no danger to Colombo in contact sports, but did foresee serious emotional problems if he was prevented from participating in sports. He then criticized the AMA guidelines as outmoded and in need of revision.

An otologist advised the school's medical officer that while he supported the AMA's regulation, he thought Colombo could play with a protective helmet.

The New York court made reference to a case that was decided against a boy with one eye, but ultimately led to legislation that will affect future cases. In *Spitaleri* the court remarked:

Clearly, the concern of the AMA and of the school physician as well as those physicians who hold the view that he should be permitted to play, is the always present danger of injury to the remaining organ which, if it should occur, would result in irreversible and permanent injury.[30]

It was ironic that the only time a court reversed a doctor's decision, in a similar situation, occurred in the same school district as presented here. In *Pendergast v. Sewanhaka Central High School District #2,* the circumstances were quite different, however, since the plaintiff had one testicle. In that instance the court observed that:

> An exercise of discretion cannot be based merely on the nature of the disability, i.e., the fact that one of the paired organs is missing. The loss of a testicle is not comparable to the loss of one of other paired organs such as eyes, ears, or kidneys.[31]

It explained that:

> The disability which results from the loss of one eye is functional in terms of participation in athletics. Lack of depth perception can increase the risk of further injury not only to the remaining sight, but to the other parts of the body. The inability to hear strongly directional sounds on the impaired hearing side could have similar consequences in some sports.[32]

While the court in Colombo sympathized with the boy's disappointment and frustration, it believed that

---

30. *Supra* note 14.
31. Pendergast v. Sewanhaka Central High School, Dist. No. 2 (Supreme Court, Nassau County, 1975).
32. *Id.*

the doctor's action was neither arbitrary nor capricious. It observed that participation in sports presented the danger of three risks to the impaired hearing athlete, namely:

1. The risk of injury to the ear in which there is only partial hearing and to which further injury could result in irreversible and permanent damage — in this case, total deafness;
2. The risk to other parts of his body by reason of his failure to perceive the direction of sound;
3. The risk of injury to other participants.

The court felt that the risks involved were too high to overrule the school doctor's decision. It denied participation in contact sports to Colombo.[33] It is interesting to note that the revised American Medical Association's guidelines no longer include impaired hearing as a disqualifying physical condition for sports participation. (See Appendix A)

The New York Legislature has attempted to protect the rights of the handicapped or physically impaired athlete to participate in sports of all types. At the same time, the Legislature tried to waive by statute the liability of the physicians and school district. The *Spitaleri* ruling may be questioned and tested in the future in court.

A new issue may be raised by the legislation and that is the liability of the physicians who sign the affidavits supporting the impaired athletes request to play.

A university official commented in a letter that the *Spitaleri* ruling may, in fact, not protect the physician at all. He made the following observation when he said:

_____

33. *Supra* note 28.

Despite the statement in the supporting memorandum that the physicians who provide supporting affidavits, would be released from liability, the bill as drawn does not provide any such blanket protection.[34]

He then expressed his concern for all such physicians when he warned that:

A physician who has been negligent in diagnosing a student's physical condition would not be immune from a malpractice action for injuries occurring as a consequence of his negligence.[35]

It is possible that various state legislatures will attempt by judicial fiat to enact statutes meeting the federal requirements for the handicapped and at the same time protecting school officials. It is also possible that the statutes may be confusing and unable to adequately protect those for whom it is designed. Further litigation may well set precedent and legal parameters for all to follow.

The Emotionally Impaired Athlete

The vast number of cases pertaining to the handicapped participant deal with physical impairments. A Texas case, however, illustrates the potential for involvement by the emotionally-impaired participant.

John Doe spent several days in a psychiatric ward of a hospital for violent behavior which his parents could

---

34. Letter from Louis Welch, The State Education Department of the University of the State of New York at Albany, Mar. 10, 1977.
35. *Id.*

not control.[36] During 1977 he lived at home with his parents and played football at Friendswood High School. Later that year, physicians diagnosed his father's condition as terminal cancer. From that time on John became unusually violent toward his parents and even threatened them with a loaded shotgun. He received psychiatric treatment but his emotional problems increased until his therapist recommended that he live with his maternal grandparents.

His grandparents were named "managing conservators" and he enrolled at Alvin High School for his senior year. John's therapist encouraged him to play football at Alvin, not Friendswood, because she felt it was necessary for his emotional health. Both school principals agreed with the therapist, but the University Interscholastic League ruled that John was not eligible to play football that year. They cited the rule that stated:

a. a student changing schools whose parents or guardians do not reside in the school district is ineligible for varsity contests.
b. a student living with a guardian is eligible only if the guardianship is of one year's standing.
c. where both parents are still alive, the UIL will not acknowledge the existence of a legal guardianship.

The rule was designed to prevent athletes from "shopping around for a school or a coach."

John's attorney alleged that the regulation was a violation of Section 794 of 29 U.S.C.A. that prohibits

---

36. Doe v. Marshall, 459 F. Supp. 1190 (S.D. Texas 1978).

federally funded programs from discriminatory practices against the handicapped.

The United States District Court (S.D. Texas) reviewed the testimony and concluded that the harm to John if denied the opportunity to participate in football would be "enormous." It reasoned that participation in football during John's senior year could:

> make the difference between the young man's growing up into a productive, happy individual, or, on the contrary, being institutionalized for the balance of his life.

The court observed that the U.S. Code statute obligates the school district to consider:

> the needs of each handicapped student and devising a program which will enable each individual handicapped student to receive an appropriate free public education.

It therefore issued an injunction prohibiting the UIL from barring John from football during his senior year at Alvin High School.

IN MY OPINION

The father of a high school athlete in Illinois took exception to my use of the word "handicapped" in describing the physically impaired athlete, and rightfully so. He listed the accomplishments of his daughter, who has been deaf since birth, and they read as follows:

> Athletically she has competed in swimming, diving, bowling, softball, tennis, volleyball, basketball and track, soccer, girls' athletic association, has two presidential fitness awards, and has qualified as a Red Cross Senior Lifeguard. During the course of these activities

she has set individual records for our high school as well as won individual honors in non-school sponsored sports. By the end of the present school year she will have earned four letters in tennis, one in volleyball, one in basketball and two in track.

He asks the question — "is she handicapped? If so, perhaps all of our students are handicapped."

Paul Smiley, the football coach at Gallaudet, was interviewed by the United Press International. He mentioned Dan Fitzpatrick, a 6'2", 255 pound defensive guard and team captain as a possible professional football player in the NFL and another student, a quarterback, who was named the Outstanding Deaf Athlete in the United States in 1977. The athlete turned down many offers from "hearing colleges to attend Gallaudet." Smiley candidly concluded his interview by expressing his opinion that:

> People that graduate from this college are in all walks of life. They can do anything and football is no exception. And, if anybody thinks deaf people can't play football, I'd like them to come here and line up against Mr. Fitzpatrick.

Morris "Mo" Udall, the Arizona senator who was a democratic candidate for the United States presidency, led the campaign to reinstate Mike Borden to the Ohio University basketball team. Udall has only one eye, but successfully participated in collegiate and professional basketball. He challenged the defendants to list the names of any previous athletes with one eye who became blind through sports competition. *None were listed!*

The examples of athletes with physical impairments could go on and on. They are convincing and compelling, but they represent only one side of the coin.

A highly respected football coach and athletic trainer recently related a situation that still troubles him. He recruited an outstanding linebacker only to discover that the athlete had only one kidney. The coach supported the team physician's recommendation to exclude the athlete from all collision sports. The coach offered to let the athlete become his assistant trainer and promised to honor his athletic grant for the four years he attended the university. The athlete accepted his offer and made a valuable contribution to the football program.

Two years later the football coach was elevated to an administrative position and a new coach was hired. The student-trainer immediately requested and was granted permission to go out for football. The former coach, with no bitterness or criticism of anyone, stated his feelings in simple terms when he declared that he would have lost his job before he would have permitted the student to suit up for football. "Football is a great game," he said, "but only a game and not worth, for one minute, the health, safety and future welfare of any student."

The coach's sentiments were almost identical to those of a highly respected team physician for both high school and college athletes. The physician questioned the callous attitude of many parents who have physically impaired children who want to participate in sports. Many parents virtually demand that he sign an affidavit enabling their son or daughter to take part in sports, no matter what the future consequences appear to be. He doubts that Section 504 of the Rehabilitation Act will result in activity that is in the best interest of our young people. "After all," he exclaimed, "how can you legislate morality, ethical conduct, or safety for our people?"

It is clear, however, that PL 94-142, § 504 will require every institution that engages in physical education, athletics and intramurals to permit any handicapped student to try out and participate in the activities.

It will take time to evaluate the results of the Act but it is my opinion that it has done little to protect the athlete from possible irreversible injury or school officials and coaches from liability suits.

It is apparent that state high school athletic associations will revise their regulations regarding the handicapped athlete and that more states will follow the example of the New York State Legislature in enacting statutes that permit participation in sports by protecting the school official and coaches from liability.

I doubt seriously if the statutes will be valid if tested in court if they attempt to provide immunity to school officials and physicians even when gross negligence occurs. The problem is as confusing and complex as any in sports today and it will take judicial decisions to set the legal parameters for all to follow.

Until that time comes, I plan to take the following action if a handicapped athlete goes out for a collision or contact sport.

I will have a conference with all the people involved, including the athlete and parents, the team and family physicians and the coach of the sport in question. We will discuss the consequences of participation and possible injury and consider alternatives such as non-contact sports or an association with the sport such as manager or trainer.

If the athlete and the parents are in agreement with the opinion of the physicians and it is determined that the athlete can benefit from participation in sports we will sign a statement to that effect. We will keep the notes of the meeting on file stating that such a meeting was held and that all parties were aware of the situation and possible consequences resulting from injury and still chose to participate. It will be helpful to have all the parties present sign the statement and keep the record on file for future reference in the event of a lawsuit.

Above all, the school officials and coaches must use sound judgment and extreme care to avoid negligent conduct.

These suggestions are not intended to offer absolute solutions to a controversial and difficult problem, but should illustrate an area that needs some study. The situation is admittedly difficult and until it is resolved by judicial decisions, all parties should proceed with extreme caution.

CHAPTER 4

Discrimination and the Athlete

Toleration of individual differences is basic
to our democracy, whether these
differences be in religion,
politics, or lifestyle.[1]

Athletes are suing in record numbers against any discriminatory practice that denies them the right to participate in sports because of their appearance, marital status, or sex.

Congress passed the Civil Rights Act of 1871 to protect emancipated blacks with the guarantees of the Federal Constitution. There was a lack of litigation under this Act for almost three quarters of a century, but recently there have been thousands of cases which involve section 1983 of the Act, in 42 U.S.C.A., which provides:

> Every person who, under color of any statute, ordinance, regulation, custom, or usage, of any State or Territory, subjects, or causes to be subjected, any citizen of the United States or other person within the jurisdiction thereof to the deprivation of any rights, privileges, or immunities secured by the Constitution and laws, shall be liable to the party injured in an action at law, suit in equity, or other proper proceeding for redress.[2]

---

1. Bishop v. Colaw, 450 F.2d 1069 (8th Cir. 1971).
2. Zeller v. Donegal School Dist. Bd. of Educ., 517 F.2d 600 (3d Cir. 1975).

The flood of litigation under this Act compels our courts to interpret the rights guaranteed by the Fourteenth Amendment. Athletes are becoming aware of their rights today, not only under the Fourteenth Amendment, but also under the First, Fourth, Fifth, and Ninth. (See Appendix B for a list of these Amendments). Athletes are sensitive to issues that affect due process, personal rights and equal protection and exhibit a willingness to seek judicial remedy when they feel their rights are violated.

Hairstyle Codes

One of the most controversial issues in sports in the early seventies centered around athletes' hair. In 1971 alone, 104 cases related to hair were reported, with school officials winning 58 to the students' 46.[3] While the intensity of the issue has abated, the issue itself refuses to go away. The people involved in sports are still confused over the inconsistency of judicial rulings on hair and the courts' failure to set standards to follow after countless cases.

As a rule the courts in the First, Fourth, Seventh and Eighth Circuits tend to favor the student in hair cases while the District of Columbia, the Fifth, Ninth and Tenth Circuits generally rule that the hair issue does not warrant federal judicial action. There is no reference to the attitude of the courts regarding the issue in the Second, Third or Sixth Circuits.[4]

Several outstanding cases illustrate both sides of the controversy.

---

3. HERB APPENZELLER, ATHLETICS AND THE LAW, The Michie Co., Charlottesville, Va., 1975.
4. *Supra* note 2.

In California, a group of track athletes at Redwood High School refused to comply with the athletic department's regulation that each athlete be neat and well-groomed, clean shaven, with the hair off the collar and at a reasonable length. The penalty for refusing to comply was automatic suspension from the sport.[5]

The California court upheld the athletic department's regulations, but emphasized that each case needs individual consideration based on its own merits according to the background and setting of the situation. It found no evidence to prove that the athletic department's regulation was "arbitrary or capricious." [6]

A Vermont court viewed the issue in a different way when three tennis players at Brattleboro High School challenged a rule they believed violated their constitutional rights.[7] The high school had a code that regulated extracurricular activities, such as athletics. The athletic department formulated regulations that were intended to promote good morale and team spirit. It specified among other things:

> For males, hair must be cut tapered in the back and on the sides of the head with no hair over the collar. Sideburns should be no lower than the earlobe and trimmed.

The Vermont court warned against conformity and uniformity which, it noted, students experience soon enough when they graduate and go into the world. It ordered the school officials to reinstate the three boys

---

5. Neuhaus v. Torrey, 310 F. Supp. 192 (N.D. Cal. 1970).
6. *Id.*
7. Dunham v. Pulsifer, 312 F. Supp. 411 (D. Vt. 1970).

to the tennis team without penalty and raised a question that many athletes also ask, namely:

> Why every sport could not have its own rules on hair length which could be reasonably related to performance in that particular sport.

The court concluded with a familiar quote:

> The Constitution does not stop at the public schools like a puppy waiting for its master, but instead it follows the student through the corridors, into the classrooms and onto the athletic field.[8]

Two more recent cases indicate again the lack of agreement among the courts on the issue of "hairstyles."

The School Board of Berthold Public School District No. 54 in North Dakota formulated a hair and dress code that set limits on the length of a male's hair.[9] If an individual failed to comply with the code, he could not represent the school in interscholastic competition. The code included participation in the band, choir, and organizations such as Future Farmers of America (FFA).

Before the code was written formally, there was an identical set of rules that were unwritten but still enforced. On several occasions, when the rules were unwritten, the school superintendent asked the plaintiff, Mark Dostert, to cut his long hair. Mark always trimmed his hair, but managed to leave just enough hair over his ears so that he never fully complied with the regulations.

---

8. *Id.*
9. Dostert v. Berthold Pub. School Dist. No. 54, 391 F. Supp. 876 (D. N.D. 1975).

The issue became so intense that several students attacked Mark and cut his hair with a pair of scissors. The boy's parents became angry and informed the police. The superintendent informed Mark that he could participate in all of the extracurricular activities but that he could not represent them in public competition. Mark had participated in basketball, the school band and the Future Farmers organization. Mark sued the superintendent and school board for allegedly violating his rights. The defendants argued that they were not guilty of any unconstitutional acts for the following reasons:

1. Since students have no constitutional rights to participate in extracurricular activities as opposed to academic programs, a school can impose hair policy as a condition of participation.

2. The band director and the FFA advisor asserted that judges in band and FFA contests might take long hair into consideration in marking down the school in general appearance.

3. The basketball coach claimed that long hair can interfere with one's play on the basketball court.

4. The football coach declared that a hair policy was necessary in building successful teams, in that it contributed to the discipline, dedication and unity of team members.[10]

The United States District Court, Northwest Division, relied on *Bishop v. Colaw,* in which the Eighth

---

10. *Id.*

Circuit Court maintained that a student in public high school has the protection of the Constitution to govern his appearance.[11] It recognized, however, that "personal freedoms are not absolute, they must yield when they intrude upon the freedoms of others." But the court noted that school officials had the obligation of "proving that they are protecting the educational purpose of the school when they infringe upon a student's freedom."[12]

In this case, the court criticized the defendants' argument that extracurricular participation was a privilege and not a right. It reasoned that while the school could deny Mark participation in the activities, the question of privilege versus right was not the issue. Instead the complaint centered, in the view of the court, around the fact that the school infringed on the plaintiff's right to determine his own appearance.

The court disregarded the arguments that the FFA's performance in competition would be graded down because some of the students had long hair. Neither the band director nor the director of the FFA could give any specific instances to support their contention that points had ever been taken away in competition for this reason. Even if points could be deducted, the court reasoned that the plaintiff could comb his hair under his band cap or wear a short-hair wig if necessary.

The basketball coach admitted that the plaintiff's hair was not objectionable but remarked that it did violate the school's hair code and declared that "the line had to be drawn somewhere." He agreed that Mark could solve the problem by wearing a hair band.

---

11. *Supra* note 1.
12. *Supra* note 1.

The football coach emphasized what has become one of the traditional arguments by coaches who justify appearance codes by insisting:

> If everyone sacrifices the right to determine his own appearance, the team will be that much more dedicated and unified. Teamwork will be enhanced. Everyone on the team will feel equal and become more integrated into the team. The team will have a high morale and be more spirited.

The coach continued:

> On the other hand, if someone can get away with breaking a rule, the other team members will lose respect for the coach and question why they themselves should sacrifice for the team. *Thus the rule becomes more important than its actual content.* (Emphasis added.)[13]

The court considered this statement as highly speculative and denounced the over-emphasis on winning that prevails in sports. It maintained that:

> Winning should not be the "be-all and end-all." And it certainly should not be of more importance in the educational process than the teaching of toleration of individual differences.

The United States District Court, Northwest Division, then supported the opinion that athletics and discipline are as important as rules of health are to training. But the court explained that while a coach must be obeyed without question during competition, there is a limit to a coach's right to control the lives of his team members. It stressed that:

> A coach may not demand obedience to a rule which does not in some way further other

13. *Supra* note 9.

proper objectives of participation and performance. It is bootstrap reasoning indeed to say that disobedience of any rule weakens the coach's authority or shows a lack of desire on the part of the competitor thus justifying obedience to any rule however arbitrary.[14]

The court explained that any reasonable rule that advances an educational purpose should be obeyed but contended that an arbitrary one could not be tolerated. It concluded that the school superintendent and School Board failed to justify the "hair rule" and could not, therefore, prohibit the plaintiff from participation in public and interscholastic competition.

The lingering problem regarding "hairstyles" and sports participation is complex and while various courts see it differently, questions continue to arise concerning the issue, such as:

1. Can school authorities legally prohibit a student who fails to comply with "hair" codes from participation in sports?

2. Is the right of a student to wear any particular "hairstyle" a right protected by the Federal Constitution?

3. Do the courts or school authorities have the right to decide the "hairstyle" issue?

A Pennsylvania case presents the "hairstyle" dilemma as well as any, and clearly raises the most troublesome aspect of the problem as it comes before the courts.

Brent Zeller was not allowed to participate in high school soccer because he refused to comply with the school's "hairstyle" regulation. Zeller charged

---

14. *Supra* note 9.

discrimination on the part of the soccer coach, athletic director, school superintendent and School District and sued all of them.[15]

The United States Court of Appeals for the Third Circuit researched a number of earlier cases as it struggled to answer the various legal questions that were raised during the trial. The court referred to the flood of cases involving section 1983 of the Civil Rights Act of 1871. The court noted that the proliferation of cases regarding the charge that federally guaranteed rights were violated was becoming so cumbersome that the number of cases might be compared to branches of a tree that could cause the tree to topple by its weight.

In turn, the weight of so many cases might seriously dilute the protections of the Constitution. It reflected that:

> We have a genuine fear of "trivialization" of the Constitution. If this should occur, some of the monumental accomplishments in defining human rights and liberties may be compromised, and the protections accorded those rights and liberties threatened.

The court then concluded that it wanted schools, not courts, to handle the question of "hair" codes by expressing the following opinion:

> The federal court system is ill-equipped to make value judgments on hair lengths in terms of the Constitution — whether an athletic code requiring that hair be "neatly trimmed" would not pass muster, whether one putting the limit on hair twelve inches below the collar would pass, or whether one drawing the line at four

---

15. *Supra* note 2.

inches below the collar would be a more
difficult decision.

The Pennsylvania Court made a final statement that
appears representative of the attitudes expressed by
those courts that steadfastly maintain that "hair codes"
have no place before the federal bench:

> There are areas of state school regulations in
> which the federal courts should not intrude . . .
> we conclude that student hair cases fall on the
> side where the wisdom and experience of school
> authorities must be deemed superior and
> preferable to the federal judiciary's. We decline
> to cast our conclusion in the form of a neat
> stylized label — to pitch our decisions into the
> jurisprudential pigeonhole of abstention.[16]

It then affirmed the school's hair code.

Former Secretary of Health, Education and Welfare,
Joseph Califano, in a statement regarding Title IX,
emphasized that issues such as hair and dress are local
in nature and should be left to the discretion of local
officials. Califano commented that:

> We are today also publishing for public
> comment an amendment to the Title IX
> regulation that would take HEW out of the
> business of examining the rules imposed by
> local authorities on the way students may dress
> or wear their hair. The purpose of this action is
> to keep the federal government out of issues
> most Americans feel are handled with more
> common sense at the local level.[17]

It appears that hair code cases will continue to plague
athletes, coaches and school officials until the courts

---

16. *Supra* note 2.
17. Joseph Califano, *Title IX Guidelines Propose Equal
    Expenditures,* BUSINESS OFFICER, Jan. 1979.

find agreement on the problem and set standards that will serve as a guide for all to follow.

Marital Status

Many married students are often denied the opportunity to participate in extracurricular activities, including athletics. These students view such a prohibition as discriminatory and a violation of their rights.

For years school officials have attempted to limit teen-age marriages, and, in some instances, marriages of athletes at the collegiate level. The number of outstanding collegiate athletes who were married soon broke down the barriers that existed in the fifties and early sixties and coaches changed their rules to meet the times.

School boards in high schools, however, continue to set restrictions against sports participation for married athletes in the hope that this policy will be a deterrent to marriages.

A. Landmark Case in Texas

The case of Jerry Kissick in the Garland Public High School in Texas probably was the landmark case regarding a married athlete's attempt to participate in sports.[18] The case and decision have been used by courts to guide them in similar situations.

The Garland Independent School District adopted a regulation that was designed to discourage teen-age marriages with the restriction that:

> married students or previously married students to be restricted wholly to classroom

---

18. Kissick v. Garland Independent School Dist., 330 S.W.2d 708 (Tex. Civ. App. 1959).

work; that they be barred from participating in athletics or other positions of honor. Academic honors such as valedictorian and salutatorian are excepted.

Jerry Kissick was a high school football player who at the age of 16 married a 15-year-old girl. He testified that he planned to continue to play football with the hope of obtaining a college scholarship for his athletic ability. He charged that the school district issued a rule which was retroactive and thereby unreasonable and discriminatory.

The court considered the fact that a year before the rule was put into effect 62 students were married. One-half of the group dropped at least ten points in their academic grade average while 24 did not return to school or dropped out during the year.

The Texas court voted to uphold the Garland School District's regulation. It reasoned that:

> Boards of Education rather than courts are charged with the important and difficult duty of operating the public schools ... the Court's duty, regardless of its personal views, is to uphold the Board's regulations unless they are viewed as being arbitrary or unreasonable.

B. Texas Revisited

Edward Bell was excluded from football because the School District had a regulation that prohibited married students from taking part in extracurricular activities.[19] Bell sought a temporary injunction and when this was denied, appealed the case to the Court of Civil Appeals in Texas.

---

19. Bell v. Lone Oak Independent School Dist., 507 S.W.2d 636 (Tex. Civ. App. 1974).

Bell argued that the rule is "arbitrary and sets up an unreasonable classification that is invalid under 42 U.S.C.A. section 1983 and the Fourteenth Amendment to the Federal Constitution." Part of the rule states:

> The married student cannot be elected to an office, or if already elected, must resign; cannot be appointed to an office; cannot participate in athletics, pep squad, class plays, social events such as junior-senior banquet, football banquet, etc., must take a full schedule and participate in classroom activities without undue absences.

Bell claimed that the rule above sets up a special category of students who are treated in a different manner than the rest of the students. The court commented that:

> If the same rule provided that a particular race or color of person would be ineligible to play football, the state courts and the federal courts would promptly strike the rule down as being discriminatory towards a class of individuals. The same logic applies to married students' participation in extra-curricular activities.

The court made some important statements that will no doubt set standards for future cases. It pointed out that the state as public policy encourages marriage rather than "living together unmarried." Yet, it commented, here was a rule that actually punishes "a student for entering into a status authorized and sanctioned by the laws of this state."

It also declared that it was taking the opposite position from the landmark case of Kissick.

The Texas court then made some pertinent observations when it said:

> It may be that an education is not a guaranteed right under our Federal Constitution. It may

further be that a school cannot constitutionally be required to provide a student with an athletic program, but if the state and local school provide free public education and an athletic program, it must do so in a manner not calculated to discriminate against a class of individuals who will be treated differently from the remainder of the students, unless the school district can show that such a rule is a necessary restraint to promote a compelling state interest.

It asserted that it could not argue with *Kissick,* but ruled instead that the trial court was in error for failing to issue Bell a temporary injunction. It enjoined the Lone Oak Independent School District from excluding Edward Bell from the football team because he was married.

Justice Cornelius concurred with the decision and added some worthwhile comments that courts should be able to base future decisions on when similar cases come before them. He compared the present issue to use of highways in declaring:

It may be conceded that a state has not federal constitutional obligation to provide paved highways for its citizens, but having voluntarily provided paved highways for its citizens through the use of public funds and state action, the state cannot then exclude married persons from using such highways merely because they are married. Marital status has no rational relationship to the use of the highways.

Justice Cornelius believed that a school might prohibit some students from sports and be justified if such a rule applied to "size, the physical health, the age, the scholastic standing, etc.," but he insisted that:

There is no rational relation between the status of being married and participation in athletics.

The justice concluded:

> The United States Supreme Court has held that the right to marry subject to reasonable regulations by the state, is not only a constitutionally guaranteed right, but is a "fundamental constitutional right."

It is clear that the sentiments in *Kissick* barring married students from athletic participation have been struck down as a violation of Section 1983 of the Civil Rights Act. The issue may finally be resolved in other states, but from the judicial opinion in *Bell* it appears Texas may have settled the issue.

Sex — Title IX Regulations

For years women's sports has been relegated to a secondary position in many athletic programs on the secondary and collegiate level. In 1972 Title IX, Public Law 92-318 of the Education Act was enacted to provide equal opportunity in athletics for women. It stated:

> No person in the United States shall be excluded from participation in, be denied the benefit of, or be subjected to discrimination under any education program or activity receiving federal financial assistance ....[20]

Title IX received national attention because of the implications for women's sports. The advocates of Title IX realized that the statute would raise questions that might take months or even years to answer. They pointed out that some issues regarding scholarships or grants-in-aid, physical education and curricula might be

---

20. Public Law 92-318 of the Education Act of 1922.

so complex that they might only be resolved by court action.[21]

Casper Weinberger, the Secretary of Health, Education and Welfare in 1975, remarked that the Title IX regulations required institutions to offer equal opportunities in sports but not necessarily equal expenditures. He predicted that the statute would assist those institutions which were moving toward compliance in good faith and warned others that continued to discriminate against women:

> I have just one message: We can wait no longer. Equal education opportunity for women is the law of the land — and it will be enforced.[22]

Several key sections were interpreted by HEW officials because of their importance to sports. They included considerations such as:

1. Whether the sports selected reflect the interests and abilities of both sexes; provisions of supplies and equipment; game and practice schedules; travel and per diem allowances, coaching and academic tutoring opportunities and the assignment of pay to the coaches and tutors; lockerrooms, practice and competitive facilities; medical and training services, housing and dining facilities and services; publicity.

---

21. *NACUBO Special Report 75-4,* National Association of College and University Business Officers, Washington, D.C., June, 1975.
22. *Higher Education and National Affairs,* American Council on Education, Washington, D.C., Vol. XXIV, No. 23, June 6, 1975.

2. When selection is based on competitive skill or the activity involved is a contact sport, separate teams may be provided for males and females, or a single team may be provided which is open to both sexes.

3. If a school offers basketball for men and the only way the institution can accommodate the interests and abilities of women is by offering a separate basketball team for women, such a team must be provided.

4. If there are not enough women interested in a specific sport to have a separate women's team, the institution must allow women to compete for the men's team if the sport is a noncontact sport such as track. Women may be precluded from participating on a men's team in a particular sport. A school may preclude men or women from participating on teams for the other sex if athletic opportunities have not been limited in the past for them, regardless of whether the sport is contact or noncontact.

5. To the extent that a recipient awards athletic scholarships or grants-in-aid, it must provide reasonable opportunities for such awards for members of each sex in proportion to the number of students of each sex participating in interscholastic or intercollegiate athletics.[23]

Many women participants, encouraged by Title IX, sought judicial action to obtain equal opportunity in sports. Several cases indicate the variety of litigation that followed the 1972 Act.

The Supreme Court of Indiana examined a rule that prohibited girls and boys from playing on the same

---

23. *Id.*

team in high school or competing against each other in athletic contests against other schools. After it declared the Indiana High School Athletic Association's rule unconstitutional in *Haas v. South Bend Community School,* the association modified its rule to read:

> Girls may participate, with or against boys only when:
>
> 1. the school being attended does not have a girls' program in that sport and,
>
> 2. they follow the contest rules and season rules established for boys and limited to the girls' program in that sport.[24]

This 1972 decision was important for girls who wanted to compete in sports that were previously unavailable to them.

In another Indiana case, Elizabeth Ruman attended Munster High School which had a girls' tennis team as well as a boys' team.[25] Ruman instituted a lawsuit to compel the high school to let her try out for the boys' tennis team and if she qualified, to play on the boys' team.

The Lake Superior Court denied her request for a preliminary injunction and Ruman appealed the decision. The Court of Appeals of Indiana, Third District, also turned down her petition. The court found that the rule classifying girls was not a violation of equal protection guarantees as was the original rule in *Haas v. South Bend.*[26] The court noted that Munster

---

24. Haas v. South Bend Community School Corp., 289 N.E.2d 495 (Ind. 1972).
25. Ruman v. Eskew, 333 N.E.2d 138 (Ind. App. 1975).
26. *Supra* note 24.

High School provided tennis teams for both girls and boys. It held that the high school complied with the modified rules of the Indiana High School Athletic Association.

Many cases, like the two above, went before the courts in various states. The majority allowed girls on a boys' team if a team was not provided for girls. Most states objected to girls participating on boys' teams in contact sports and the courts usually supported their objection.

In 1978, however, Carl Rubin, an Ohio judge, in a widely publicized decision, supported the efforts of two girls to play on the boys' basketball team.[27] The facts of the case are interesting and will undoubtedly be cited by future litigants.

Two girls tried out and made the boys' high school basketball team but the Board refused to let them play. Instead the Board created a girls' basketball team so the girls could play interscholastic basketball.

Judge Rubin disagreed with the action of the Board and stated:

> Although some women are physically unfit to participate with boys in contact sports, it does not "necessarily and universally" follow that all women suffer similar disabilities. Babe Didrikson could have made anybody's team. Accordingly, school girls who so desire, must be given the opportunity to demonstrate that the presumption created by the rule is invalid. They must be given the opportunity to compete with boys in interscholastic contact sports if they are physically qualified.

---

27. Yellow Springs Exempted Village School Dist. Bd. of Educ. v. Ohio High School Athletic Ass'n, 443 F. Supp. 753 (S.D. Ohio W.D. 1978).

Rubin and the United States District Court (S.D. Ohio) reasoned that the rules that prohibit girls from trying out for mixed gender competition go beyond the state level and are unconstitutional. It then commented:

> It has always been traditional that "boys play football and girls are cheerleaders." Why so? Where is it written that girls may not, if suitably qualified, play football? There may be a multitude of reasons why a girl may elect not to do so. Reasons of stature or weight or reasons of temperament, motivation or interest. This is a matter of personal choice. But a prohibition without exception based upon sex is not.

The court and Judge Rubin viewed such a practice as unfair and a violation of the provisions of the Fourteenth Amendment declaring:

> It may well be that there is a student today in an Ohio high school who lacks only the proper coaching and training to become the greatest quarterback in professional football history. Of course the odds are astronomical against her, but isn't she entitled to a fair chance to try?[28]

The court then denied the defendants' motions and ordered the Association to permit the girls to compete on the boys' team without punishment or sanctions against the school and coach.

Susan Leffel and Nina Kelly sought a permanent injunction against the Wisconsin Interscholastic Athletic Association (WIAA) and their school officials to prevent them from enforcing a regulation that prohibited them from participating on the boys' teams

---

28. *Id.*

in interscholastic athletics.[29] The girls claimed that the WIAA regulation violated their right of equal protection under the Fourteenth Amendment. The girls were granted permission to institute the suit as a class action, representing the female students at De Pere High School who wanted to participate in baseball, but the school did not sponsor a girls' team and denied them the opportunity to go out for the boys' baseball team.

The class action suit also represented females at Washington High School who were not permitted to qualify with the male students for the varsity swim and tennis team. There was a swim team for the female students, but no girls' tennis team.

After Title IX was enacted into law, the WIAA modified its rules to read:

> The Board of Control shall prohibit all types of interscholastic activity involving boys and girls competing with each other except:
>
> a. *as prescribed by state and federal law*
> b. *as determined by Board of Control's interpretations of such law.*

The defendants contended that their regulations complied with Title IX and that they would be valid unless Title IX is ruled unconstitutional.

The United States District Court did not agree with the defendants and declared that:

> Title IX merely created an administrative remedy, subject to judicial review to enforce the prohibition of sex discrimination in educational programs receiving federal financial assistance.

---

29. Leffel v. Wisconsin Interscholastic Athletic Ass'n, 444 F. Supp. 1117 (E.D. Wisc. 1978).

It remarked that Title IX does not limit the individual's right to sue when the Fourteenth Amendment is violated. The court viewed the issues as follows:

1. Have the defendants violated the equal protection clause by denying female high school students the opportunity to qualify for a position on a boys varsity interscholastic team engaged in a contact sport where no separate team is provided for girls, or where the separate team does not have a comparable program?

2. Does the equal protection clause of the Fourteenth Amendment require that female high school students be permitted to attempt to qualify for a position on a boys' varsity interscholastic team where the boys team has a higher level of competition than the corresponding girls' team?

The court reasoned that the WIAA's rule, while not intentionally imposed on the girls did, nevertheless, treat girls differently than boys and thereby violated the equal protection clause of the Fourteenth Amendment.

On the issue of contact sports, the court referred to *Craig v. Boren* in which the U.S. Supreme Court set the standard for gender classification when it declared:

Classification by gender must serve important governmental objectives and must be substantially related to achievement of those objectives.[30]

---

30. Craig v. Boren, 429 U.S. 190, 97 S. Ct. 451, 50 L.ed.2d 397 (1976).

In the instant case, the defendants argued that its governmental objective was the prevention of injury to the female athlete because of the anatomical and physiological differences between boys and girls. The plaintiffs responded that this reasoning was "too weak to withstand equal protection scrutiny." [31] The court agreed that the exclusion of girls from all contact sports did violate the Fourteenth Amendment. It offered three remedies for the WIAA to eliminate discrimination:

1. provide coeducational teams
2. drop all varsity interscholastic competition
3. establish separate girls' teams for contact sports with programs comparable to the boys'

The court conceded that the state public high schools are not compelled by the Constitution to provide interscholastic competition in athletics. But, it commented:

> If they choose to do so, this educational opportunity must be provided to all on equal terms. [32]

It insisted that the school officials and the WIAA may not afford an educational opportunity for boys that is not available or denied the girls. The court, therefore, granted the plaintiffs summary judgment and ordered the defendants not to exclude the plaintiffs and the class they represent from participation in any varsity sport that is open to boys. [33]

---

31. *Supra* note 29.
32. Brown v. Board of Educ. of Topeka, 347 U.S. 483, 74 S. Ct. 686, 98 L.ed. 873 (1954).
33. *Supra* note 29.

Sex and the Rules of the Game

In addition to cases in which females sue to obtain equal opportunities in sports competition, another issue has been raised in the courts. The difference in rules for boys and girls in a particular sport has been the object of recent lawsuits.

Victoria Ann Cape, a high school junior at Oak Ridge High School in Tennessee, sued the state athletic association for promulgating separate rules for girls' basketball.[34] Tennessee was one of five states that failed to adopt the National Federation of State High School Athletic Association's rules which are modeled after standard rules for boys in which the game is played on a full court.

Cape insisted that split court rules hampered her possibilities of obtaining an athletic scholarship and the trial court concurred by stating that:

> There was no national relationship between the limited state objectives and the chosen sex-based classifications.

The Tennessee Secondary School Athletic Association appealed the trial court's decision to a higher court.

The United States Court of Appeals for the Sixth Circuit reviewed the testimony and, particularly, the Association's claim that the rules it adopted for girls were necessary:

1. To protect those student[s] who are weaker and incapable of playing the full-court game from hurting themselves.

2. To provide the opportunity for more student athletes to play in basketball games.

---

34. Cape v. Tennessee Secondary School Athletic Ass'n, 563 F.2d 793 (6th Cir. 1977).

3. To provide the opportunity for awkward and clumsy student athletes to play in basketball games.

4. To provide a "more interesting" and "faster" game for the fans.

5. To ensure continued crowd support and attendance (gate receipts) because these fans are accustomed to a split-court game.

Cape contended that the rules violated her rights of equal protection guaranteed under the Fourteenth Amendment of the Federal Constitution. The United States Court of Appeals did not agree with the plaintiff, nor the decision of the lower court, because it thought that there was a physical difference between males and females which is "reflected in the sport of basketball by how the game itself is played." The court also made a statement which will surely be challenged by many men and women alike when it observed:

It takes little imagination to realize that were play and competition not separated by sex, the great bulk of the females would be quickly eliminated from participation and denied any meaningful opportunity for athletic involvement.

The court then reversed the district court's decision by emphasizing that it found no evidence of discrimination in the rules and suggested that Cape work within the Association to resolve issues of this nature. It concluded:

Since there are such differences in physical characteristics and capabilities, we see no reason why the rules governing play cannot be tailored to accommodate them without running afoul of the Equal Protection Clause.[35]

In a similar case, Cheryl Jones, a female basketball player in Oklahoma, challenged the Oklahoma Secondary School Activities Association (OSSAA) in court because it provided a different set of rules for the girls than for the boys.[36] She argued that the difference in rules prevented her from receiving the necessary opportunity to promote her skills so that she could obtain a college scholarship or use the skills as a professional basketball player. Jones sought a temporary and permanent injunction by claiming that the difference in rules constituted a violation of 42 U.S.C. 1983 and the Fourteenth Amendment of the United States Constitution. She also contended that playing half-court basketball deprived her of fun and kept her from setting up plays, fast breaking and taking part in the strategy of the sport.

The OSSAA pointed out that 1209 high school girls' basketball players disagreed with her petition and wanted it defeated. The defendants also declared that Jones failed to seek administrative review and could, therefore, not avail herself of the protection of Title IX.

The United States District Court (W.D. Oklahoma) noted that physical education in Oklahoma is provided on an elective basis. Students who elect physical education in grades seven through twelve meet for 150 minutes per week. Some schools are larger than others and are able to offer opportunities in tennis and swimming because they are able to provide tennis

---

35. *Id.*
36. Jones v. Oklahoma Secondary School Activities Ass'n, 453 F. Supp. 150 (W.D. Okla. 1977).

courts and swimming pools. Smaller schools are unable
to provide such facilities and often cannot provide its
students with sports such as football because of limited
student enrollment. Although these students are denied
certain activities, it is illogical to rule that they are
denied equal protection under the law or that the
schools must build tennis courts, swimming pools or
provide the opportunity for certain sports such as
football. The court noted that, like the plaintiff, these
students will also be deprived of the chance to develop
skills in some sports that are available to others in the
state. The court cautioned that:

> *Brown v. Board of Education of Topeka* cannot
> and must not be stretched to such lengths as to
> require every program, every rule, every
> facility and every policy in every school to be
> the same.

The court observed that every school in the state will
sponsor a girls' basketball team during the school year.
The OSSAA claimed that this participation satisfies the
requirement of *Brown* since the opportunity for
participation in basketball is open to all. The court
emphasized that:

> It will not recognize a violation of constitutional
> rights when based upon an athletes' assigned
> position on a team or when an athlete disagrees
> with his/her coach.

It stated that while Oklahoma's rules may be out of
step with those in other states and may not necessarily
be in the best interest of the girls, nevertheless, it felt
that the judgment of those "who play, coach and
administer interscholastic basketball, and not the
federal court" should make the decision on what rules
to use. It, therefore, favored the OSSAA.

Governor Robert Ray of Iowa angrily replied to a request by HEW to review Iowa's girls' basketball rules to determine if they were discriminatory. Ray declared:

> We get a total of $25 million from Title IX (federal school programs) and they think they can order anything and everything from Washington.[37]

Iowa, like Tennessee and Oklahoma, maintains six-girl basketball which requires three girls to play offense on one half of the court and the other three to play defense on the other half. Opponents of the six-girl rule contend that the rule prevents girls from developing skills that would prepare them for college, professional or international basketball. As such they believe it is discriminatory.

Governor Ray disagreed and pointed out that more girls participate in basketball in Iowa than boys. He urged HEW officials to come to Iowa to watch the girls' state tournament. He also suggested with tongue in cheek that:

> Maybe they should require boys to play six-man basketball so they could be equal to girls.[38]

Equal Per Capita Expenditures

On December 6, 1978, then HEW Secretary Joseph Califano declared that women in sports still fail to receive a "fair share of athletic resources, services and benefits." [39] Califano observed that the number of women participating in sports continues to grow despite the inequities they receive. He pointed out that while

---

37. The Raleigh News and Observer, July 1, 1978.
38. *Supra* note 17.
39. *Supra* note 17.

the enrollment of women in college increased 39% from 1971 to 1976, the number of women participating in intramural and intercollegiate sports actually increased 100% in the same period. In a statement intended to clarify the Title IX regulations, Califano stated:

First, there must be equal expenditure of money per person involved in intercollegiate athletics.
Second, there must be comparable standards set where there are elements that are not easily measurable.
Third, colleges must have policies and procedures for upgrading women's athletics such as showing how they will upgrade [any] women's club team to a varsity team.[40]

Jean Peeler, an attorney for HEW, in an attempt to further clarify the equal per capita expenditure provision explained that:

If a college gives out 95 full athletic scholarships to men for football, the guidelines do not mean that college must also give out 95 full scholarships to women.

Peeler continued by saying:

It does mean, however, that if a college has 200 male varsity athletes and spends $200,000 on scholarships for an average of $1,000 per scholarship per male athlete, that college must spend an average of $1,000 on athletic scholarships for women. So, if that college has 50 women in varsity sports it must spend $50,000 on women's athletic scholarships.

Also, if a college spends $300 for each football helmet that does not mean it must spend a

---

40. *Id.*

similar amount for a piece of equipment for
women. But it does mean that if tennis racquets
cost $40 each, a college with women's tennis
must spend the money to make racquets as
available to the women as the helmets are to the
football players.[41]

Margaret Polivy, legal counsel for AIAW, approves
of the equal per capita/comparability standard, but
questions the suggested justifications included in the
regulation that poses ambiguities which:

> may be perceived by some as loopholes to
> effectively exempt any nonlegitimate expenses
> of some sports which are not required or
> justified by the nature of the sport. For
> example, differences justified by 'nature,'
> 'scope,' or 'level' of competition could easily be
> used to justify continued inequity to female
> student athletes.[42]

Polivy separates "financially measureable" items
such as scholarships, recruitment, equipment and
supplies, travel and per diem, publicity, etc." from
"financially unmeasurable" items. She includes among
these:

1. Opportunity to compete and practice
   (facilities and game schedules must be
   equally convenient for men and women).
2. Opportunity to receive coaching (ratio of full
   time coaches or equivalent is substantially
   equal for men and women) and academic
   tutoring (available on a nondiscriminatory
   basis).

---

41. *Supra* note 17.
42. *HEW Proposed Policy Interpretations of Title IX,* National
    Association for Girls and Women in Sport, Washington,
    D.C., Dec. 7, 1978.

3. Provision of locker room; practice and competitive facilities (may either share time on existing facilities or upgrade women's facilities).

4. Provision of medical training services and facilities (insurance may vary by sport but must offer similar benefits to men and women; medical and training services and facilities must be available to both); and

5. Provision of housing and dining services and facilities (separate dorms may be provided men but not women and vice versa but cannot offer additional services or benefits to one but not the other).[43]

Polivy listed the basic concept for compliance to the athletic regulations of Title IX when an institution can show that it:

1. "has eliminated discrimination in financial support and other benefits and opportunities in its existing athletic program; and

2. "follows an institutional policy that includes procedures and standards for developing an athletic program that provides equal opportunities for men and women to accommodate their interests and abilities." [44]

Califano made it clear that revenue sports such as football are not exempt from the regulations. He remarked that the various attempts to eliminate revenue-producing sports from the guidelines have consistently failed. He promised a policy that is "both

---

43. *Id.*
44. *Supra* note 42.

practical and consistent with the law" and concluded that "once a final interpretation is issued, we intend to enforce it." [45]

Patricia Harris replaced Califano as Secretary of Health, Education and Welfare in August, 1979. The controversy over the equal per capita interpretation of Title IX continues without resolution. The United States Commission on Civil Rights changed its position after receiving new information. The commission now recommends that:

> Colleges and universities be required to spend the same amount per athlete for male and female sports programs.[46]

Terry Sanford, the president of Duke University, offered a counter-proposal for Title IX compliance that has the support of over 138 colleges and universities. Sanford's plan attempts to place the responsibility for Title IX compliance upon the individual institution. See Appendix C for the Alternative for Title IX Compliance.

On December 4, 1979, Patricia Harris, Secretary of HEW, issued the long-awaited policy interpretation of Title IX as it relates to intercollegiate athletics. Harris admitted that the guidelines are "not writ in stone" and promised to be the first to admit it if they do not serve the purpose intended and change the policy.[47]

---

45. *Supra* note 17.
46. *The Chronicle of Higher Education,* Sept. 17, 1979.
47. *HEW News,* U.S. Dept. of HEW, Washington, D.C., Dec. 4, 1979. The Policy Interpretation can be found in Appendix H.

IN MY OPINION

Although we thought the issues of married athletes and "hairstyles" in sports were dead, they refuse to go away. We want clear, definitive judicial decisions to base our rules on but the courts simply refuse to grant us this luxury. Some courts prefer to pass the problem back to the local school districts for resolution while others insist that regulations that restrict individual freedoms are legitimate matters for the courts to consider. These issues will continue to plague us, but probably at a reduced level as the courts in various parts of the nation continue to treat them with little uniformity.

Sex discrimination in sports poses various questions that instantly raise emotions ranging from lavish praise to biting criticism. It is interesting to note that both Secretaries of Health, Education and Welfare, Casper Weinberger in 1972, and Joseph Califano in 1978, vowed to enforce Title IX since it was the "law of the land." To date, not one institution has been denied one dollar although 600 schools have been charged with non-compliance with the Title IX regulations.

On December 6, 1978, Califano hit the sports world with his bombshell interpretation of Title IX that demands "equal per capita expenditure" for men and women to achieve compliance. His statement was intended to clarify the already confused regulations, but merely touched off nationwide debate. The National Collegiate Athletic Association (NCAA) led the opposition to the "per capita" funding by charging that the Department of Health, Education and Welfare (HEW) was illegally interpreting the regulations. The NCAA pointed out that Secretary Weinberger declared in 1972 that "equal opportunity" not equal expenditure was all that Title IX required. The critics of Title IX's latest interpretation join the NCAA in deploring HEW's apparent unwillingness to recognize the enormous burden the regulation puts on institutions already beset with financial problems. Some sports authorities predict that compliance to the "equal per capita expenditure" interpretation will cost the 726 NCAA member schools anywhere from $60,000,000 to a quarter of a billion dollars per year. Opponents of "per capita" regulations insist that the law should not include sports programs since they do not receive federal funds, but other federally supported programs in the schools instead.

Both critics and proponents of Title IX agree on one thing — the law is written in a manner that invites loopholes and inconsistencies. They claim that the regulations contain words that are ambiguous and confusing such as "nature," "scope," or "level" of competition. They argue that straight talk and clear regulations could be understood and would be obeyed.

Weinberger and Califano both admitted that the issues in Title IX are so complex that court action would be needed to set the parameters for compliance. It appears that this will happen when the final interpretations are made and the courts will be filled with Title IX litigation.

Most school officials claim that they have attempted to meet the guidelines of Title IX in good faith. They deplore the vagueness and lack of clarity in the regulations that prevent compliance based on understanding. In addition, the students who sought redress for alleged violations wonder how long it will take HEW and the Office of Civil Rights (OCR) to investigate and penalize violators of the law.

Patricia Harris summarized the Policy Interpretation of Title IX as it pertains to intercollegiate athletics. The announcement surprised and disappointed many people who expected strict per capita requirements. The interpretation appeared to be the result of more than 700 comments from "representatives of colleges and athletic associations." The interpretation seems to take into account the diverse views of the various groups and reflects a flexibility that will be welcomed by many groups. The emphasis is not on equal per capita expenditures in all aspects of the sports program but rather on equitable measures to provide opportunities for all athletes.

The emphasis is on financial athletic assistance. In Harris' words:

> If 70 percent of a school's athletes are male, they are entitled to 70 percent of the financial aid dollars their school makes available.

An institution has flexibility in determining its program as long as it can justify that its rationale is based on nondiscriminatory factors.

The next few years will determine the effectiveness of the regulations as measured by HEW's ability and determination to enforce the law. Sports participants everywhere are waiting, the battle lines are drawn, and the courts are waiting to settle the issue, if needed, so we can get on with the game.

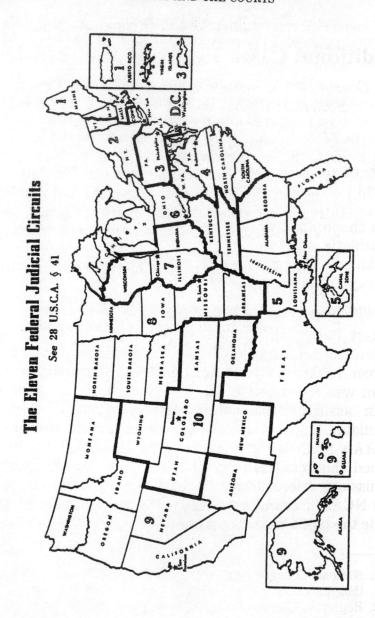

Legal Research, Writing and Analysis: Some Starting Points, William P. Statsky, West Publishing Co., St. Paul, Minnesota, 1974.

CHAPTER 5

Additional Cases Involving the Athlete

*Courts cannot make rules to govern amateur
athletics; all they can do is apply legal
precedents to rules promulgated by
associations involved.*[1]

There are a number of unusual cases relating to the
sports participant that, while not listed in a particular
category, have an important effect on sports litigation.
This chapter will review judicial decisions that pertain
to athletic scholarships, athletic-related injuries and
workmen's compensation, eligibility, the right to
privacy and defamation of character.

Scholarships

Mark Begley, an outstanding Tennessee High School
athlete, signed an athletic grant to play basketball at
Mercer University in Macon, Georgia.[2] The four year
grant was worth $11,208.00.

An assistant basketball coach at the university
calculated Begley's average to be sufficient to meet the
NCAA's predicted grade point average of 1.6. Begley
signed his contract in January, but in July an
admissions officer found an error in his point average.
The NCAA's average was based on a maximum of 4.0
while the boy's high school operated on the basis of 8.0.

1. National Collegiate Athletic Ass'n v. Gillard, 352 So. 2d 1072
   (Mo. 1977).
2. Begley v. Corporation of Mercer Univ., 367 F. Supp. 908
   (E.D. Tenn. 1973).

The university informed Begley that he did not qualify for the scholarship and he sued for damages. The contract had been signed in Tennessee and came under its state laws. The United States District Court declared:

> It is ... the rule where one party is unable to perform his part of the contract, he cannot be entitled to the performance of the contract by another party.

Since Begley could not meet the guidelines of the NCAA, the court dismissed the case against the University and any subsequent liability.

Gregg Taylor signed a grant-in-aid contract to play football at Wake Forest University.[3] Taylor signed the agreement to remain eligible under Conference and institutional rules. The agreement, in like manner, protected the athlete, if injured, from severance of the grant.

Wake Forest University did not have a written policy on grants-in-aid at the time Taylor signed the Conference contract, but a policy was adopted soon afterwards. A statement was included in the policy that required attendance at practice to keep a grant-in-aid. The athletic director testified that such a regulation had been part of athletic policy for the thirty years the school had granted athletic scholarships.

A review of the facts in the case revealed the following information. Gregg Taylor entered Wake Forest and played football that fall. After the first semester, his academic average dropped below the standard required by the university.

---

3. Taylor v. Wake Forest Univ., 191 S.E.2d 379 (N.C. 1972).

Gregg decided to forego spring football practice so he could bring his grade point average, based on a 4.0 scale, up to the acceptable standard. He notified his football coach of his plans and succeeded in attaining a 1.9 average which was well beyond the 1.35 average required the freshman year.

Gregg then decided to pass up football during the fall season of his sophomore year and achieved a 2.4 average. He did not report for spring practice his sophomore year either and was notified that his refusal to participate in football would be reviewed by the Faculty Athletic Committee. The committee recommended that his grant be terminated and the scholarship committee approved this action. His grant was therefore terminated at the end of his sophomore year.

Gregg returned to Wake Forest for his junior and senior years and graduated in 1971. He and his father sued the University to recover the $5,500 which they claimed was the cost of his final two years. The plaintiffs contended that participation in football hindered Gregg's academic progress and declared that he acted "in good faith in refusing to participate in the football program."

The North Carolina Court of Appeals upheld the action taken by the university. It believed that Wake Forest kept its part of the contract, but Gregg did not. It noted that he was not injured and could have met his obligations. Failing to do so was a violation of the agreement he signed.

Athletic Injuries and Workmen's Compensation

Although there are only a few cases on record involving athletic injuries and subsequent action for workmen's compensation, the potential for litigation is present under certain conditions. John C. Weistart, Professor of Law at Duke University, and Cym H. Lowell, a member of the Georgia Bar, point out in *The Law of Sports* that a collegiate athlete should not be classified as an "employee" of an institution because he or she receives some type of financial aid.[4] They admit, however, that an athlete may become an "employee" and eligible for workmen's compensation benefits if he or she enters into a relationship with an institution in which athletic service is exchanged for financial aid.[5] Three cases relating to football injuries present different aspects to sport injuries and claims for workmen's compensation benefits.

Ernest Nemeth sustained an injury while participating in football at the University of Denver.[6] At the time he was injured, Nemeth was employed by the university to work on the tennis courts which were located on campus. He ate all his meals in the school cafeteria and the cost of the meals was deducted from the amount of money he was paid for the campus job. As payment for his room on campus, Nemeth worked in the boiler room and cleaned the sidewalks. Nemeth and other athletes were paid monthly while regular students received hourly wages for work at the stadium or field house.

Nemeth injured his back during spring football practice and contended that he was entitled to benefits under workmen's compensation since he was allowed to

---

4. JOHN C. WEISTART AND CYM H. LOWELL, LAW OF SPORTS, Bobbs-Merrill Co., Inc., Indianapolis, Ind., 1979.
5. *Id.*
6. University of Denver v. Nemeth, 257 P.2d 423 (Colo. 1953).

take time off from his job to practice football. The University's attorney disputed Nemeth's claim that he was employed for football by insisting that Nemeth's job was to "keep the tennis courts free from gravel and litter." The attorney stated that Nemeth received "free meals and a job" because he was a student and not because he played football.

Witnesses at the trial reported that it was common knowledge that the students who excelled in football got the meal tickets and jobs. The football coach supported their testimony by freely admitting that any player who was cut from the squad immediately lost his meal ticket and campus job.

The Supreme Court of Colorado commented that the University was engaged in big business since its enrollment numbered over ten thousand students and it employed hundreds of workers. It ruled that Nemeth's injury did result from his employment and he was therefore entitled to the benefits of workmen's compensation.

Ray Dennison, playing his first football game for Fort Lewis A&M, was fatally injured against Trinidad State Junior College.[7]

Dennison was employed at a local service station on a part-time basis while he was attending college. The school's football coach offered him a campus job that would pay him the same salary but enable him to play football. Dennison eagerly accepted the job, which required 20 hours of work a week and allowed him the time necessary to play.

---

7. State Compensation Ins. Fund v. Industrial Comm'n, 314 P.2d 288 (Colo. 1957).

The football coach indicated that Dennison was not under a contract to play football nor was his job related to his ability as a player. He testified at the trial:

> Ray wanted to play football and he had a job at a filling station that would require more time. I asked him if he could get a job that would make him as much as he made at the filling station at different hours, would he play football and he said yes.

Unlike Nemeth in the previous case, Dennison's job did not depend on his ability to play football; he merely substituted jobs so he could pursue a sport he enjoyed.

The lower court awarded Dennison's widow workmen's compensation benefits but the Supreme Court of Colorado reversed the decision. The higher court held that since an employer-employee relationship did not exist, no claim could be made. It expressed its sentiments regarding sports injuries and subsequent claims for workmen's compensation when it asserted:

> The burden is always on the claimant to establish to a reasonable certainty that the accident arose out of and in the course of employment. We cannot believe that the legislature, in creating the compensation fund, intended that it be in the nature of a pension fund for all student athletes attending our state educational institutions.

Edward Van Horn was returning from Ohio to California on an airplane after participating in an intercollegiate football game for California State Polytechnic College.[8] The airplane crashed and Van Horn was killed.

---

8. Van Horn v. Industrial Accident Comm'n, 33 Cal. Rptr. 109 (Cal. App. 1963).

Van Horn's widow and her children sought payment under the Workmen's Compensation Act and the question raised by the court was whether he was an employee of the college because he received an athletic scholarship to play football.

The Industrial Accident Commission denied death benefits because it did not believe that a recipient of an athletic scholarship was providing services within the guidelines of the Workmen's Compensation Act. The plaintiffs appealed the decision to the District Court of Appeal, Second District, Division I, California.

During the trial the coach testified that the college's Booster Club contributed money for the athletic department to use for its athletes. The coach reported that he tried to give financial help to the married athletes so that the cost of off campus housing could be equalized to that of the athletes living on campus. An athlete was required to maintain a 2.2 grade average and enroll for 12 units to receive financial assistance.

The plaintiffs claimed that the deceased had entered into a contract of employment with the college when he agreed to accept a football scholarship. The defendants argued that the deceased voluntarily played football and the scholarship was merely a gift.

The court did not agree with the commission's finding that the scholarship was awarded for the entire year and could not be taken away even if the athlete failed to participate in sports. It declared that a person could only receive a scholarship if he was on the team and recommended by the coach. It also disagreed with the commission's conclusion that it would be detrimental to public policy to impose such a burden on a college to protect its scholarship athletes by Workmen's Compensation. Instead, the court declared that:

> The Workmen's Compensation Act is, in effect, a socially-enforced bargain which compels an employee to give up his valuable right to sue in the courts for full recovery of damages under common-law theories in return for a certain, but limited award.

It also commented:

> The theory of the compensation act as to death cases is that the dependents of the employee killed through some hazard of his employment shall be compensated for the loss of the support they were receiving from him at the time of his death.

It therefore annulled the order and remanded it back to the commission for further action.

In *Nemeth* and *Van Horn* the court found that a contractual relationship existed between the athletes and their institutions. The courts, therefore, declared that the athletes were eligible for Workmen's Compensation benefits. In Ray Dennison's case, however, the Colorado court took an opposite view of the situation. It held that the institution had not compensated him to play football and therefore denied his widow benefits under the Workmen's Compensation Act.[9]

Eligibility

A. Overage Athlete

Edgar Barrett III, playing for New Hanover High School of Wilmington, North Carolina, collided with an

---

9. *Supra* note 4.

opposing player from Rose High School of Greenville, North Carolina.[10] Barrett died from the injury he received in the game.

The father of the deceased accused the school authorities of negligence in filing an eligibility list that contained an error which ultimately caused the death of his son. The boy who collided with his son was 20 years of age; ineligible to participate in sports under the rules of the state athletic association and the State Department of Public Instruction.

The Superior Court of Pitt County granted the defendants summary judgment and the plaintiff appealed. Justice Martin of the North Carolina Court of Appeals explained summary judgment when he said:

> The purpose of summary judgment can be summarized as being a device to bring litigation to an early decision on the merits without the delay and expense of a trial where it can be readily demonstrated that no material facts are in issue.

The trial court did not believe that the defendant's incorrect filing of the ineligibility list was the proximate cause of the boy's injury and resulting death. It granted the defendants summary judgment and its decision was upheld by the court of appeals.

B. Red-Shirting in High School

Patrick Murtaugh was prohibited from participating in high school sports because he had attended school for more than eight semesters.[11] Murtaugh and his father

---

10. Barrett v. Phillips, 223 S.E.2d 918 (N.C. App. 1976).
11. Murtaugh v. Nyquist, 358 N.Y.S.2d 595 (N.Y. Sup. Ct. 1974).

took the case to court, alleging that the rule in question was arbitrary. The rule provides that a boy could be eligible for participation in sports for only eight semesters from the time he entered the ninth grade. It allowed an exception for "illness, accident or other such circumstances acceptable to the league or section."

The rule was put in to prevent "red-shirting," the practice of holding an athlete back for one grade so he can compete his fifth year when he is older and supposedly stronger. The rule makers were afraid that a student who "red-shirted" possibly could injure a younger student.

Since Murtaugh did not meet the criteria for an exception for an illness or accident, the Supreme Court, Special Term, Sullivan County, decided that the regulation was reasonable and not arbitrary and favored the school authorities.

C. Rule Violation

Larry Gillard, a football player at Mississippi State University, bought clothes at a one third discount at a Mississippi clothing store. The discount was arranged by a friend of the athletic department. His actions subsequently were included among 20 accusations of rule violation directed at the Mississippi State University's Athletic Department.[12]

The NCAA notified the athletic department that it was under investigation and it made every effort to observe due process in its dealings with the university. It invited the school's officials to attend the hearings and extended the same invitation to Gillard.

---

12. *Supra* note 1.

After the hearings, Gillard was declared ineligible for future participation in football at the university. Football Coach Bob Tyler acknowledged that the alumnus involved in the infractions had been informed that he had to break all relationships with Mississippi State's athletic program. Tyler then explained that Gillard was unaware that he was doing anything illegal and made a special appeal to the NCAA committee to consider the following:

> With the burden of the total penalty imposed on our program, i.e., probation, loss of scholarships, admonishment of coaches, severance of alumni, the loss of a young man from the squad simply adds greater difficulty to restructuring goals and morale in connection with our squad. On behalf of this fine young athlete, I feel that his future as a football player and as a student would be greatly damaged.

The NCAA considered the letter and notified Tyler that Gillard would be ineligible for only the remainder of the 1975 year (his sophomore year). The committee stipulated that Gillard not lose his scholarship or any benefits he was presently receiving. It advised Tyler that he and the university could appeal the decision, but no appeal was made.

The day after Gillard received notification of the NCAA's ruling, he filed for an injunction in the Chancery Court of Oktibbeha County. Along with the officials of Mississippi University, he alleged that his rights had been violated by the NCAA. The chancellor (judge) issued a writ of injunction which ordered the NCAA not to interfere with Gillard's participation in intercollegiate athletics. The chancellor stated that Gillard's right to participate in athletics was "constitutionally protected" and the NCAA had violated that right. He declared that:

> The internal rules, regulations and operations of the association could be voided by the court because Gillard personally, was not a member of the association.

Gillard was then granted a permanent injunction which enabled him to play football his final two years at the university. The NCAA appealed the decision.

The Supreme Court of Mississippi reviewed the facts and referred to several important cases that were relevant to the present case. It listed several key points in these cases:

1. the privilege of participating in inter-scholastic athletics must be deemed to fall . . . outside the protection of due process.[13]
2. engaging in extra-curricular activities is a privilege which may be claimed only in accordance with the standards set up for participation.[14]
3. participation in interscholastic athletics is not a property right but a privilege.[15]

The court emphasized that Gillard's rights were protected, but that the university failed to take advantage of the remedies available to it when it refused to appeal every NCAA decision.

It stated that the university should have pursued administrative remedies before it went to court.

---

13. Parish v. National Collegiate Athletic Ass'n, 506 F.2d 1028 (5th Cir. 1975).
14. Scott v. Kilpatrick, 237 So. 2d 652 (Ala. 1970).
15. 68 Am. Jur. 2d *Schools,* § 244.

The supreme court then reversed the lower court's ruling by concluding:

> the courts cannot "make rules" to govern amateur athletics. All we can do is to apply legal precedents to the rules promulgated by the associations involved.[16]

D. "Educational Exploitation"

Eight athletes threatened legal action against their basketball coach and California State University at Los Angeles for alleged "educational exploitation." [17] The athletes entered the university under a special program for minority students. They are seeking awards of $14 million for what they claim are abuses that include the following charges:

1. They were directed to enroll in courses such as "Theory of Basketball" and "Backpacking" to remain academically eligible for sports participation.
2. Their athletic scholarships were in reality loans which they were required to pay back.
3. The state withheld their income tax when they refused to pay their loans.
4. The institution refused to send their transcripts to other schools until they paid the loans.
5. The basketball coach arranged to have a person take the college board examination for one of the athletes.
6. One of the players was told to play under a false name because he was reportedly ineligible to play under his own name.

---

16. *Supra* note 1.
17. The Los Angeles Times, Mar. 28, 1979.

The university denied all the allegations as did the basketball coach who termed the charges "180 degrees wrong." The coach had taken the coaching job at California State University at Los Angeles when the program was at a low point. He had only two and one-half basketball scholarships while his competitors had between 12-18 grants each. The coach wanted to improve his program and sought alumni support for scholarships. He even cashed in his high school retirement and used the $9,000 for scholarships. In addition he used the money he made for teaching a course and operating a summer camp to supplement the scholarship fund. He hoped to build a winning program that would attract alumni interest and result in the financial backing of his basketball program. The team's record improved considerably and it participated in the NCAA Western Regionals playoffs. For various reasons the program deteriorated and the alumni support he sought failed to come. In 1978 the coach resigned in apparent frustration and disappointment. He commented when he resigned:

> I had attempted to resign a year earlier. I was very tired, I guess would be the word . . . When the season was over I was not eager to go out and recruit to replace the athletes I had lost. The thought of having to go out six or seven nights a week, to go to your house, to your house, to your house, to attempt to convince you and your youngsters that our place would be the place for them to go to, just got to the point that I wasn't interested in doing it any more.

On the other hand, the attorney for the athletes characterized the situation as a "classic kind of exploitation" and one that has made the athletes victims of wasting from four to six years of their lives. One of the athletes, who was suspended from the team and described by the coach as wanting to get back at him, declared:

> I'm not in this for money or for any vindication of myself but to put college sports back into proper perspective.[18]

Right of Privacy

Joe Namath, former star quarterback for the New York Jets, claimed that Time Incorporated, publisher of *Sports Illustrated,* violated his rights to privacy by using his photograph to promote the sale of subscriptions.[19] Namath sued for $2,250,000 in damages.

During the trial Namath testified that he received income "in excess of several hundred thousand dollars" for endorsing various commercial products. He admitted that his photograph was used on many occasions and that he did not object to its use by newspapers and magazines. However, he argued, he was denied substantial revenue by the publishers of *Sports Illustrated,* who used his photograph without first obtaining his written permission.

The Supreme Court, Special Term, New York County considered the facts and observed that:

> plaintiff seeks damages, not for violation of his right of privacy but because he was deprived of substantial income from a property right. He earns substantial income for endorsement of

---

18. *Id.*
19. Namath v. Sports Illustrated, 363 N.Y.S.2d 276 (N.Y. Sup. Ct. 1975).

many products. The contention is that this
defendant should not be permitted to use his
name or photograph without his written
consent and without remuneration to him.

The court then agreed that it understood the
plaintiff's desire to be paid for advertisements that use
his name or photograph to sell subscriptions but noted
that:

This he cannot accomplish under the existing
law of our state and Nation. Athletic prowess is
much admired and well paid in this country. It
is commendable that freedom of speech and the
press under the First Amendment transcends
the right to privacy. This is so particularly when
a petitioner seeks remuneration for what is
basically a property right — not a right to
privacy.

It dismissed the case.

Defamation of Character

The late Neil Johnston, a professional basketball
player for the Philadelphia Warriors, sued the publisher
of *Sports Illustrated* for a statement in its publication
which he charged damaged his career as a coach.[20]

Sports Illustrated selects a "Sportsman of the Year"
annually and in this particular year it honored Bill
Russell of the Boston Celtics. George Plimpton, a well
known feature writer, wrote an article on Russell. In
the article, Plimpton interviewed Arnold "Red"
Auerbach, who coached Russell, and quoted Auerbach
as follows:

That's a word you can use about him — he
(Russell) destroyed players, you take Neil

---

20. Time, Inc. v. Johnston, 448 F.2d 378 (4th Cir. 1971).

Johnston — Russell destroyed him. He destroyed him psychologically as well, so that he practically ran him out of organized basketball.

Johnston was coaching basketball at Wake Forest University and, when the article was published, sued for libel, charging that the article injured his career as a basketball coach.

The United States Court of Appeals used the case of *New York Times v. Sullivan*[21] to interpret the "constitutional rule of privilege." On the basis of the *New York Times* decision, the court agreed that the plaintiff (Johnston) was a public figure and that the alleged defamatory article was related to legitimate public interest. Public figures were described as:

Those persons who, though not public officials, are involved in issues in which the public has a justified interest, and includes artists, athletes, business people, dilettantes, anyone who is famous or infamous because of who he is or what he has done.

The court of appeals then added the following people to the list of public figures:

A college athletic director, a basketball coach, a professional boxer and a professional baseball player.

Johnston recognized that he was a public figure at the time he played basketball, but declared that the article was written twelve years after the event took place. He failed to see how he could be considered a public figure

---

21. New York Times Co. v. Sullivan, 376 U.S. 254, 84 S. Ct. 710, 11 L.ed.2d 686 (1964).

when he was no longer playing basketball and argued
that the *New York Times* criteria no longer protected
the publisher.

The court disagreed when it observed that the
passing of time does not necessarily change the status
of a public figure. In fact, it said:

> No rule of repose exists to inhibit speech
> relating to the public career of a public figure
> so long as newsworthiness and public interest
> attach to events in such public career.[22]

It concluded that Johnston was still a public figure
and the article involving Russell's selection as
Sportsman of the Year an event of public interest. It
commented that a publisher can seek the protection of
New York Times:

> So long as the press correctly quotes another's
> statement about a matter of legitimate public
> interest, does not truncate or distort it in any
> way, and properly identifies the source.[23]

It ruled that the article did meet these specifications
and as such was not libelous. It dismissed the case in
favor of the magazine and its publishers.

IN MY OPINION

It is clear that the overwhelming number of cases
pertaining to sports litigation centers around the
participant who seems willing to sue for almost any
reason.

---

22. *Supra* note 17.
23. *Supra* note 17.

Arnold Beisser, in *The Madness in Sports,* characterizes society's attitude toward the present-day sports participant by commenting:

> These modern-day gladiators continue to be idolized and imitated, their comments serving as potent forces for selling everything from deodorants to political candidates.[24]

As such, sports participants often seek judicial redress when they feel that they are exploited for various reasons or criticized unfairly in the news media. The cases discussed in this chapter involving Joe Namath and the late Neil Johnston support Beisser's assessment of today's athlete. The courts, however, consider athletes to be public figures who are newsworthy. It seems that the courts tolerate unfavorable publicity because the athlete is of interest to the public as long as the statements are correctly quoted and the sources identified.

It appears that money will be the dominant factor in sports litigation. Collegiate athletes will, in all probability, continue to sue to gain or keep athletic scholarships. A new source of revenue for the injured scholarship athlete may be the little-heralded area of workmen's compensation. There seems to be very few cases involving collegiate athletics outside of the three mentioned in this chapter, but a case pending in Indiana may soon change this. The Indiana case involves a football player who was injured seriously during practice at Indiana State University. As a result of his injury, he is now a permanent quadriplegic. The student

------

24. ARNOLD BEISSER, THE MADNESS IN SPORTS, The Charles Press Publishers, Bowie, Md., 1977.

received a reported $15,000 from his athletic insurance at the University to apply toward his medical bills. Because of the high cost of medical treatment, he is seeking additional funds from workmen's compensation. As a scholarship athlete, he believes he is covered by its benefits. The case has been called a potential landmark case by sports authorities who predict that its outcome could possibly change the awarding of athletic scholarships as we now know them. It is still pending.

It may well be that judicial decisions will affect the athlete and the future of sports more than any other organization, coach, or rules that presently shape the athlete's welfare.

CHAPTER 6

The Administrator

Athletic directors can't win. They are asked to run a
$3-million business (an intercollegiate athletic pro-
gram may have, say 23 sports). And a recent
study showed that 97 percent of all universi-
ties operate athletics in the red. Imagine.
Twenty-three sports, 23 coaches, all
shouting for more, more, more
money.[1]

The individual or group of individuals that
administers sports are part of over five million people
who are charged with administrative duties.[2] The
responsibilities seem to increase each year and are
overwhelming in scope. Sports administrators are
accountable for the organization of the sports program,
the athlete's health, budgets, insurance, contracts,
eligibility, scheduling, crowd control, transportation,
officials and other endless lists of duties. For each area
of responsibility there are records of lawsuits in which
administrators are the defendants.

Sports administrators, other than the coach, include
the athletic director, the supervisor, principal, and, in
some instances, policy making groups such as the
school board or board of trustees. As a rule

---

1. ATHLETIC ADMINISTRATOR Vol. 13, No. 1, Fall 1978 National
   Association of Collegiate Directors of Athletes, Cleveland,
   Ohio.
2. Charles A. Buckner, ADMINISTRATION OF HEALTH AND
   PHYSICAL EDUCATION PROGRAMS INCLUDING ATHLETICS,
   5th ed., The C. V. Mosby Co., St. Louis, Mo., 1971.

administrators are generally one step away from direct contact with the athlete and manage to avoid liability. Occasionally the administrator may even be considered to be an officer and enjoy the protection of governmental immunity. However, they are usually treated as school employees and have little reason to be complacent with regard to liability for their own negligence and that of their subordinates. Some public school boards and boards of trustees on the college level are clothed in immunity regardless of the circumstances of the case in question.

While there is a trend away from the time-worn doctrine of immunity, courts and legislative bodies are reluctant to abrogate this traditional doctrine as long as the agency performs a function that can be viewed as governmental.

In Montana, a woman was injured when she fell on defective stairs on her way to the stands to watch a basketball game.[3] The Montana court decided that the school and administrators acted in a governmental capacity and were thereby protected by immunity from suit. The court commented that basketball was similar in the school program to debating societies, band concerts and art exhibits. The fact that admission was charged made little difference to the court.

One of the judges disagreed, wondering how a person could collect damages for an injury at a theatre but not for similar conditions at a basketball game. He pointed out that:

> Most of the states, in attempting to decrease the severity of the rule, have adopted the

---

3. Rhoades v. School Dist. No. 9, Roosevelt County, 142 P.2d 890 (Mont. 1943).

governmental-proprietary test. This test is an arbitrary one, but the general trend of the decisions is to declare more and more functions proprietary rather than governmental so as to allow recovery.[4]

Governmental Immunity Versus Proprietary Function

The question of whether an activity in sports qualified as a governmental or proprietary function was the issue in a tragic Michigan case in which one boy died and another was permanently disabled.[5] David Lovitt and Brian Cecil, two high school football players, were overcome by the heat during a strenuous practice session in July. The plaintiffs sued the football coaches for allegedly requiring the boys to practice strenuously when the weather was "particularly severe." They also sued the administrators for hiring the coaches and failing to properly supervise them. The trial court granted the defendants summary judgment and the plaintiffs appealed.

The plaintiffs contended that football was not a legitimate part of the school's physical education program since it became proprietary in nature when admission was charged for the games. The school's athletic director disputed this claim by testifying that the football program had operated at a deficit for the past five years.

The plaintiffs stated that they realized that the administrators could be protected by governmental immunity if the court upheld the doctrine and ruled that football was not a proprietary function. However, they

---

4. *Id.*
5. Lovitt v. Concord School Dist., 228 N.W.2d 479 (Mich. App. 1975).

argued that the football coaches could not share such protection. The Michigan Court of Appeals supported their contention. It found that the lower court erred when it favored the coaches and dismissed the case. It ruled, instead, that the administrators were not guilty of negligence but that the coaches had "violated a private duty to avoid negligently injuring these particular students." It therefore reversed the decision and remanded it back for a new trial. The case was settled before it came to trial for the amount of insurance coverage the plaintiffs had at the time of their injuries.

It has become common practice for schools to rent their facilities to outside groups for various fees. Some do this as a gesture of good will while others attempt to gain revenue. The question of liability frequently arises when an individual leasing the facility is injured.

In Kansas an elderly woman entered a school building her organization had rented.[6] The building was dark and she fell down the unlighted stairs in the community center. She sued the school's administrators for negligence in causing her injuries.

The Board of Education had a written policy that permitted individuals or groups to use the building for a small fee. In this instance only $3.00 was charged.

Once again the question of governmental versus proprietary function became the issue. The court referred to a previous Kansas case in which it was said:

> When there is an activity or function in a
> private or proprietary capacity for the special

---

6. Smith v. Board of Educ. of Caney School Dist. No. 34, 464 P.2d 571 (Kan. 1970).

or immediate profit, benefit, or advantage of
the city or town, or the people who compose it,
rather than for the public at large, then the city
or town is in competition with private enterprise
and is accountable for the torts of its employees
the same as any private corporation or
individual.[7]

The court considered the above rule and found that a
$3.00 rental fee could not be interpreted as a
"commercial enterprise." It then made a timely
comment that has implications for schools that permit
outside organizations to rent its facilities when it said:

> We must not place a too narrow restriction on
> the use of school buildings. They are occupied
> little enough during the course of a year. School
> buildings are maintained for educational
> purposes. Education embraces either mental,
> moral or physical powers and faculties.
> Education is not limited to children. The middle
> aged or the aged may also benefit. We would
> not say that a school board encouraging, or a
> school building used for, debate societies,
> musicals, home makers, home demonstrations,
> etc. is extending activities beyond those
> anticipated in our schools and educational
> system insofar as the activities do not interfere
> with the usual educational program and are not
> commercial in nature.

It therefore affirmed the lower court's ruling in favor
of the school and the administrator.

Charitable Immunity

Charitable immunity applies to private institutions
and is similar to governmental immunity. The majority

---

7. Stolp v. Arkansas City, 303 P.2d 123 (Kan. 1956).

of colleges and universities have been deemed to be charitable in nature in the past. There is a trend, however, toward the abrogation of the doctrine of charitable immunity, but it is not widespread at this time. The courts have the problem of determining whether a college or university qualifies for immunity.

William Bodard was a student at Culver-Stockton College in Missouri.[8] Culver-Stockton was a church-related four-year institution. Bodard assisted the athletic department by voluntarily marking lines on the athletic fields. Bodard sued the college when caustic lime stored in a dispenser without a top "expelled into his eyes causing an injury." The court dismissed the case and Bodard appealed to the Supreme Court of Missouri.

Culver-Stockton had enjoyed the protection of charitable immunity throughout the years, but the State of Missouri abrogated the doctrine after the injury to the plaintiff. The plaintiff argued that the abrogation of the doctrine was "substantive and not procedural" and should not be applied to his case. He also pointed out that since the college had taken out liability insurance it could not claim the protection of immunity. Finally, he argued, charitable immunity did not apply in his case since the uncovered lime represented a nuisance leaving the college vulnerable to suit.

The Supreme Court of Missouri did not support the plaintiff's contentions. It reasoned that the college was engaged in educational pursuits and athletics was part of the student activities. The students did not pay the

---

8. Bodard v. Culver-Stockton College, 471 S.W.2d 253 (Mo. 1971).

full cost of their education and therefore the college could not be in a business enterprise removing its charitable status.

On the plaintiff's claim that the storing of lime in a container without a top constituted a nuisance, the court defined a nuisance as:

> A condition and not an act or failure to act by the person responsible for the condition and it does not depend on the degree of care used, but rather on the danger, indecency or offensiveness existing or resulting even with the best of care.

It held that a nuisance did not exist and it affirmed the judgment of the lower court in dismissing the charges against the college.

Rules and Regulations

Today's athletes often resent regulations restricting their freedom. As a result, the administrator is in a difficult position when rules of conduct are challenged by athletes and their parents.

A Nebraska case attracted nationwide attention when five senior athletes were expelled from the boys' and girls' basketball teams for violating training rules.[9] The athletes sought and received a permanent injunction prohibiting the school from denying them participation on the teams. The school officials appealed the case and school people everywhere waited for the decision to learn what guidelines the court would set regarding good conduct rules and extracurricular participation.

By the time the case came to court the athletes had graduated from high school and tried to get the case

---

9. Braesch v. DePasquale, 265 N.W.2d 842 (Neb. 1978).

dismissed since it was *moot*. The school officials refused to drop the case because the issue involved was of such great public interest. The court agreed and decided to hear the case.

Three boys and two girls were seniors at Arlington High School in Nebraska. Before the basketball season began the respective coaches required each student and their parents to sign a statement that read as follows:

> DRINKING, SMOKING OR DRUGS: Do not come out for basketball if you plan on using any of the above. Any use of them will result in the immediate expulsion from the squad.

The five students and at least one or more of their parents signed the statement.

On a Saturday evening during the season the five students were at a party with other students who were not on the basketball teams. The five athletes drank liquor at the party. Several days later the boys' basketball coach heard about the party and called his players in to discuss it. When the boys admitted they broke the training rules, he consulted with his principal and then dismissed the players from the team. He met with the boys, the principal and the parents and then excluded them from future participation. The principal supported his action and then informed the players and their parents that a letter would follow confirming the decision.

The girls' basketball coach then met with the two girls involved in the incident and they admitted that they also drank alcoholic beverages at the party in violation of the rule. The principal followed the same procedure as he did with the boys.

The athletes and their parents were notified by letter that they could file an appeal. The plaintiffs initially requested a hearing, but then elected instead to bypass it for a court hearing. They were granted a restraining order prohibiting the school officials from excluding them from participating with their respective basketball teams. The district court changed the temporary injunction to a permanent one a month later stating that the students had a "constitutional right protected by the due process clause of the state and federal constitutions" to participate in interscholastic basketball.

The Supreme Court of Nebraska realized that the issue involved was important to many people and made an exception to hear it contending:

> In the context of disciplinary action in the field of interscholastic athletic competition, almost no case could reach this court for decision before it became moot if we refused to decide all cases where no actual controversy still exists between the parties at the time of appellate hearing and decision.

The court noted that recent decisions varied regarding the question of whether athletic participation was a privilege or a constitutional right. It recognized the fact that while the state of Nebraska provided students with the opportunity to engage in athletics, there were far less constitutional decisions concerning sports than academic programs. It raised the question of whether the school, in light of constitutional implications, could legitimately deny the students the opportunity to participate in sports. The court then considered whether the defendants had observed due process and referred to the *Goss v. Lopez* [10] case in

10. Goss v. Lopez, 419 U.S. 565, 95 S. Ct. 729, 42 L.ed.2d 725 (1975).

which the United States Supreme Court set guidelines for suspending students for disciplinary reasons. In *Goss* the Supreme Court held that a student subject to suspension be given due process that included:

> oral or written notice of the charges against him, and, if he denies them, an explanation of the evidence the authorities have and an opportunity to explain his side of the story.

It is obvious, the court concluded, that expulsion from athletics requires no additional provisions. The Nebraska Supreme Court then reviewed the administrator's action toward due process in this case and remarked that:

1. The plaintiffs had specific advance notice of the rule of conduct involved and notice of the date, time, and place of the violation charged.
2. Each of the plaintiffs admitted his or her violation of the rule.
3. In addition to the informal procedures and meetings, which met all rudimentary requirements of due process, the plaintiffs were given the right to appear at a formal hearing with a right to present evidence, cross examine witnesses, and be represented by counsel.

The court then commented that the plaintiffs ignored the school officials' effort to provide a hearing and chose instead to seek an injunction from the court. It reasoned that the plaintiffs could have presented their argument to the school board claiming that the rule was arbitrary and the penalty too severe. The board had the authority to reduce or change the penalty and, as such, the plaintiffs failed to exhaust their administrative remedies when it bypassed the board for the court. It then concluded that:

> The rule involved in this case, even though the penalty of expulsion for the season might be deemed severe by some persons, clearly serves a legitimate rational interest and directly affects the discipline of student athletes. It cannot be said that the prescribed penalty was an arbitrary and unreasonable means to attain the legitimate end of deterrence of the use of alcoholic liquor by student athletes.

It reversed the action of the district court in granting the athletes injunctive relief and favored the administration instead.

Insurance

The high cost of medical services for injured athletes has been a major concern of many sports administrators. Insurance representatives explain that public schools and colleges are not required to furnish medical insurance coverage to athletes. A problem arises, however, when an athlete is injured because someone employed by the school has been negligent. In this instance, insurance protection becomes important for the school. Some institutions provide insurance for its athletes, others act as a conduit so students can purchase insurance protection at their own cost, and others simply leave the problem to the parents and individual athletes.

While there seems to be a lack of litigation involving insurance claims and sports participation, a recent case is noteworthy for the questions it poses and the response of the court to questions raised.

Mark Friederich was a student at Mt. Carroll High School in Carroll County, Illinois and a member of the football team.[11] Friederich was injured in a football game and as a result sustained a permanent disability to the extent that:

> He will never throughout his lifetime, be able to engage in occupations requiring physical effort.

The school board had the discretion to purchase medical and hospital insurance, but chose to act as a conduit by which students participating in sports could obtain, at their own expense, medical protection.

The plaintiff declared that since he was required to buy insurance so he could participate in interscholastic athletics, the school board had the duty to:

1. Provide adequate insurance coverage.
2. Explain to the student athlete that disability insurance was not provided.

The Circuit Court of Carroll County denied his petition and favored the defendant whereby the plaintiff appealed the verdict to the Appellate Court of Illinois.

The appellate court reviewed the facts and maintained that the school board was not required to purchase insurance, but could merely act in a clerical capacity enabling the students to obtain coverage at their own expense. It doubted that the students could have purchased such medical coverage on their own. The court said:

> The procuring of medical and hospital insurance for the benefit of a student, and at his expense, appears to be one of many instances of an attempt by a public body to provide for a

---

11. Friederich v. Board of Educ. of Community Unit School Dist. # 304, Carroll County, 375 N.E.2d 141 (Ill. App. 1978).

possible contingency in a reasonable and economical way, without undue burden on the individual or his parents.

The court considered the plaintiff's allegation that the board had the obligation to furnish "adequate" insurance coverage. It felt that the word "adequate" was subjective and did not set a reasonable standard for the board to follow. Actually, it remarked, "adequate" depends on the particular need of an individual and this cannot be determined in advance. By plaintiff's contention, it surmised, "adequate" means "adequate in my case" which happens to be 1 million dollars.

The court dismissed the plaintiff's contention that the board owed each athlete an explanation that they did not have disability coverage. The court commented that the plaintiff was a senior in high school and should have understood the type and amount of coverage he bought. It agreed that the plaintiff was neither misinformed nor misled by the board regarding his insurance coverage. It therefore upheld the lower court's decision and dismissed the complaint.

Victoria Ann Shriver was a student at Kansas State University.[12] She went to a place that had been designated by the Athletic Council as the spot where tickets for the upcoming football game would be put on sale. She "crawled into a sleeping bag and settled in for a long wait." Suddenly, after a large crowd had gathered, an announcement came over a loudspeaker that the place to acquire tickets had been changed by the Athletic Council. The crowd immediately rushed toward the new site and the plaintiff was trampled on

---

12. Shriver v. Athletic Council of Kansas State Univ., 564 P.2d 451 (Kan. 1977).

and severely injured. The injured woman sued the Athletic Council for negligently causing her injuries. The court did not agree and granted the Athletic Council summary judgment. The plaintiff appealed the judgment to the Supreme Court of Kansas.

Two issues emerged that included the following:

1. Is the Athletic Council an instrumentality of the University, and, if so, does it enjoy governmental immunity?
2. If it is judged an instrumentality of the University, does the purchase of liability insurance waive its right to immunity?

The Supreme Court of Kansas considered the various facts such as:

1. The Athletic Council is operated as another department of the University.
2. Its funds are handled and administered by the University fiscal offices and are kept in the University's bank account.
3. The budget of the Council is prepared according to the same criteria as those in other University departments.
4. Its salary levels follow the same criteria as those in other departments of the University.
5. It is subject to the policy and control of the University.

The court concluded "that the Athletic Council is an instrumentality of Kansas State University" and is protected by governmental immunity according to the Kansas statutes. In addition, the court ruled that the Athletic Council had not waived immunity because it purchased liability insurance that was paid for with non-state funds. The statutes provided that governmental immunity could be waived, but only up to the limits of the insurance policy. As such, the Athletic Council cannot use the defense of immunity to prevent paying damages to a person who is injured because of its negligence. Instead, the plaintiff could collect damages up to the amount of the insurance if the court so ruled.

The court, therefore, reversed the lower court's decision in dismissing the case.

Discrimination

When previously segregated high schools integrated, many problems faced the administrators. The administrator was often charged with discrimination in hiring of personnel, the lack of equal budgets, salaries, etc. One of the less publicized issues that frequently developed was the argument over the selection of a symbol or mascot for the newly integrated school. In some instances the designated symbol became a highly explosive issue. Such was the situation that developed in Escambia High School in Escambia County, Florida.[13]

Escambia County was under a court order to desegregate its schools into a system operated on a non-racial basis. The court was delegated to oversee the operation of the school district. During 1972-1973, approximately four years after integration had begun, the school experienced serious disruptions involving interracial fighting. The police had to be summoned and they remained for the rest of the school year. The school was forced to close twice because of the racial tension that erupted.

---

13. Augustus v. School Bd. of Escambia County, Florida, 507 F.2d 152 (5th Cir. 1975).

Among the sources of discontent by the eight percent of the student body's black students were the symbol of the previously all-white school, the Confederate Battle Flag and the nickname of "Rebels." The student body had overwhelmingly voted in 1973 to use the symbol and nickname.

These symbols became the issue in court and the United States District Court for Northern Florida approved an injunction that prohibited the following:

1. The use of the name "Rebels."
2. The display of the Confederate Battle Flag on school premises with certain exceptions.
3. The wearing of the flag on the clothes of any student while the student attended a school-sponsored activity.

The court noted that the symbols had an "irritating" effect on the black students and increased existing tension between the races. The court conceded that the majority of white students did not associate the symbols with anti-black feeling, but viewed them as symbols of the high school only. It determined, however, that the continued use of the symbols would add to the tensions that were already present.

The court then considered several pertinent questions such as:

1. Should a federal court interfere with the day-to-day operation of schools?
2. Is it appropriate for a court to consider the name an athletic team chooses as its symbol?
3. Is it not more suitable for students rather than courts to select its symbols?
4. Should a minority obtain a court order to change a name and a symbol?

It was obvious that the overriding factor in the
situation was the violence and disruption that took place
at the school and the court's mandate to oversee the
operation of the school during the transition period.

The white students were upset by the court's action
and argued that their rights under the First and
Fourteenth Amendments had been violated. The court
referred to previous cases in which the courts were
consistent in ruling that students lose their First
Amendment guarantees when the exercise of that right
causes violence and disruption of the educational
process.[14]

The students also pointed out that the court
intervened before the school board could take action
itself. It also reminded the court that the school board
had adopted a policy that:

> prohibited the use of the involved symbols to
> harass or intimidate teachers or other students,
> directing their use and display only in good
> taste and directing the policy's enforcement
> and providing sufficient lawmen to protect all
> students.[15]

The district court recognized that the decision
banning the symbols did not curtail violence in the
school since two confrontations took place after the
injunction eliminating the symbols was made. The court
referred to a case in which a district court judge advised
school authorities to eliminate symbols that were
offensive to a racial majority. He cautioned the school

---

14. HERB APPENZELLER, ATHLETICS AND THE LAW, The Michie
    Co., Charlottesville, Va., 1975.
15. *Supra* note 13.

authorities that certain symbols were not appropriate for public institutions. He listed a few such as:

> The Nazi Swastika, the hammer and sickle, the hooded white-sheet of the Ku Klux Klan, the clenched fist, etc.[16]

The judge then made an interesting comment on the students' vote on the adoption of symbols when he caustically said:

> Tyranny by the majority is as onerous as tyranny by a select minority — An exercise in democracy which results in offense to a sizeable number of the participants should be carefully reconsidered by the student body.[17]

The United States Court of Appeals decided to modify the lower court's decision and send it back for reconsideration. It felt that the school board should be given the opportunity to devise a plan that would permit the court to avoid intervention into the daily operation of the school. It changed the permanent injunction to a temporary one until the case could be reviewed.

One of the judges took exception to the decision and made comments that are relevant to the problems administrators face in similar situations. He declared:

> When the federal courts undertake to regulate the conduct of students and spectators at football games, (such as cheering and pennant waving) and the nickname (the "Rebels") by which the team is called, in my opinion they have, indeed, strayed far beyond their

---

16. Banks v. Muncie Community Schools, 433 F.2d 292 (7th Cir. 1970).
17. *Id.*

constitutional functions and created a new kind
of tyranny, i.e. "tyranny of the courts." [18]

The judge also took exception to the action of a small
minority that can affect change through the courts. He
criticized such tactics when he viewed with alarm the
practice that enables:

> The will of the vast majority (concededly a
> "landslide student vote") to be overridden at
> the behest of a small minority (here less than
> eight percent of the students were black), then
> the concept of our so-called democratic system
> might as well be scrapped. If small minorities
> know they can attain their goal by saying "do
> thus and so because we find your actions
> offensive to us" and can obtain a federal
> injunction if the majority do not bend to their
> demands, then federal jurisdiction will have
> been stretched far beyond its intended
> constitutional limits. *Civil rights should mean
> civil rights for all — not merely for a militant
> or threatening minority.* (Emphasis added.)

The judge stated that he could see no logical
relationship between a unitary school system and the
athletic team's nickname or symbol. He pointed out that
sports has taken the lead in the advancement of
integration and he cited the racial makeup of teams in
sports to support his opinion. He concluded with a
stinging plea for the reversal of the court's injunction
by declaring:

> Until a local ordinance is enacted making it a
> misdemeanor for a spectator to give a
> spontaneous rebel yell after Escambia scores a
> touchdown or a court order decrees that only

---

18. *Supra* note 13.

United States marshalls be Escambia's
cheerleaders, I would prefer to remain on the
sidelines and let "1984" approach with dire
misgivings that the federal courts may
substitute themselves for "big brother" in that
prophetic novel fast becoming nonfiction.[19]

Administrative Organizations

Some of the major sports governing organizations
that administer amateur sports include the Amateur
Athletic Union (AAU), the Association for
Intercollegiate Athletics for Women (AIAW), the
National Intercollegiate Athletic Association (NAIA),
the National Junior College Athletic Association
(NCAA), the National Federation of State High School
Associations (NFSHA), and the various state high
school athletic associations.

Litigation involving these governing bodies seldom
challenges the actual playing rules of a particular sport,
but seems instead to concentrate on issues such as
discrimination, due process, eligibility, finances and
staffing. Most of these administrative or governing
organizations eventually go to court to defend some
regulation or practice promulgated by its group.

The following cases represent a sampling of cases
that come before the bar in the various states and
illustrate the types of issues that are currently decided
by the courts.

State High School Athletic Associations

The state high school athletic associations are
referred to by different names in the various states, but

---

19. *Supra* note 13.

their role is basically the same — the administration of high school sports on the state level. These associations devise rules and regulations to govern the sports programs on the state level and, as such, are quasi-legislative in nature. Traditionally, the courts prefer to let the associations administer the sports program without judicial interference unless they violate students' rights or act in an arbitrary or capricious manner.

A. Eligibility

The greatest number of cases relating to the state athletic associations deals with some aspect of eligibility. The following cases are typical of issues that come before the courts against the various state organizations.

1. Double Participation

Many high school athletes play on community, civic, or church teams at the same time they participate in interscholastic sports. One problem that surfaces is that some states prohibit participation by high school athletes on other teams under other sponsorship. The state of North Carolina recently abolished its rule against double participation because a large number of parents complained and state officials felt that the policy would not be upheld if taken to court.

Some state associations, however, continue to keep such rules and prefer to defend them in court. The following case illustrates what can happen in such instances.

The Louisiana High School Athletic Association (LHSAA) declared seventeen students ineligible for participation in baseball and the parents of eight of the students brought suit against the respective high schools and the LHSAA.[20] The students had been practicing with the Babe Ruth Baseball League while playing for their various high school teams. They were declared ineligible for one year and the games in which they played were forfeited and a fine levied on their particular school.

The president of the Babe Ruth Baseball League testified that many high school athletes had participated through the years in the league and admitted that he was unaware of the rule. Many high school baseball coaches watched the games, aware that the players were participating on a dual basis and one athlete testified that his coach actually encouraged him to play in the league.

The LHSAA Commissioner reported that the double participation rule had been in effect for twenty-five years and on the books in all fifty state athletic associations. He declared that the purpose of the rule was to curb excessive participation in sports to prevent problems in the students' academic area.

The 32nd Judicial District Court granted the students relief because:

> the affected players were misled by their coaches who allowed them to practice Babe Ruth [baseball] and play for their respective schools at the same time.... If any action should have been taken by LHSAA, it should have been directed against the schools, but not the innocent parties affected.

The LHSAA appealed the decision and the Court of Appeals of Louisiana, First Circuit, considered the question of whether the private association came under

---

20. Dumez v. Louisiana High School Athletic Ass'n, 334 So. 2d 494 (La. App. 1976).

state law. It noted that all the public schools that competed in sports were members of the LHSAA and that public funds supported the salaries of the coaches and the facilities. It commented that the question of whether the association was private and voluntary mattered little in this instance. The association came under state action whenever an individual alleged that his right of due process had been violated.

The court reasoned that the schools displayed posters in prominent locations explaining the regulations, thus meeting the due process requirement even if the coaches failed to inform the students of the rule. It disagreed with the lower court judge who felt that it was unfair to penalize the students and not the coaches, declaring:

> If this be proper grounds, then the hundreds of high school coaches in this state would render any rule utterly worthless. The interscholastic athletic arena would be reduced to a confused mass of participants without standards or limits.

The court reversed the lower court's decision and favored the LHSAA.

2. Non-Public Schools and State Athletic Associations

With the proliferation of non-public high schools in the different states, litigation often arises when these schools seek membership in the state associations. A case in Louisiana and one in Virginia point out the type of situation that may result in litigation.

In Louisiana, St. Augustine was an all-black private school that sought admission to the all-white LHSAA.[21]

---

21. Louisiana High School Athletic Ass'n v. St. Augustine High School, 396 F.2d 224 (5th Cir. 1968).

At the time, black schools were members of the Louisiana Interscholastic Athletic and Literary Organization. While St. Augustine did not have any white students, it had an admissions policy permitting qualified students of any race to attend. The United States District Court ordered the LHSAA to admit St. Augustine to its membership and the association appealed the decision.

The United States Court of Appeals affirmed the lower court's decision. It was apparent to the court that while the association had considerable power to regulate high school athletics, it could not deny membership to an all-black school such as St. Augustine. It concluded that once a school held membership in the association, its rights were protected by the Equal Protection Clause of the Fourteenth Amendment. The Louisiana court then made an interesting comment regarding similar athletic associations when it observed:

> The power of the Association reaches not only to the stadiums, the gymnasiums, and the lockerrooms, but into the public classrooms, the principal's office, and the public pocketbook.[22]

Denis O'Connell High School, a private school, brought suit against the Virginia High School League to gain admission to the league.[23] The league's constitution restricted membership to public schools. The United States District Court enjoined the league from denying the parochial school membership and the league appealed the decision.

---

22. *Id.*
23. Denis J. O'Connell High School v. Virginia High School League, 581 F.2d 81 (4th Cir. 1978).

O'Connell High School argued that the league's refusal to admit it to membership constituted a violation of its rights guaranteed by the Equal Protection Clause of the Fourteenth Amendment. It contended that its outstanding athletes were denied the opportunity to receive athletic scholarships because they could not compete in the league-sponsored tournaments. The league countered by claiming that while O'Connell High School had not been denied any federally protected right, its membership in the league would violate the Establishment Clause of the First Amendment. It also pointed out that the reason it limited membership to public schools was to enforce rules regarding transfer students.

The court of appeals stated that the United States Constitution does not guarantee the right of:

> education nor participation in interschool competition, nor the speculative possibility of acquiring an athletic scholarship, professional bonus or other endowment.

It disagreed with the decision of the lower court and supported the league instead. It contended that private schools can attract students from a wider area than the public schools and, if allowed to join the league would create transfer problems. The court reasoned that a student could choose a private or public school on the basis of its athletic program, in violation of the "spirit of the League." It believed that the LHSAA's transfer rule was adopted to prevent overeager coaches and fans from recruiting school children for their programs. The court referred to *Chabert v. LHSAA,* in which a Louisiana Court of Appeals decried such unethical recruiting practices by declaring:

Past history, and especially recent events, have shown the unconscionable actions to which some individuals will resort in order to insure themselves of a superior athletic program.

The court continued:

Illegal recruiting of promising young athletes is the gravamen of this recurring problem. Not only is the atmosphere of fair competition irreparably clouded, but many times the lives of the athletes themselves in that athletics becomes primary and academicism secondary under the overbearing scrutiny of those who would entice through illicit means.[24]

The court, in the instant case, reversed the district court's decision and favored the league instead. It believed that the opportunity of students to transfer to schools of their choice would increase the problems of recruiting if private schools could join the Virginia High School League.[25]

One justice dissented, concluding that the league did violate the Equal Protection Clause of the Fourteenth Amendment. He pointed out that in Louisiana the athletic association embraced both private and public schools in its membership and successfully enforced a no-transfer rule.[26]

A 17-year-old student at a private school in Texas was suspended from participation in sports for misconduct during a football game.[27] His school was operated by

---

24. Chabert v. Louisiana High School Athletic Ass'n, 312 So. 2d 343 (La. App. 1975).
25. *Supra* note 23.
26. *Supra* note 23.
27. Stock v. Texas Catholic Interscholastic League, 364 F. Supp. 362 (N.D. Tex. 1973).

the Catholic Diocese and was a member of the Texas Catholic Interscholastic League (TCIL). The TCIL had adopted the same rules for its members as the public schools association and the University Interscholastic League. Besides the student's prohibition from future sports participation, the TCIL declared the private school ineligible for district football honors the following year. The school appealed the TCIL decision as arbitrary. The TCIL modified its decision and allowed the student participation in winter and spring sports after the following football season. The participation was to be based on the student's principal and counselor's recommendation that he had improved in sportsmanship.

The student sued the TCIL, claiming that his right of due process had been violated. The United States District Court did not share his sentiments, observing instead that:

> Nowhere in the Constitution is there any guarantee of a right to play football. If that right exists, therefore, it is ancillary to some other right.[28]

It favored the TCIL and dismissed the case.

3. Transfer Students

Our society is characterized by mobility among its citizens. Students now transfer more often than in previous years. Many state athletic associations have rules that prevent a transfer student from engaging in sports immediately. This prohibition becomes an issue that is frequently litigated in court. Three cases demonstrate questions that are raised.

---

28. *Id.*

Leonard Chabert transferred to Vanderbilt School which was outside the parish in which he lived and was immediately declared ineligible for sports participation by the Louisiana High School Athletic Association for one year.[29] He sought a temporary injunction against the LHSAA and the 32nd Judicial District Court, Parish of Terrebonne, granted it. The LHSAA appealed the order.

The court of appeals considered a number of related transfer cases and concluded that such a rule was essential to prevent the evils associated with the unethical recruiting of high school and even grade school athletes. The court recognized that the rule had been in effect since 1920 and uniformly applied to all students. It rationalized that the rule was designed to curb recruiting ills by regulating transfers and although it imposed a hardship on the plaintiff, was not unconstitutional. It affirmed the lower court's decision reversing the order permitting the student to play and upheld the association's rule declaring him ineligible for one year.

John Albach challenged a New Mexico Activities Association's rule prohibiting a student from playing immediately when transferring from a home district to a boarding school and vice versa.[30] Albach charged the NMAA with promulgating a rule that violated his civil rights. The United States Court of Appeals found that sports participation is not a protected civil right unless the student's guaranteed rights are violated. It also decided that, whenever possible, the federal courts

---

29. *Supra* note 24.
30. Albach v. Odle, 531 F.2d 983 (10th Cir. 1976).

prefer that schools supervise and regulate their athletic programs. It therefore upheld the NMAA's transfer rule and dismissed the case.

Mark Neighbors and John Mozingo transferred to school in Salina, where they resided, and were declared ineligible by the Oklahoma Secondary School Activities Association.[31] The athletes sought and were granted an injunction that prevented the OSSAA from denying them the opportunity to participate in sports immediately. The OSSAA appealed the order.

The boys testified that they realized the intent of the rule was to eliminate unethical recruiting of athletes, but argued that they should be considered exceptions because they were not recruited. They also pointed to a provision in the association's bylaws that granted exceptions to the regulation when:

> it finds the rule fails to accomplish the purpose for which it is intended, or when the rule works an undue hardship on the student.

Claude White, the Association's Executive Secretary, responded that the rule was designed to maintain stability by requiring all students to meet the same standards. White opposed granting the plaintiffs an exception to the rule.

The Court of Appeals of Oklahoma referred to *Bruce v. South Carolina High School League* in which the Supreme Court of South Carolina upheld its state athletic association's transfer rule by emphasizing:

> There are no exceptions or qualifications, nor is there any discretion vested in League officials in its application. It applies to all schools and students alike — the merits of such a rule or the

---

31. Mozingo v. Oklahoma Secondary School Activities Ass'n, 575 P.2d 1379 (Okla. App. 1978).

wisdom of its adoption are not for the courts to determine.[32]

The Oklahoma court found no evidence of fraud or arbitrary action and reversed the trial court's decision to grant the students a temporary injunction. Instead it favored the OSSAA's regulations.

4. Hardship

Student athletes frequently seek exception to eligibility rules on the basis of hardship. Simon Terrell, the Executive Director of the North Carolina High School Athletic Association, reported that his association heard over 60 "hardship" cases over the years and waived about one half of the cases. He explained that the instances usually pertain to sickness or auto accidents where students have been advised to drop out of school.[33] Several cases are examples of hardship situations.

Leonard Smith's widowed mother became ill and he dropped out of the spring term at school to help at home.[34] He returned to school in the fall and took extra courses to make up the lost work. Smith participated in football, soccer and track and had hopes of obtaining a football scholarship to attend college. The Georgia High School Association ruled that he was ineligible under its rules, which limit participation in sports to four consecutive years or eight semesters.

The plaintiff contended that the rule denied him his guaranteed right to a free education under the Georgia

---

32. Bruce v. South Carolina High School League, 189 S.E.2d 817 (S.C. 1972).
33. Greensboro Daily News, Nov. 2, 1978.
34. Smith v. Crim, 240 S.E.2d 884 (Ga. 1977).

law. The Supreme Court of Georgia contested his argument, remarking that he had competed during his eligible years but now desired to have additional eligibility. In answer to Smith's claim that the rule violated his right of equal protection under the law, the court disagreed by explaining:

> Although the rule appears harsh in this case, the general goals of keeping high school interscholastic activities competitive and safe by allowing children of relatively equal maturity to compete, of insuring that as many children as possible are able to participate by limiting the number of eligible years for each student, and of protecting students from exploitation by coaches seeking to obtain transfers, to 'red shirt' or to delay a student's normal progress in school are met by the rule.[35]

It upheld the trial court's decision supporting the Georgia High School Association.

While the Georgia Supreme Court's decision is convincing, two Florida cases assume the opposite position and point out the position other courts may take in similar circumstances.

Dennis Lee attended school in California until the eleventh grade when he moved to Florida. Lee stayed out of school in Florida to support his family and, a year later, enrolled in Hialeah Miami Lakes High School. His principal informed him that he was ineligible for sports since Florida High School Activities Association (FHSAA) rules limit athletic participation to four consecutive years in high school.

Lee appealed to the FHSAA and based his case on hardship. He explained that he felt he could earn a

35. *Id.*

college athletic scholarship if he played his senior year. The FHSAA refused to grant Lee an exception and he sought judicial relief in court. The Court of Appeals of Florida, Third District, viewed the association's action as arbitrary and reversed the association's order that dismissed the student's complaint.[36]

In like manner, the District Court of Appeals of Florida affirmed a circuit court's order granting Aaron Bryant injunctive relief against the FHSAA's eligibility rule.[37] Bryant contended that participation in high school sports had improved his academic work and his "attitude, self-confidence, discipline and maturity." The court credited participation in sports with Bryant's rehabilitation from past problems. It concluded that "red-shirting" was not involved and therefore favored his participation in sports.

5. Out-of-Season Participation

Post-season play not sanctioned by state athletic association rules and summer camps that specialize in a particular sport are a constant source of litigation. Three cases, one regarding post-season play in New Hampshire, and camp cases in Missouri and Texas illustrate the problems that come before the courts.

George Hawksley, a senior at Groveton High School in New Hampshire, sought a court order to compete in soccer and basketball.[38] The issue related to Hawksley's participation in a basketball tournament sponsored by the Order of De Molay following the regular high school

---

36. Lee v. Florida High School Activities Ass'n, Inc., 291 So. 2d 636 (Fla. App. 1974).
37. Florida High School Activities Ass'n, Inc. v. Bryant, 313 So. 2d 57 (Fla. App. 1975).
38. Hawksley v. New Hampshire Interscholastic Athletic Ass'n, 285 A.2d 797 (N.H. 1971).

season. Hawksley testified that he played with the principal's knowledge and approval. The rules of the association, however, declared him ineligible for one calendar year.

The New Hampshire court did not believe a restraining order granting Hawksley permission to play was necessary because the regulation of one calendar year would terminate in December, making him eligible for basketball once again.

A Missouri court upheld the Missouri State High School Activities Association's rule declaring a student who attended a summer sports camp for more than two weeks ineligible for future high school participation.[39] The rule did not exclude the student from attending a generalized sports camp where several sports were taught, but only one that specialized in a particular sport for more than two weeks. The case was a notable one which set a precedent for other summer sports camp litigation.

In 1978 Greg Kite and his parents took exception with the University Interscholastic League's regulation that declared that he would lose eligibility for one year if he attended a basketball camp.[40]

Kite was an exceptional basketball player and an "A" student. At 6'11", he was regarded as one of the top scholastic basketball players in the United States. He planned a career in medicine and professional basketball and felt that the camp would enable him to meet those goals. Kite saved his money to attend the camp because he wanted the chance to play against other talented and tall players and to receive instruction

39. Art Gaines Baseball Camp, Inc. v. Houston, 500 S.W.2d 735 (Mo. App. 1973).
40. Kite v. Marshall, 454 F. Supp. 1347 (S.D. Texas 1978).

from NBA players such as Boston Celtic Dave Cowens and Houston's Rudy Tomjanovich. During the trial, testimony indicated that Kite would compete against more 7' tall players in one week than he could the entire year. Kite's parents supported his desire to attend the "Superstar" camp because they too believed it would help develop the skills necessary to obtain a college scholarship.

The United States District Court, S. D. Texas, considered a wide variety of judicial decisions pertaining to the question of an individual's rights under the constitution. It noted that the UIL was unique since it is "the only one of the 50 states with a rule so broad and prohibitory as the one here in issue."

The plaintiffs recognized the reason for this type of rule, which originally was designed to restrict activity such as that which occurred at a camp in Colorado where a high school basketball team spent a large part of the summer with the high school coach. The team had a very successful season following their summer experience. Many states, afraid of a "Colorado Summer," devised rules regarding summer camps to prevent similar situations from happening. However, most state associations permitted students to attend generalized sports camps or allowed attendance at a specialized camp for one week. Others did not object to attendance as long as the athlete's coach was not present at the camp.

The director of the UIL contended that educators, not courts, should change the summer camp rule. The court, however, granted Kite a temporary injunction enabling him to attend the camp without the threat of losing eligibility. It reasoned that to do otherwise would cause the athlete and his parents to suffer material harm. The

Texas court hoped, however, that the UIL would solve the problem before the case went to court for further intervention. It justified its decision when it stated:

> Certainly the right of a family to make decisions concerning the education of its own children is one of our most precious freedoms. The right of an individual to develop his talents to the utmost is one of our most precious freedoms.

It then concluded that:

> The fact that Texas is the only one of the 50 states which has adopted a rule as broad, pervasive and prohibitory as the Texas rule here under challenge is almost conclusive proof of fatal deficiency in that precision of regulation which is the touchstone where fundamental rights are involved.[41]

IN MY OPINION

It has often been said, and I tend to agree, that an administrator may be the loneliest person in the world. While the administrator faces pressures from many publics, a new adversary has entered the arena — the courts!

An athletic director, at a sports conference in Florida, listened to the confusing rhetoric of a session on Title IX. He became incensed and frustrated and suddenly jumped up and shouted over the microphone to the athletic directors:

> Your college presidents should fire all of you at once and replace you immediately with attorneys.

---

41. *Id.*

Consider the plight of two athletic directors, one in the Atlantic Coast Conference and the other in the "Big Ten" Conference who are representative of the typical sports administrator.

The athletic director in the "Big Ten" regretfully fired his football coach after a 5-6 season. The fact that he had three consecutive winning seasons meant little when the attendance at home games dwindled to less than 40,000. The athletic director admitted that a 6-5 season could not have saved the coach's job unless a bowl bid went with it. He lamented the fact that economic factors dictated such action.

The other athletic director is a widely respected administrator who works hard to keep his program competitive in the prestigious Atlantic Coast Conference. From 1972 until 1978, his time and energy have been diverted by sports-related lawsuits that include:

1. An athlete quit participating in football and sued to keep his scholarship.
2. The parents of a boy who died in a summer sports camp accident at the University sued for $23 million.
3. The golf coach was replaced and offered an administrative position. He turned it down and sued instead for $443,000.
4. The football coach was removed after a 1-10 season but was offered another position in the athletic department. He chose to sue, instead, for $151,381.

It is obvious from this chapter that those who administer sports programs will be sued for any and all reasons — it is inevitable. The administrator must become familiar with sports law and consider the legal parameters regarding his program.

The job isn't easy or glamorous, but the effort will pay off in the knowledge that everything possible has been done to protect the welfare and safety of all who participate in the sports program.

CHAPTER 7

The Coach

*I have always resented coaches who filed suit, but
now I feel that I do not have any alternative
— I am not eager to plead the situation
through the media. The courts
will suffice.*[1]

Coach "Chuck" Mills

Coaches occupy a unique position in today's society
because they are highly visible and perhaps, more than
most professionals, subject to extreme praise or
criticism. Most coaches place a low priority on
sports-related lawsuits preferring, instead, to spend
their time on fundamentals and strategies. For years
they had little to fear from the courts since people just
did not sue coaches. Today, however, sports and the
courts present a totally new arena for coaches. It may
well be that modern-day coaches will spend many hours
preparing for their most important contest ever, one
that will be contested in the courtroom and not on the
playing field.

The majority of lawsuits involving coaches deal with
some area of employment. Coaches frequently go to
court when discrimination is attributed to racial or
sexual bias. They also seek judicial relief in cases
pertaining to tenure, dismissal, divisible contracts and
defamation of character.

----

1. Greensboro Daily News, Aug. 5, 1978.

Issues Relating to Employment

A. Racial Discrimination

An interesting case took place in Arkansas when Othello Cross, a highly successful black coach, sued the school board for allegedly bypassing him as head football coach and athletic director.[2] He asked the court to rectify the situation by promoting him to both positions and granting him back pay from 1964 until 1974.

The school district, reportedly, had ignored the Supreme Court's mandate of 1954 to end dual schools and continued to maintain racially segregated schools. In 1968 the district was under a court order to desegregate its schools. All-black Townsend Park High School became an integrated junior high school and formerly all-white Dollarway High School became the integrated senior high school. Dollarway High School needed a head football coach and it hired a white coach as head coach and Cross as his assistant. When the head coach resigned in 1973, he recommended Cross as his successor. The superintendent traditionally hired the teachers and coaches, but, in this instance, sought help from the school board because:

> The job was so important to the community and because he feared that appointment of a black coach would provoke adverse community reaction and scare off white athletes.

During the trial several facts were revealed, such as:

1. The board did not have written criteria for employment.

---

2. Cross v. Board of Educ. of Dollarway, Arkansas School Dist., 395 F. Supp. 531 (E.D. Ark. 1975).

2. The superintendent used educational experience, enthusiasm, ability to get along with people, and knowledge of the game as qualifications for the position of head coach.
3. The superintendent decided to go outside the system to find a coach because there was friction within the staff.

The court noted that the board had passed over Cross a second time to hire a coach whose record of 7-22-1 at a lower level of competition did not match Cross's 68-14 mark. The court refused to accept the argument that Cross could not get along with people or that he was not enthusiastic. It surmised, instead, that Cross had been denied the dual position of head football coach and athletic director because of racial discrimination. The court speculated that Cross would have been named to both positions if he had been white. It therefore ordered the board to promote him to both positions at once or pay him the salary that the jobs would pay as long as he remained in the district. It also directed the board to reimburse Cross $4,410.00 in back pay.

A school system in Alabama was in the process of desegregating its school system. Mr. Alexander, a black football and basketball coach at the school that was eliminated in the process of consolidation was not hired as head football coach at the main school, Etowah High School.[3] He was given the basketball job, however, and the district court entered a consent decree that promised him that he would be given preference over any white coach for the position of head football coach or athletic director. The preference would be his as long

---

3. Lee v. Attala City School Sys., 588 F.2d 499 (5th Cir. 1979).

as the other candidates' qualifications were equal or less than his.

A year later, Etowah High School came under the jurisdiction of the Attala City Board of Education. The football coach resigned and approximately 10 to 12 candidates applied for the position. The Board of Education assumed the responsibility for the consent decree relating to Alexander. The board appealed to the court of appeals to permit it to hire a coach they felt had superior qualifications to those of Alexander. The board stated that its criteria for the coaching position were as follows:

1. the educational background of the applicants
2. the type of certificate possessed by each candidate
3. the applicant's total experience in education
4. the applicant's experience as a head football coach
5. the win-loss record of the applicant
6. the applicant's experience at the college level

The board petitioned the court to permit them to hire Charles Randall Hearn rather than Alexander and cited Hearn's superior qualifications as the overriding factor. Alexander had a master's degree in educational administration, but Hearn had two master's degrees and 36 hours toward a doctorate. Alexander had twenty-three years' experience and a Class A certificate. Hearn, however, had twenty-five years' experience and a AA certificate which was the highest awarded by the State of Alabama. Hearn also had eight more years' experience as a coach than Alexander, had been selected to coach the Alabama All Stars and received Coach of the Year honors twice. In addition, Hearn's coaching record was outstanding while Alexander's was not known. Hearn had also coached on the college level, while Alexander's experience was at the secondary school level only.

The court recognized that Alexander's qualifications were acceptable, but concluded that Hearn's made him "exceptionally well qualified." It ruled that the Attala City School System could employ Hearn since his qualifications were superior to Alexander's and awarded the job of head football coach to Hearn.

B. Sex Bias

Three separate cases originating in Pennsylvania involve allegations that women coaches were the victims of discrimination regarding compensation for coaching in comparison to their male counterparts.

Mary Johnson and Elizabeth Pollock were paid a yearly supplement of $324.00 for coaching women's basketball.[4] The men's basketball coaches were paid the following supplements:

Varsity	*Junior Varsity*
$ 972.00 first year	$756.00 first year
$1080.00 second year	$864.00 second year
$1296.00 third year	$972.00 third year

The women coaches based their suit on their coaching supplements, not their teaching salaries. They filed their case with the Pennsylvania Human Relations Commission, arguing that while they coached as many athletes and played as many games as the men, they received less compensation. Although it was not mentioned during the trial, four men also coached women's basketball for the same supplement of $324.00 per year.

---

4. Jackson v. Armstrong School Dist., 430 F. Supp. 1050 (W.D. Pa. 1977).

The United States District Court sympathized with the plaintiffs and commented that the training of women in the fundamentals of basketball was probably more difficult than the coaching of men. But the court disagreed with the plaintiff's claim of unfair treatment under Title VII of the Civil Rights Act. The court explained that the women's claim was not valid since the male coaches of women's basketball also received supplements identical to the women coaches. It concluded:

> Here plaintiffs are not discriminated against because of their sex. They are treated equally with the men who coach women's basketball. Allowing their claim, as stated, to stand would not only emasculate the statutory language but would embrace construction that renders the sex of the employee immaterial to the claim.

In a similar salary dispute, two women coaches sued the Hampton Township School District because they were not paid the same coaching stipend as the men.[5] Terry Kenneveg coached swimming and basketball and Cathy Lane coached gymnastics and volleyball from 1974 until 1977. They also based their claim on Title VII of the Civil Rights Act.

Once again the court held that Title VII was not applicable since there was no evidence of discrimination, but only a different salary scale allotted for coaches of women's sports.

Linda Jean Richards, a women's tennis coach, received $300.00 a year less than the men's tennis coach.[6] She described her duties and responsibilities as

---

5. Kenneveg v. Hampton Township School Dist., 438 F. Supp. 575 (W.D. Pa. 1977).
6. School Dist. of Township of Millcreek v. Commonwealth Human Relations Comm'n, 368 A.2d 901 (Pa. Commw. 1977).

equal to his. She filed her suit under the Pennsyvania Human Relations Act and the commission favored her. The school district appealed the decision to the Commonwealth Court of Pennsylvania.

Richards scheduled three fall tennis matches and sixteen in the spring, but only three matches met the approved standard of the Pennsylvania Interscholastic Athletic Association's regulations. The following year the supervisor of athletics scheduled ten matches and all were approved by the PIAA. The boys scheduled seven more matches than the women, which led the court to conclude that the schedule for the women was not comparable to the men's. It also commented that Richards had scheduled twenty-two matches voluntarily but when her salary demand was denied, cut the number to eight.

The Pennsylvania court observed that Richards accepted the women's tennis position with full knowledge of the salary she would receive. Since she increased the number of matches on her own volition, the court held that she was not entitled to additional pay. In reversing the commission's earlier decision, it refuted her charge of discrimination by the school officials.

Mary Alice Hill was hired to administer the women's intercollegiate sports program, intramurals, coach track and field, and teach physical education at Colorado State University. After three years she was dismissed because she allegedly failed to complete her doctorate, had excessive absences from class and caused friction with other staff members. Hill sued the administrators and the university, basing her defense on the claim that they discriminated against her in violation of Title VII.[7] She sought damages and the District Court of Colorado ruled in her favor by awarding her $50,000 in compensatory damages and $15,000 in punitive damages. The defendants appealed the decision.

The entire athletic department was staffed by males who had dual responsibilities to teach in the physical education department and coach in the athletic department. The United States District Court, D. Colorado, found that the "dual appointment system was used for males and it was not available for females."

It observed that:

> The men who coached the football, basketball, track and field and other teams for the male athletes were free from any pressure from the academic departments to obtain advanced degrees.

The defendants defended their position by stating that:

> the athletic programs for males and females were so different that the less favorable conditions of the plaintiff's employment were justified by the lack of comparability of the position of coaches and administrators in the two programs.

The court reasoned that such differences in the two programs violated the provisions of Title VII that prohibits "gender classifications and double standards."

Mary Hill had been hired at a salary of $10,500, but when she was replaced, a woman's athletic director received $20,800. The court concluded that Hill should

---

7. Hill v. Nettleton, 455 F. Supp. 514 (D. Colo. 1978).

receive that amount in back pay and therefore upheld the award of the lower court of $50,000 in compensatory damages.

Mavis Enstad taught English and was the women's track coach. In addition, she supervised the cheerleaders and pom-pom girls. After one year her duties as track coach were eliminated. She received a reemployment contract in which she was assigned the coaching duties of the girls' basketball team. She accepted the contract, but decided not to coach the basketball team. The North Central Board of Education informed her that her counter-offer was not acceptable and told her that unless she accepted the entire contract it would employ another person in her place. She refused and the board hired another teacher to replace her. Enstad sued the board and asserted that she was not qualified to coach girls' basketball.[8]

The Supreme Court of North Dakota observed:

> A rule of reasonableness must be implied in the continuing contract law so that the law does not become a sword or subterfuge in the hands of the district, defeating the intent of the legislature to create job security. All parts of an offer for reemployment, curricular and extracurricular, must be within the education, professional preparation, and experience of the teacher. The offer may not be of such extended hours or other adverse conditions as to make the offer unreasonable and hence unacceptable.

The court voted that Enstad had taught the fundamentals of basketball in her physical education classes, taken a college course in basketball, and played

8. Enstad v. North Cent. of Barnes Pub. School Dist. No. 65, 268 N.W.2d 126 (N.D. 1978).

basketball in high school and college. It found her qualified to coach girls' basketball and also observed that the state of North Dakota does not require specific qualifications to coach sports in the schools. The Supreme Court of North Dakota therefore affirmed the District Court's ruling in favor of the school board.

C. Tenure and Dismissal

The majority of court cases involving the coach come under the heading of tenure and dismissal. Many coaches insist that they are teachers and should be protected by teacher tenure acts. Situations that center around dismissal raise questions of due process and the legality of divisible contracts. When a coach is fired or his salary is reduced, the school official's authority to sever the contract is often challenged and the court usually becomes the arbitrator in such a situation.

When coaches lose their jobs, a common allegation is made regarding a lack of due process. In most instances in which due process is an issue, the provisions and guaranties of the Fourteenth Amendment are cited by the litigant.

A case that illustrates the charge of due process violation occurred in Florida in 1972.

John Parker, a law student and part-time assistant for the Florida University Athletic Department, became embroiled in a campus-wide controversy that led to his dismissal.[9] Parker became the spokesman for a group of disgruntled athletes who formed an organization known as the League of Florida Athletes. The athletes tried to alter the athletic department's rules regarding dress and grooming.

---

9. Parker v. Graves, 340 F. Supp. 586 (N.D. Fla. 1972).

Parker wrote several articles in the school paper criticizing the athletic department's rules. After the articles appeared in the school paper, Parker's supervisor recommended his dismissal. The assistant athletic director charged Parker with failure to enforce regulations concerning dress codes, grooming and quiet hours in the athletic dormitory. The athletic director met with Parker in the presence of a university official and dismissed him for conduct disloyal to the athletic program. He contended that Parker's personal views seriously conflicted with his assignment in the athletic department.

The controversy took place during a disappointing football season and increased tension among athletes and coaches alike. While some athletes supported the articles, others bitterly resented them and insisted that they did not reflect the views of all the athletes. In addition, the unfavorable publicity created by the articles caused prospective athletes to turn down visits to the campus and adversely affected the recruiting of prospective athletes.

Parker instituted a lawsuit claiming that he had been denied his right of free speech and expression as guaranteed by the First Amendment. The United States District Court, however, viewed the plaintiff's conduct as divisive since it created:

> Serious disciplinary problems and discord within the University Athletic Association which disrupted the orderly and efficient administration of the athletic department.

The court held that the plaintiff was disloyal to the athletic director by failing to carry out the responsibilities for which he had been employed. It did not believe that his right of free speech had been violated. It favored the defendants by concluding with a statement from the United States Supreme Court's decision in *Epperson v. Arkansas* in which the high court said:

> Courts do not and cannot intervene in the resolution of conflicts which arise in the daily operation of school systems and which do not directly and sharply implicate basic constitutional values.[10]

In Wisconsin a basketball and cross country coach taught driver education. He received $10,472.00 for teaching and $980.00 for his coaching duties.[11] At the end of the school year the superintendent issued him a new contract to teach, but not to coach. The superintendent told him that he had taken this action because of numerous complaints with his coaching, but refused to disclose the nature of these complaints. The coach was granted a hearing and disputed the charges against him. He sued the school district for allegedly failing to provide him due process and raised the following questions:

1. Is the refusal to disclose the reasons for dismissal a violation of the Due Process Clause of the Fourteenth Amendment?
2. Did the school board violate state law by failing to give him a notice in writing that he would not be assigned an extracurricular activity?

The court referred to a previous case in which a librarian was fired. In that instance the Supreme Court

---

10. Epperson v. Arkansas, 393 U.S. 97, 89 S. Ct. 266, 21 L.ed.2d 228 (1968).
11. Richards v. Board of Educ. Joint School Dist. No. 1, City of Sheboygan, 206 N.W.2d 597 (Wis. 1973).

of Wisconsin made a strong statement regarding a school board's power to dismiss a non-tenured employee. It emphatically said:

> The right to hire carries the concomitant right to fire — this power may be exercised by the board arbitrarily and without cause.[12]

The question in the coach's case was whether the school board violated his rights by issuing him a contract that did not include coaching duties. The school district noted that the coach was employed as a teacher for which he was certified but that he was not required to be certified to coach. It reasoned that he was therefore not entitled to a hearing.

The court commented that the school board had not maligned the coach's reputation in any way and that he was free to seek employment elsewhere. It affirmed the action of the school board in retaining him to teach driver education, but releasing him as the basketball coach.

A fascinating case took place in Arkansas in which the Arkansas Activities Association investigated a report that a football coach had illegally conducted off-season football drills.[13] After the investigation, the association placed the high school on probation with the stipulation that it could not compete against member schools unless it fired the head football coach.

The coach sued the association because it enforced a rule that was allegedly vague and too broad, thereby violating his right of due process. He pointed out that the rule did not specify that a coach could be fired for

---

12. State ex rel. Wattawa v. Manitowoc Pub. Library Bd., 39 N.W.2d 359 (Wis. 1949).
13. Wright v. Arkansas Activities Ass'n (AAA), 501 F.2d 25 (8th Cir. 1974).

violating the provision regarding off-season practice. The district court agreed with the coach and so ruled. The association immediately appealed the decision to a higher court.

The association based its argument on previous judicial decisions in which municipalities were found not to be "persons" and subsequently received immunity from lawsuits. The judge took exception to this interpretation by stating that the association was not created by state statutes and therefore could not claim the protection of immunity.

The United States Court of Appeals supported the judge by ruling that the association, just as a person, was subject to the provisions of Section 1983 of the Civil Rights Act. It held that the association was also involved in state action which made it subject to regulations regarding violations of rights protected by federal law. It found the Arkansas Athletic Association to be guilty of arbitrary action toward the coach and urged it to warn coaches of possible penalties in the future. The court felt that it was not an unfair burden to expect the association to clarify the regulations that would state that individuals, as well as institutions, could be penalized for rule infractions.

In Delaware a head football coach and his assistant requested a hearing before the school board to protest their dismissal as coaches.[14] After the hearing the board voted once again to terminate their coaching contracts. The assistant coach decided to pursue the case by seeking an injunction to prevent the board from hiring

---

14. Leone v. Kimmel, 335 A.2d 290 (Del. Super. 1975).

a coach to replace him. His petition was denied when the judge explained:

> As to coaching positions, it is established that no hearings are required under Delaware statutory law and none are required by the Constitution in connection with the awarding of contracts for extracurricular football coaching.

The Superior Court of Delaware refused to grant the coach the same protection granted teachers since coaches are "not regularly employed." In upholding the school board's right to hire and fire any coach once the contract for a given year had been completed, it made a comment with far-reaching implications when it remarked:

> If coaches could not be relieved of their contract period without specific charges and a formal hearing or other special formalities usually afforded in teaching contracts, a new and very interesting field of contract law might develop.

Ellis Williams, a coach, became unhappy at not being named athletic director when the position came open and from that time on reportedly refused to support the administration.[15] When the school board reluctantly decided to terminate his contract, he sued the board for "Constitutional impermissible reasons." He contended that the board voted not to rehire him because he protected students under his care from faculty mistreatment, that he objected to verbal abuse from spectators against an athlete (who was his son) and that his right of free speech had been violated.

The school board emphatically replied that Arkansas law vested power in the school board to do whatever it considered best for the benefit of its students.

---

15. Williams v. Day, 412 F. Supp. 336 (E.D. Ark. 1976).

The United States District Court of Arkansas did not agree with the coach's contentions either and commented that he was unhappy and discontented because another man was given the position he wanted. It concluded that from the time he had been denied the athletic director's job, he showed a lack of control and refused to cooperate with the school officials and in general "created an intolerable situation for the athletic director, the principal, the superintendent and the school board." The court reasoned that the plaintiff apparently decided that he would leave sooner or later, but wanted the public to recognize the injustice that was put on him. The board realized that he was a popular coach and tried to retain him until it became aware that the situation had deteriorated.

The federal court upheld the school board's decision not to renew his contract and remarked:

> It is a sad story. But it is the type that confronts school boards, unfortunately, on not infrequent occasions, the type which usually involves the entire school community. This particular school community has finally resolved the problem. It cannot be said that it did so in an unfair or arbitrary manner. The matter should therefore remain at rest.

A coach in Maine who had earned tenure after four outstanding years of service to the school system was dismissed as "unfit to teach" and "unprofitable to the school." [16] The coach denied the charge that he was unfit to teach or unprofitable to the school and instituted a lawsuit against the school committee.

---

16. McLaughlin v. Machias School Comm., 385 A.2d 53 (Me. 1978).

The coach (plaintiff) organized a pick-up game of basketball in the gymnasium after soccer practice had been cancelled. He was attempting to take a shot at the basket when a student pushed him from behind. The plaintiff then turned around and:

> with a single blow of an open hand struck the student on his right cheek bone. The blow caused closure of the student's mouth and, in consequence, the student lost one of his teeth and suffered serious damage to another tooth. He also sustained a bloody nose and a black eye.

The plaintiff testified that he had not intended to injure the student, but the student argued that he was deliberately hit in anger.

The school superintendent stated that a teacher and coach had to set an example for his students and felt that the coach could not carry out his responsibilities in an effective way after the unfortunate incident. The plaintiff replied that the school committee had acted in an unlawful manner in dismissing him and questioned whether he had been given due process.

The Supreme Judicial Court of Maine referred to a previous case and several statements pertinent to the instant case. In *Fernald v. City of Ellsworth* the court made several strong statements regarding the conduct of coaches when it observed:

> The example set by a coach or physical education teacher is critical to his "overall impact" on impressionable young athletes, particularly at a time when the malady of violence jeopardizes the benefits to be derived from teaching competitive sports.[17]

---

17. Fernald v. City of Ellsworth Superintending School Comm., 342 A.2d 704 (Me. 1975).

The court added that the coach had the responsibility of aiding the student in the control of emotions that come into play during competitive games. It noted that the teaching of sportsmanship is hindered when the coach fails to set a good example for his students to follow. It then concluded:

> The teacher's actions may speak more loudly than his words. In addition, a single act of violence in the setting of a competitive sport may cause serious injury or provoke a violent response.[18]

The court in the instant case then considered the plaintiff's contention that due process was violated by the school committee's action to dismiss him. It pointed out that the plaintiff's attorney did not object to any of the procedures involving his client. As such, it reasoned:

> The failure to raise issues of procedural due process at the hearing before the School Committee ordinarily constitutes a waiver of those issues.[19]

The court denied the coach's appeal and favored the action of the school committee.

D. Divisible Contracts

A constant source of confusion among coaches results from contracts that include teaching responsibilities along with coaching duties. In a day when there is an unparalled growth in sports programs and a concomitant lack of qualified coaches, the school administrator faces a serious dilemma. Can a teacher-coach give up his coaching duties for the

---

18. *Id.*
19. *Supra* note 17.

classroom and still retain his position? Can a teacher
refuse to accept extra-curricular responsibilities
legally? Can a teacher-coach be dismissed as coach and
have the coaching salary cut from the total
compensation?

Several provocative cases provide answers to these
and other questions regarding the coach's status.

The Asbury Park School Board traditionally assigned
extra-curricular duties to its teachers at the close of the
school year. For some unknown reason, the board
waited until the beginning of the school year to delegate
extra-curricular duties.[20] Twenty-eight teachers who
had extra-curricular responsibilities the previous year
refused to accept the assignments. All twenty-eight
planned to teach, but not to take responsibility for
supervision of the extra activities. The board named the
teachers and the Asbury Park Education Association as
defendants in a suit and sought a court order to require
the teachers to accept the assignments. The Superior
Court of New Jersey relied on a California case in which
a teacher challenged the school district's right to
require its teachers to supervise football and basketball
games without extra compensation.[21] The teacher called
the assignment of duties unprofessional, unreasonable
and unfair. The court did not agree and countered with
a strong statement that supported the school board's
policy when it said:

> Teachers are engaged in professional
> employment. Their salaries and hour of

---

20. Board of Educ. of City of Asbury Park v. Asbury Park Educ.
    Ass'n, 368 A.2d 396 (N.J. Super. Ct. Ch. Div. 1976), modi-
    fied, 382 A.2d 392 (N.J. Super. Ct. App. Div. 1977).
21. McGrath v. Burkhard, 280 P.2d 864 (Cal. App. 1955).

employment are fixed with regard to their professional status and are not fixed upon the same basis as those of day laborers. The worth of a teacher is not measured in terms of a specific sum of money per hour. A teacher expects to and does perform a service. If that service from time to time requires additional hours of work, a teacher expects to and does put in the extra hours, without the thought of measuring his or her compensation in terms of a given sum of money per hour.

The court then continued to comment on a teacher's responsibility to the students by adding:

A teacher's duties and obligations to students and the community are not satisfied by closing the classroom door at the conclusion of a class. The direction and supervision of extra-curricular activities are an important part of his duties — All of this is, of course, subject to the test of reasonableness.

The court then referred to a decision in New York in which a court endorsed a principal's policy of assigning teachers extra duties without extra pay. The New York court decided that the regulation was valid when it commented:

There are many activities that are part of instruction but, by their very nature, may be performed after the close of the regular school session. The athletic program, for instance, takes place under such circumstances. It has nevertheless, over the years been always regarded as part of the school curriculum — *Coaching in athletic sports is teaching.* It, therefore, does not follow that because an activity is conducted after regular class hours, it is not part of the school curriculum.[22] (Emphasis added.)

The New Jersey court suggested that it might be more appropriate to change the term extra-curricular to extra-classroom. It felt that teachers had the obligation to carry out such duties, and that:

> For this court to require less would be to lend its hand to the subversion of the educational process.[23]

While teachers do have the freedom to resign from such assignments, the court reasoned that twenty-eight such resignations constituted an illegal strike, contrary to the best interest of students. It therefore ordered the teachers to return to their extra-curricular assignments.

In an unusual action the defendant Asbury Park Education Association appealed the unfavorable decision to the Appellate Division of the Superior Court of New Jersey.[24] The higher court noted that the issue was moot since the year in question was over. It did, however, rule that the issue of whether teachers could resign from extra-curricular duties lay within the jurisdiction of the Public Employees Relations Commission which had the ability to settle the issue. It observed that "this important issue should have been transferred to that administrative body" and not to the court.

Two coaches, in separate but similar cases in Minnesota, challenged the school board's right to fire

---

22. Parrish v. Moss, 107 N.Y.S.2d 580 (N.Y. App. Div. 1951).
23. *Supra* note 20.
24. Board of Educ. of City of Asbury v. Asbury Park Educ. Ass'n, 382 A.2d 392 (N.J. Super. Ct. App. Div. 1977).

them as coaches while retaining them to teach. Both claimed that they had coached for years and thereby acquired tenure under the Minnesota statutes which grants tenure to teachers after a probationary period of three years. In addition, the statutes stated that teachers who exhibited competence and good conduct could not be released without a hearing. In *Chiodo v. Board of Education*,[25] the coach admitted that the word "coach" was not included in the statute, but he pointed to *Webster's Dictionary* in which a coach is described as "one who instructs players in the fundamentals of a competitive sport." He maintained that a gymnasium could be classified as a classroom where instruction takes place. The defendants argued that coaching sports could not be classified as classroom instruction. Chiodo declared that he had to be certified to coach in the state of Minnesota and therefore met the requirements of the statutes.

The Supreme Court of Minnesota considered cases in other states relating similar circumstances and found that, in every instance, the courts denied the coach's request for tenure. The Minnesota court likewise held that Chiodo could obtain tenure for teaching but not for coaching.

Another Minnesota case involved a basketball coach-teacher who was released from his coaching duties with an accompanying cut in salary of $1,650. Donald Stang went to court to regain his position as coach.[26] The Minnesota court affirmed the school

---

25. Chiodo v. Board of Educ. of Special School Dist. No. 1, 215 N.W.2d 806 (Minn. 1974).
26. Stang v. Independent School Dist. No. 191, 256 N.W.2d 82 (Minn. 1977).

board's decision because Stang failed to exhaust the administrative remedies available to him through the arbitration board. It felt that this was the proper action to take, not court action.

In the state of Utah a situation similar to those of Chiodo and Stang resulted in a lawsuit. Lee Brown had earned the reputation of a good teacher and successful coach.[27] He informed the school board that he planned to continue to teach, but would not coach wrestling or football anymore. The school board accepted his written letter as a total resignation of both positions and Brown sued to regain his teaching position.

The district court ruled that his contract to teach and coach could not be divisible unless both parties mutually consented to it. It found that Brown voluntarily terminated his contract and could not rely on the Utah's Orderly School Termination Act to protect him.

He appealed the decision to the Supreme Court of Utah which noted that he had originally listed an interest and ability to coach when he filed his application to teach and coach with the school board. The Supreme Court of Utah held that his contract to teach and coach was not severable and supported the board's action in accepting his letter as a total resignation.

The number of cases in which the courts rule that a teaching-coaching contract is nonseverable is overwhelming. But, as is true in so many instances, the courts often take different directions in similar situations.

Robert George coached football in a community that had little appreciation or tolerance for losing seasons

27. Brown v. Board of Educ. of Morgan County School Dist., 560 P.2d 1129 (Utah 1977).

and even less for losing coaches.[28] After two dismal
seasons, in which only two victories were recorded, the
coach was informed that he could stay on and teach
mathematics, but that he could no longer coach the
football team. He accepted the decision until he learned
that his salary would be cut by $2,000.00. He contended
that his contract called for a salary of $9,300.00. The
school board was just as adamant in its determination
not to pay someone to do nothing. It ignored his protest
and hired another person to replace him in the
classroom and on the football field.

The plaintiff was out of a job except for occasional
days when he could substitute teach. He sued the school
board for damages and the Oregon court ruled that
while the school board could replace him as coach it
could not reduce his salary once it had contracted to pay
him another amount. It awarded George $7,300.00
which represented his loss of wages from the time he
was released until the present.

E. Defamation of Character

A college track coach took exception to an article that
appeared in a prominent magazine and sued for libel.[29]
The parts of the article entitled "The Angry Black
Athlete" that offended the coach included the following:

> It is a mess that extends from Niagara to the
> University of California from Michigan to the
> University of Texas at El Paso. Sometimes the
> racial issue is inflamed by a coach's get tough

---

28. George v. School Dist. No. 8R of Umatilla County, 490 P.2d
    1009 (Ore. App. 1971).
29. Vandenburg v. Newsweek, Inc., 507 F.2d 1024 (5th Cir.
    1975).

policy. "I could give in to a lot of Negro demands," says one Southwestern coach, "and keep my team intact. But someone has to hold the line against these people."

The article went on to say:

> At El Paso track coach Wayne Vandenburg threatened to kick six athletes off the team if they joined the boycott of the New York Athletic Club indoor meet in February. The club was charged with discriminatory membership policies. Vandenburg won and the athletes competed. But two months later after a talk with Harry Edwards, the same athletes refused to enter a meet at Brigham Young University in Utah because of Morman doctrines against blacks. Vandenburg promptly dropped champion long-jumper Bob Beamon and five others from the squad.

A jury awarded Vandenburg $130,000.00 in damages, but ten months later a trial court ruled that he had failed to prove his case. Vandenburg promptly appealed the decision to a higher court.

The United States Court of Appeals, Fifth Circuit, considered Vandenburg to be a public figure according to the *New York Times* standard as discussed in the previous defamation cases in Chapter 4. This standard sets the guidelines for recovery in such cases and states:

> He may recover for injury to reputation only on a clear and convincing proof that the defamatory falsehood was made with knowledge of its falsity or with reckless disregard for the truth.[30]

---

30. New York Times Co. v. Sullivan, 376 U.S. 254, 84 S. Ct. 710, 11 L.ed. 686 (1964).

The court of appeals then made several comments that offer guidelines for future litigation in defamation cases, such as:

> The New York Times test represents recognition that the freedoms of press and speech are essential to that wide-open discussion of public issues deemed so important by our founders to the continued existence of our governmental system. Further, the test is recognition that erroneous statement is inevitable in free debate, and that it must be protected if the freedoms of expression are to have "breathing space" that they "need to survive."[31]

The court continued to set the legal parameters of defamation by saying:

> The public figure or public official has generally placed himself in a position inviting comment and has meaningful opportunity to rebut the alleged libel, so state interest in protecting the individual from damage is less compelling.[32]

In reviewing the background of the incident, the court discovered that a protest group urged the black athletes who had been invited to the track meet to boycott the sponsoring New York Athletic Club. Nine black athletes ignored the picket lines to compete and six represented the University of Texas at El Paso. Their coach, Wayne Vandenburg, testified that he gave his athletes the choice to compete or not and they chose to participate in the meet. He insisted that he put no pressure on them.

----

31. *Id.*
32. *Supra* note 30.

Later that year, Vandenburg suspended several athletes who refused to take part in a track meet against Brigham Young University. The athletes reportedly talked prior to the meet with Black Power leader Harry Edwards.

The author of the article depended on statements from Harry Edwards and a sports director of a San Francisco radio station for the information he needed to write the article.

After considering the testimony of all parties, the court commented on a writer's ability to write controversial articles when it declared:

> When the story is not "hot news," . . . the investigation must be more thorough, and "actual malice may be inferred when the investigation . . . was grossly inadequate in the circumstances . . . ."

> Evidence of actual malice must be clear and convincing, more than a preponderance . . . .
> . . . [A] reporter, without a 'high degree of awareness of their probable falsity,' may rely on statements made by a single source even though they reflect only one side of the story without fear of libel of prosecution . . . ." [33]

The court found that the track coach failed to prove that the reporter, who wrote the article, used malice as described by the *New York Times* standard. It affirmed the lower court's decision in favor of the magazine.

One of the most highly publicized cases involving coaches and the press occurred in the March 23, 1963 issue of the *Saturday Evening Post.* In that issue a reporter wrote that Wallace Butts, the athletic director

---

33. *Supra* note 29.

at Georgia University, had given information regarding the Georgia team to Alabama Coach Paul
"Bear" Bryant. According to the story, an insurance
salesman had been inadvertently included in the
conversation between the two men. The article's
apparent conclusion was that the two men had
"conspired to fix the outcome of the game."[34]

The jury ruled against the magazine and awarded
three million dollars in punitive damages, which was
reduced by a judge to $400,000.

The question of whether Butts was a public figure
became an issue and the Supreme Court agreed that
under the *New York Times* rule, Butts so qualified.
However, the Supreme Court also found that the article
came under the *Times* rule regarding malice. The
magazine lost its case and discovered that "hefty
awards can be made if libel is found."[35]

Michael Laskey in *Law and the Writer* comments that
the *New York Times* rule has been modified by the
courts and concludes:

> The matter is not yet settled, however, and the
> question of what constitutes a libelous
> publication is certain to be fought in the courts
> for years to come.[36]

IN MY OPINION

How often when we hire coaches and require them to
teach in the classroom do we emphasize our desire for
effective teaching in addition to competent coaching?

---

34. Kirk Polking and Leonard S. Meramus, *Law and the Writer,*
    WRITER'S DIGEST, F. & W. Publishing Corp., Cincinnati,
    Ohio, 1978.
35. *Id.*
36. *Supra* note 34.

But do we honestly mean what we say, or are we merely giving lip service to the teaching aspect of the classroom? How many times has a qualified and dedicated teacher who also coached been relieved of his job because his won-lost record was not as impressive as his teaching? No matter that the coach inherited a bankrupt program or one decimated by unpredicted injuries to key players. The simple and realistic fact is that losing coaches, who happen to be excellent teachers, do not remain at their jobs very long. If they do, they are the exception not the rule.

On the other hand, how many winning coaches with shoddy teaching performance in the classroom are tolerated by an admiring community and passive administration? When this is permitted to happen, the students become the losers.

Too often well-meaning but misguided booster clubs dictate the fate of a coach as championship teams become an obsession and anything less is unacceptable. Unhealthy pressure passes from the administrator to the coach, and on to the athlete.

An example of a booster club's reaction to the firing of a popular, winning coach, took place when Arizona State University fired football coach Frank Kush. Kush was named as a defendant in a $1.1 million lawsuit instituted by Kevin Rutledge, a former Arizona State player. Rutledge alleged that Kush struck him after he punted poorly in a game. Athletic Director, Fred Miller, stated that he was "completely convinced" of Kush's innocence until he learned that Kush was reportedly pressuring both coaches and players to remain silent about "what they had seen." [37]

37. Greensboro Daily News, Oct. 16, 1979.

The Sun Angel Foundation, a booster organization for Arizona State's athletic program, responded immediately by demanding the reinstatement of Kush until the issue was resolved. The booster group also urged the firing of Athletic Director Miller. The booster club also informed university officials that it was "suspending plans to build a golf course at ASU and cannot consider enclosing the south end of Sun Devil Stadium." [38]

A questionnaire was sent to the fifty states and six United States territories to determine the status of coaches with regard to tenure and due process. 94% responded to the 1978-1979 survey and the results are an indication of the problem that confronts the coach today. (See Appendix D for the responses by the states and territories.)

Summary of Survey

1. Coaches in your state or territory can be granted tenure.
   Yes — 10   No — 44

2. If given tenure, how many years must be served on a probationary status?
   1 year to 5 years

3. A teacher who coaches can give up coaching to only teach and not lose his or her job.
   Yes — 44   No — 10

4. Coaches are granted formal hearings when relieved of their coaching duties.
   Yes — 35   No — 19

The survey reveals that only six states and four territories grant coaches tenure with the probationary

---

38. Raleigh News and Observer, Oct. 17, 1979.

period ranging from one year in American Samoa to five years in Florida. While a majority of states report that a teacher may relinquish coaching duties and remain on the teaching staff, several states qualify their answer. Kansas cautions that a coach who resigns coaching responsibilities may lose the contract. The Attorney General in Iowa indicates that he favors one contract and discourages separate contracts for teaching and coaching.

The survey points out that nineteen states do not extend due process to coaches. Guam points out that its coaches are all hired on a part-time basis and therefore do not qualify for the privileges offered to full-time employees.

California reports a shortage of coaches and suggests several ways to meet the problem such as:

1. When new teachers are hired and want to coach, do not permit them to stop coaching after tenure unless mutually agreed between principal and coach.

2. Eliminate year-round coaching — limit coaching to length of prescribed sport season (coach is then available to coach more than one sport).

3. Permit non-credentialed personnel to serve as head coaches.

The lack of tenure and due process may well be a large reason for the abuses that exist at all levels of sports today. Overemphasis on sports continues because too often the pressure to win is the ultimate goal of the people in authority. Coaches soon realize that the winning coach and not the successful teacher, is rewarded in today's educational system.

Unfortunately, a large number of educators do not believe that a coach is a teacher or that coaching is teaching.

I strongly disagree! Evidently the New Jersey Court in the Asbury Park case agreed with me. When twenty-eight teachers decided to give up their extra-curricular responsibilities, the court quickly enjoined them from resigning. The court recognized the importance of sports in the total life of the students. In fact, the court held it to be so important that it ruled that extra compensation was not required since supervision of extra-curricular activities are part of a teacher's job.

But, on the other hand, when a school board can decide to release a coach of his coaching duties, then coaching is no longer considered teaching and the coach is regularly denied the protection given teachers.

In 1978 the Minnesota legislature responded to *Chiodo* and *Stang* by enacting a statute to answer the questions that went unanswered during the judicial hearings. The statute reads as follows:

> Before a school district can terminate the coaching duties of a teacher, the teacher shall be notified in writing of the reasons for the proposed termination. The affected employee then may request a hearing before the school board. After the public hearing, the board may terminate the teacher's coaching duties, but the reason for the termination must be "based upon competent evidence in the record."

This is a step in the right direction because it offers the coach simple but fair due process. If more states adopt this policy, many abuses will be eliminated. It is time that we honestly evaluate our educational goals and put the proper emphasis on coaching so that our young people can receive the very best training possible by secure, dedicated coaches.

CHAPTER 8

The Official

To err is human, to forgive is divine, but to complain about officiating is football —now, then and forever.[1]

An angry 6'2", 200-pound lineman, at a small New Jersey college, repeatedly asked an official to watch his opponent for illegal play.[2] When the official failed to act on the alleged violations, the frustrated player shouted an obscenity at him and was immediately ejected from the football game. As the distraught player was leaving the field, he impulsively hit the official from behind. The official was carried off the field on a stretcher and taken to a nearby hospital. The official sued the college, its athletic director and football coach for allegedly permitting the athlete to act in such an unsportsmanlike manner.

In Vigo, Spain, a crowd of over 20,000 fans became upset with the officiating at a soccer match and threw their rented cushions on the field to protest the conduct of the game.[3] The town's mayor may have set a precedent when he fined the referee $670 for behavior that allegedly irritated the fans and endangered the safety of the spectators.

In a time of instant replay, officials and their decisions are subject to the scrutiny of millions of viewers, backed by the camera's eye. The official has

---

1. William O. Johnson, *It's Open Season on the Zebras,* SPORTS ILLUSTRATED, Oct. 9, 1978.
2. Daily Reporter, Hanover, N.J., Mar. 6, 1975.
3. *The Review of the News,* SPORTSMAN, Mar. 6, 1974.

become the object of intolerant derision. William O. Johnson, writing in *Sports Illustrated,* may have summed up the official's dilemma when he inquired:

> The question is whether a mere human being — or seven mere human beings (the current size of an officiating crew) — can bring law and order to a vast field populated with 22 speeding giants joined in hand-to-hand combat.[4]

Yet the official is, like other professionals, sued for alleged negligence that causes injuries and he himself sues for damages when alleged discrimination and defamation exist.

Injuries Attributed to Negligence

Kenneth Hinton, a 16-year-old basketball player in the state of Washington, sued many parties for an injury that caused him to become a permanent quadriplegic.[5] Hinton sued his coach and the opposing coach, the school district, the state athletic association, the officials' association and an unusual party in a lawsuit, the officials. He sued the officials for negligence based on the allegation that they failed to curb the rough play or stop the game when it got explosive and out of hand. The plaintiff and his parents sought $1 million in damages.

During the trial, testimony revealed that Hinton was fouled by an opposing player with only one minute and six seconds remaining in the game. He was thrown over the opponent's shoulder and landed on his head. His injury was diagnosed as a fracture of the cervical

---

4. *Supra* note 1.
5. Hinton v. Pateros School Dist. No. 122 (No. 29847, Superior Court of Washington County of Chelan, 1976).

vertebrae and he was paralyzed from the neck down. The plaintiff contended that the official neglected to:

Exercise proper discretion, supervision and control and allowed the game to degenerate into an abusive, physical contest, and his negligence was a proximate cause of the injury.

The injured plaintiff claimed that the state athletic association was also derelict in its duty for failing to train the officials in the state uniformly. Such failure, he argued, left the officials in the various counties confused regarding the rules and without standard guidelines to follow. This led to rough play and confusion, he stated.

In addition, the plaintiff pointed to a rule that prohibited a coach from taking a team off the court to protest some action during the contest. Since the penalty was severe, the plaintiff charged the association with negligence for promulgating a rule that led to his injury. He commented that his coach should have taken the team off the basketball court when the action got too rough and highly volatile. The fear of penalty probably kept the coach from such action, he surmised.

The superior court judge granted the defendants summary judgment and the plaintiff appealed to a higher court. While the case was pending, the defendants agreed to an out-of-court settlement for approximately $35,000. All the defendants, except the opposing player, contributed to the settlement. The student did not have insurance coverage or the financial means to pay any costs of the award.

In the same state, Roger Anderson and Steve Carabba were wrestling in the 145-pound division.[6]

---

6. Carabba v. Ancortes School Dist. No. 103, 435 P.2d 936 (Wash. 1968).

Anderson was winning the match easily and at the end of the third period was using alternating half nelsons to try for a pin. They were wrestling in a corner when the referee spotted a separation in the mat and tried to close it. He took his eyes off the competitors long enough to fix the mats. During this split second, Anderson apparently put a full nelson on Carabba with just a few seconds left in the match. (This was the testimony of several witnesses.) It was also reported that Anderson then lunged when the buzzer sounded and broke the hold on the plaintiff. As a result, Carabba sustained crippling injuries that left him paralyzed from the neck down.

The plaintiff attempted to recover $500,000 for the injuries received during the wrestling match on the grounds that the school district was negligent through its agent, the referee, on the following counts:

1. Failing to supervise the contestants in an adequate manner.

2. Permitting his attention to be diverted from the action of the boys.

3. Allowing an illegal and dangerous hold to be used by one of the participants.

4. Allowing the hold to be applied for a substantial period of time.

The lower court favored the school district and the plaintiff appealed. The higher court denied the school district's contention that the referee was not its agent and ruled that as a matter of law, he was. The court also maintained that while Carabba participated in the sport on a voluntary basis, he could not be held to assume the risk of another's negligence. It did not find evidence to support the school district's claim that Carabba was guilty of contributory negligence.

The judgment was reversed and the case ordered to be retried. It was finally settled out of court in favor of the injured boy.

Injuries to an Official

Athletic administrators are generally held to be responsible for the safety of officials that call the games at their site. A well known case illustrates the type of incident that is possible during an athletic contest.

An umpire was assaulted after a baseball game because, supposedly, he ejected the home team's manager from the game in the ninth inning.[7] The spectators verbally abused the umpire and challenged him to fight. The umpire was escorted from the field by two policemen and a fellow umpire. A fan managed to push through the protective group and hit the umpire on the head. The umpire sued the baseball team, the manager, and the spectator who struck him.

The Superior Court of Wake County, North Carolina, rendered "default judgment against the fan," and "struck certain portions of the complaint." The umpire appealed.

The Supreme Court of North Carolina then considered the facts in this unusual case. The umpire argued that he was due damages because the injuries he sustained were the result of the manager's attempt to arouse the anger of the spectators against him. He referred to the rules and regulations that govern professional baseball to prove his point. These rules set the following guidelines for the protection of officials.

---

7. Toone v. Adams, 137 S.E.2d 132 (N.C. 1964).

1. The home team shall provide police protection sufficient to preserve order at a game.

2. They authorize the umpire to remove managers, players, spectators, or employees from the game or field for a violation of the rules or unsportsmanlike conduct.

3. They declare that his "decisions which involve judgment" shall be final and that players or managers shall not object thereto.

In North Carolina where a contract between two parties is intended for the benefit of a third party, the latter may maintain an action in contract for its breach or in tort if he has been injured as a result of its negligent performance. It is agreed that a person may institute a suit if an injury results from the omission of a legal obligation. The North Carolina Supreme Court considered the plaintiff's claim that the home team officials failed to perform their duty in protecting him from irate fans, irritated by the overt action of the manager.

It made a comment that may be applicable to many spectator sports when it said:

> For present day fans, a goodly part of the sport in a baseball game is goading and denouncing the umpire when they do not concur in his decisions, and most feel that, without one or more rhubarbs, they have not received their money's worth.

It went on to speculate that:

> Ordinarily, however, an umpire garners only vituperation — not fisticuffs. Fortified by the knowledge of his infallibility in all judgment

decisions, he is able to shed billingsgate like water on the proverbial duck's back.

It then questioned the umpire's contention that the two policemen and fellow umpire were not adequate to protect the umpire from one spectator. It recognized that "hindsight" might require more escorts, but doubted the legitimacy of such a claim.

The court could not connect the actual assault by the angry spectator to the action of the manager. It therefore concluded that:

> It would be an intolerable burden upon managers of baseball teams to saddle them with responsibilities for the actions of every emotionally unstable person who might arrive at the game spoiling for a fight and become enraged over an umpire's call which the manager had protested.

It supported the superior court's decision against the spectator, but dismissed the charges against the other defendants.

Student Umpire

A physical education student at Cortland State Teachers College wore glasses, but did not use a protective shield or guard over them.[8]

During a game in class the student was waiting for his turn at bat. An argument erupted and no umpire was available to settle the dispute. The student volunteered to umpire and the players agreed as did the teacher who was present.

The student umpire stood behind a portable cage that was placed behind the batter's box to keep the balls

---

8. Hanna v. State, 258 N.Y.S.2d 694 (N.Y. Ct. Cl. 1965).

from being deflected. There was a twine netting on a metal frame. The teacher advised the student umpire to stand well back from the net, which was frayed in several places.

The "umpire" stood only one foot behind the net without a protective mask. A foul ball came through the net, shattered his glasses and cut the corner of his right eye. He went to the school infirmary where the broken glass was removed from his eye.

The student umpire sued on the basis of negligence on the part of the school in maintaining such a defective net. He testified that his vision with glasses prior to the accident was 20/20 and now was 20/30 with accompanying blurred vision. An expert witness observed at the trial that it would be dangerous to stand behind the net even if it was a new one since the ball traveled at a speed of 90 miles per hour at times.

The court was convinced that the plaintiff was an intelligent individual who was familiar with the sport of baseball. It concluded that he entered into the act of umpiring voluntarily and not by directive. It stated:

> If in neglect of his own safety, he failed to foresee the danger of standing too close to the netting, after his attention had been drawn to the apparent danger not only by prior warnings of his instructor, but by his own observations, prior to his injury, this personal neglect bars his recovery.

His act, the court ruled, constituted contributory negligence which was the proximate cause of his injury.

It dismissed the case.

Discrimination

It has become commonplace for officials to go on strike to protest alleged inequities in salary and

working conditions. During 1977-1978, basketball
officials of the National Basketball Association went on
strike and in the summer of 1979 the umpires of the
American League also struck to protest their overall
working conditions.

With Title IX legislation in effect, a new era of
litigation has begun involving officials who officiate
women's sports. These officials are not willing to
officiate women's contests for less compensation than
men's. The following case is an example of what can
result when different salary scales are maintained in
sports, involving different sexes.

Elaine Brigman was the chairperson elect of the
Central Western New York Board of Women Officials.[9]
Because of her position, she was chosen to institute a
lawsuit against the New York State Public High School
Athletic Association. Her complaint was directed
against the association's regulations regarding the
requirements for equal opportunity for women as well
as men in sports. The various school districts which
made up the association's membership were also
named as defendants.

Each school district listed its procedure for
compliance with the Affirmative Action directive. The
procedures in the various districts for different
categories were very similar. A common statement
among the districts was the one relating to officials and
a typical one included the following:

> The school district shall comply with the New
> York State Public High School Athletic
> Association's requirements for the hiring of

9. Brigman v. New York State Public High School Athletic
   Ass'n (Civil Action No. 1973-347, 1978 US District Court
   N.D. N.Y.).

qualified officials for girls' sports. When available, the school district shall participate in officials' draws or other mechanisms for the securing of certified, rated officials for girls' sports.

The plaintiff charged the school districts and the association with discrimination in the hiring and salary scale of officials employed to officiate girls' contests.

A settlement was finally reached by all the parties and the court was requested to review the conditions of the settlement to determine whether or not they were fair. The terms of the settlement provided that:

1. Defendants will make payments to certain officials of back pay with respect to certain prior girls' athletic competition.

2. Defendants will agree to pay certified officials at girls' interscholastic varsity, junior varsity and modified sports events in basketball, swimming, gymnastics, track, and cross country the same fees as are paid to certified officials at boys' sports.

3. Defendants will agree to pay counsel fees, costs and disbursements incurred in this action.

In return for these concessions, the plaintiff was asked to withdraw her complaint against the defendants. The court approved the conditions of the settlement and ordered the defendants to set a uniform salary for officials of both girls' and boys' contests.

Defamation of Character

Officials have come to expect fan reaction to their decisions and generally accept volatile spectator reaction as an inevitable occupational hazard. As such, little attention is given to criticism resulting from questionable calls. However, when the official's integrity is publicly challenged in print, the potential for litigation becomes very real.

It seems that many athletes freely criticize officials in practically all sports. A Cleveland Browns' football player blasted the officials after a close loss to the Pittsburgh Steelers by claiming that:

> The game was stolen from us. The officials are like God. They have the power to give and take away. They decided this time to take away.[10]

In like manner, some newsmen criticize officials in their write-ups.

A veteran football and basketball official in the Southwestern Conference sued a reporter and the paper he represented for allegedly damaging his reputation.[11] The article said in part that:

> One reason the Southwest Conference has trouble winning all of its non-league games — aside from the fact Texas Christian is in the conference — is that not all of the Southwest Conference games are played at home.
> Another reason is that key personnel can be stretched only so far. On most days, referee Percy Penn and his officiating crew can work only one game.
>
> Usually that one game is in Arkansas.

The article stated that Penn was not needed in Fayetteville since Arkansas easily defeated Tulsa University 31-15. It went on to discuss the use of split

---

10. *Supra* note 1.
11. Penn v. Hartzell and The Tulsa Tribune Co. (N. CT. 76-309, District Court for Tulsa County, Okla. 1976).

crews when various conference schools play each other.
It then commented:

> It now appears that having six Southwest
> Conference officials — including Percy Penn —
> working your game when you are the visiting
> team in Fayetteville is only the SECOND worst
> thing that can happen to you.

The official claimed that he had officiated for over 25
years and had acquired a "reputation of complete
honesty, absolute integrity and impeccable moral
character." He stated that this reputation existed
among "officials, players and fans" in the various
states in which he officiated. The plaintiff declared that
his reputation had been severely impaired by the article
which was widely distributed in the southwestern area
of the country. He argued that the article was libelous
and caused him much "embarrassment and
humiliation." The plaintiff contended that officials
could not keep professional standing if the general
public and participants of sports questioned their
integrity.

The plaintiff's attorneys insisted that the article was
completely false and placed their client in an untenable
position because it constituted:

> A defamation of plaintiff's character and
> exposed him to public hatred, contempt and
> ridicule, and impeached his honesty, fairness,
> integrity and virtue, and irrevocably damaged
> his reputation.

They added:

> Such statements would, in the mind of the
> ordinary reader, impute to plaintiff, a complete
> lack of honesty, integrity and virtue and
> accuses him of not being an impartial referee

and with intentionally and habitually making wrong calls as an official in order to obtain favorable results for certain participants.

The plaintiff sued for damages of $1 million for the "lifelong injury upon him" because the writer did not take the time to check on the accuracy of his statements which he circulated so freely.

The case was dismissed and the plaintiff appealed to the Supreme Court of Oklahoma. The court, favoring the defendant and ruling that the plaintiff failed to prove that the article damaged him, pointed to the fact that he had been selected to officiate in the prestigious Cotton Bowl after the article appeared earlier in the year.

IN MY OPINION

Officials live in a glass house as their every decision is subject to public scrutiny and instant replays. It is amazing how accurate they are as a rule. The pressures of each call can be seen in the emotional playoff games of professional sports. This pressure extends downward to the collegiate, scholastic and even little leagues.

Celeste Ulrich, in *To Seek and Find* epitomizes the ideal attitude toward officials when she writes:

> The official is deemed incorruptible for he is truly an objective judge who deserves respect by virtue of both his position and his talents.[12]

Compare this to the angry denunciation of an official by Notre Dame Coach Dan Devine after his team lost to USC:

---

12. CELESTE ULRICH, TO SEEK AND FIND, AAHPER, Washington, DC, 1976.

if the official made a mistake on that call, I'll
work to see that he'll never work another
game.[13]

The truth may be found somewhere between the two
statements. Certainly officials are important and their
decisions will affect the outcome of many contests. As
such, they will continue to bear the derision of unhappy
athletes, coaches and spectators when the outcome of
important contests are hotly contested.

As a result of the pressures and publicity the official
will be just as vulnerable as the player, the coach,
administrator, team physician, etc., to litigation and be
forced to have his day in court. As we see from the cases
recorded in this chapter, the official will be charged with
negligence when he fails to take action in a rough game
and, as a consequence, someone is seriously injured.

It is encouraging to note that this year in
interscholastic athletics, several games were being
played when dangerous lightning struck the stadium.
Without hesitation, the officials called the game. This is
progress, for all too many games are played when
conditions are prohibitive to the safety of all concerned.

The official is finding that the salary scale for all
contests must be equitable and no longer can the official
of boys' contests be paid more than the official of a
comparable sport for girls.

In like manner, the official is going to court when his
or her reputation is damaged by libelous or slanderous
statements.

No longer can the official find immunity from a
sports-related lawsuit; but, conversely, no longer is the

---

13. Greensboro Daily News, Nov. 1978.

official denied a day in court that may be needed to insure fair treatment in one of the most demanding and least appreciated of the many sports professions.

CHAPTER 9

The Spectator

Violent attacks by spectators or players are no longer rare or unique events, but now cause serious concern to all who attend sports events.[1]

The desire and need for financial support for the operation of sports programs has placed the spectator in a powerful position. In many instances fans are not content to sit and watch, but actually get involved in the sports events in ways that can be dangerous. The demands of a win-at-any cost attitude create problems that cause serious concern at all levels of sports.

One Atlantic Coast Conference basketball coach deplores the conduct of fans at tension filled contests when he states that:

A bad situation at one school got worse. Some of the objects they've thrown are uncalled for. The crowd had been drinking for two or three hours before the game, there was actual physical contact and it was a highly volatile situation.[2]

Spectators often stand in endless lines to purchase tickets to see their favorite teams perform. Duke University officials find that success in a program creates unusual problems. (One Duke University student camped in line beginning Tuesday for a

---

1. ARNOLD BEISSER, MADNESS IN SPORTS, The Charles Press Publishers, Bowie, Md., 1977.
2. Greensboro Daily News, Jan. 30, 1979.

Saturday game.) The problem resulted from the fact that:

> Duke received 23,000 requests for season tickets this year. Cameron Indoor Stadium seats 8,564 of the most innovative, loud and controversial fans in college basketball. And an extra 50 or so have been known to sneak in the building the day before and sleep in back rooms and closets in order to gain admission. Others climb in windows.[3]

Edwin Cady, a professor of humanities at Duke University and a faculty representative to the National Collegiate Athletic Association, describes the relation between spectators and sports as "an affair of the people" that mirrors society in the United States. He raised the question:

> Where, indeed, can you see and hear a hard hat who never finished high school and a scientist with three degrees stand side by side and sing the foolish and vulgar tune of 'alma mater' with a fervor and unction fit for a Bach Chorale sung by believers.[4]

James Michener echoes these sentiments when he writes, in *Sports in America,* that sports exist, among other things, to entertain the public.[5] But not everyone agrees that the purpose of sports should be for spectator entertainment. Arnold Beisser, a sports psychologist, rejects the fanatic spectator mania that is escalating today. He laments the trend that:

---

3. *Id.*
4. Greensboro Daily News, Nov. 12, 1978.
5. JAMES MICHENER, SPORTS IN AMERICA, Random House, N.Y., 1976.

American competitive sports prepare youth for maturity as spectators who watch rather than participate in the significant and meaningful activities in society.[6]

While the controversy over the spectator's role in sports continues, one thing is certain: the spectator shares the courtroom with other sports participants. This chapter considers several cases that pertain to spectator injuries and disruptive spectator behavior.

Injuries to Spectators

Spectators are injured at many types of sports events. Injuries occur in various sports environments and cause the owners and operators of sports facilities concern over the threat of expensive lawsuits.

A. Baseball

According to the number of cases on record, it appears that more spectators receive injuries at baseball games than any other type of sports event. The most prevalent baseball injury takes place when a spectator is hit by a ball batted into the stands. The issue usually centers around the location and use of protective screens. Four cases involving a lack of protective screens and subsequent injuries illustrate this type of case.

David Maytnier, Jr., requested a seat behind the Chicago Cubs dugout so he could see his favorite players close up.[7] The seat was in a section that was not covered by a protective screen. In the sixth inning, Bob Rush, a Chicago pitcher, warmed up in the bullpen and

---

6. *Supra* note 1.
7. Maytnier v. Rush, 225 N.E.2d 83 (Ill. App. 1967).

threw a wild pitch that hit Maytnier on the left side of his head. During the trial it was stated that:

> The seat occupied by plaintiff was in such a position that it required him to look to his right to see the pitcher and batter in the game and to see to his left to see the bullpen activity.

He sued Rush, the pitcher in the bullpen, for negligence, and the Chicago Cubs for failing to install a screen to protect the spectators.

The defendants contended that they did not owe the spectator a duty to furnish such a screen since he assumed any risk of injury when he bought a ticket to the game.

The Illinois Appellate Court, First District, Second Division, dismissed the case against the Chicago pitcher, but found the Chicago Cubs guilty of negligence for failing to provide a screen to protect spectators from wild pitches from the bullpen. It felt that it was impossible for a spectator to watch the game and the bullpen at the same time. It reasoned that the bullpen was too close to the stands for safety without a screen. The court awarded Maytnier $20,000 in damages.

A 47-year-old woman was hurt at her first baseball game when a foul ball struck her while she was sitting behind first base.[8] The area was not protected by a screen. Her husband testified that the ticket seller assured him that he had good seats, but when he entered the ballpark, he found them to be in an unsafe section. He saw the long lines of people waiting outside

---

8. Schentzel v. Philadelphia Nat'l League Club, 96 A.2d 181 (Pa. 1953).

the ballpark to purchase tickets and decided to use the tickets he had instead of exchanging them.

During the trial the plaintiff testified that she had only seen a baseball game on television and never saw a foul ball hit into the stands. Her husband stated, however, that foul balls are common and, on occasion, four or five are hit into the stands in one inning. His wife, however, blamed the Philadelphia Baseball Club for her injury, which she attributed to a lack of protective screening.

The court did not agree, but ruled, instead, that she assumed the risk of injury inherent in baseball. The court made several observations regarding such injuries when it said:

1. Negligence is never presumed, and the plaintiff has the burden of proving it.

2. The mere happening of an accident is no evidence of negligence.

3. One who maintains a place of amusement for which admission is charged is not an insurer, but must use reasonable care in the construction, maintenance, and management of it, having regard to character of exhibitions given and customary conduct of patrons invited.

4. Consent to accept hazard may be implied from conduct of one who freely and voluntarily enters into any relation or simulation which presents obvious danger, and, therefore, those who participate or sit as spectators at sports and amusements assume the obvious risks of being injured.

Evelyn Ierolino sat behind a dugout at Forbes Field watching Pittsburgh play Los Angeles.[9] She had attended baseball games for 15 years and knew that baseballs were often hit into the stands. Don Hoak hit several foul balls into the stands and one struck the plaintiff.

Justice Robert VanDerVoort posed the following question to the jury:

> Was it negligence for the defendant to invite a patron to a sports event and view a baseball game from a position where she was exposed to a hard projectile traveling 94½ feet in a split second?

The jury believed that the defendant was obligated to furnish a screen to protect the spectator. It awarded the plaintiff $10,000 in damages and the defendant appealed the verdict.

The Superior Court of Pennsylvania ruled that the trial court erred in permitting the jury to decide the standard of care required of the operator of the facility. It emphasized that a jury is not allowed to "speculate or guess," observing that spectators generally assume the risk of injury at sports events unless an exception exists when:

> numerous balls are being hit — in this case — batting practice, infield practice, pitcher warmup.

The court concluded that:

> A spectator is not expected to follow intently balls that are thrown or batted outside the

---

9. Iervolino v. Pittsburgh Athletic Co., Inc., 243 A.2d 490 (Pa. Super. 1968).

regular play of the game when his attention is fixed on the ball in regular play or when the game is not in progress.

It reversed the lower court's decision because the exceptions listed above were not applicable. Instead, it found that the plaintiff assumed the risk of being hit by a foul ball.

A fourth case demonstrates that assumption of risk is not always a successful defense in baseball cases.

Evelyn Jones accepted the Three Rivers Stadium's opening night invitation to come early and inspect the new facility.[10] She was on the concourse behind the Pittsburgh dugout when she decided to get something to eat. Someone shouted "watch" and she was hit in the eye by a batted ball. The jury awarded her $125,000 in damages and the defendant appealed.

The defendants cited a 1925 case to support their contention that batting practice has the same status as a regular game regarding liability for injury due to negligence.[11]

The plaintiff insisted that old Forbes Field had a screen in a comparable location and questioned its absence at Three Rivers Stadium. The Superior Court of Pennsylvania noted that most baseball fans try to find seats that are located in unscreened areas of the stadium. It did not believe that the area in question required screening. It held that the plaintiff did not prove any negligence on the part of the Three Rivers Corporation and reversed the earlier decision.

The Supreme Court of Pennsylvania then reviewed the plaintiff's appeal and reinstated the original award

10. Jones v. Three Rivers Management Corp., 380 A.2d 387 (Pa. Super. 1977).
11. Cincinnati Baseball Club v. Eno, 147 N.E. 86 (Ohio 1925).

of $125,000 to the injured woman by holding that the defendant's failure to provide a protective screen did breach a duty it owed the spectators who sat in that section.[12]

B. Football

Judy Sims sued the Etowah County Board of Education for an injury she sustained when the bleachers on which she sat collapsed during a high school football game.[13] She claimed that her ticket implied a contract between the school board to guarantee her a safe place to sit and watch the game. The school board based its defense on the doctrine of governmental immunity.

The Supreme Court of Alabama recognized that various jurisdictions treated governmental immunity for spectator injury at sports events in different ways. Some permitted recovery while others did not. The court commented, however, that the state of Alabama establishes a contract between the purchaser of a ticket and the proprietor of a facility when a person buys a ticket to a sports event. It declared that while the board of education can sell a ticket, it can also be held liable for injuries that result from an unsafe facility.

The court considered the question of torts to be another matter, however. It reasoned that school boards historically have been immune from tort claims. It therefore decided that while the board was immune from torts it could be held liable if the ticket holders were injured because the board failed to maintain a safe facility.

---

12. The News and Observer, Nov. 21, 1978.
13. Sims v. Etowah County Bd. of Educ., 337 So. 2d 1310 (Alaska 1976).

The sidelines at football games often are crowded with spectators, television crews, medical personnel, the press and others who place themselves in a dangerous position and frequently are injured. As this author said in *From the Gym to the Jury*:

> Little children, elderly grandmothers, enthusiastic parents, relatives, and friends crowd the sidelines to get a closer look at their local heroes.[14]

Three cases demonstrate the court's attitude toward sideline injuries in collision sports such as football.

Louise Perry, a 67-year-old grandmother of one of the football players, watched her grandson from the sidelines.[15] The game was played between the third-string squads of two high schools. The parents, relatives and friends of the players had been encouraged to attend the game and no admission was charged.

Louise Perry was standing near midfield, about one or two feet from the out-of-bounds line, when a tackler drove the ball carrier into her, inflicting serious and permanent injury. At the time of impact she was not watching the game and did not see the players moving toward her.

The trial court dismissed the case since it felt that the school district was not guilty of negligence. It ruled, instead, that she assumed the risk of injury by standing so close to the sidelines and was, therefore, guilty of contributory negligence.

---

14. HERB APPENZELLER, FROM THE GYM TO THE JURY, The Michie Co., Charlottesville, Va., 1970.
15. Perry v. Seattle School Dist. No. 1, 405 P.2d 589 (Wash. 1965).

The court of appeals supported this decision because it was of the opinion that the plaintiff had a duty to protect herself, not only against the dangers of which she had actual knowledge, but also against dangers inherent in the game. She had seen football on television and had been a spectator at previous games, which she watched from the stands. The court commented that "while it is clear that a plaintiff must know the risk before it can be assumed, it is equally clear that he cannot deny knowledge of the obvious."

A similar situation took place in Louisiana when Ruth Turner was watching her first football game. Her grandson was one of the players and at the time she was 71 years of age.[16] She was watching the game from about two yards from the sidelines at about the forty-yard line when she was hit by a ball carrier and two tacklers. She was knocked down by the violent impact, suffering a fractured vertebrae and two broken legs.

The trial court favored the school district and the plaintiff appealed the verdict. The court of appeals reversed the decision because the plaintiff was not asked to leave the sidelines by anyone in authority and was unaware of the perilous situation she was in. The court held that the school district breached a duty it owed the plaintiff when it failed to remove the spectators from the sidelines. It awarded Mrs. Turner $18,500 in damages in addition to $1,375.05 for medical expenses.

The Supreme Court of Louisiana then reviewed the case and decided that the school officials were not

---

16. Turner v. Caddo Parish School Bd., 204 So. 2d 294 (La. App. 1968), *rev'd*, 214 So. 2d 153 (La. 1968).

negligent.[17] It did not believe that anyone in this day of television could be unaware of the possibility that players occasionally run into persons standing near the sidelines such as "cameramen, officials, other players, spectators, etc."

The court held it unreasonable to require school officials to determine which spectator lacked knowledge of the sport and needed a special warning. It also noted that it would be too expensive to erect barriers along the sidelines of junior high schools since such barriers limit the function of the field and interfere with other activities. It recognized the fact that no past accidents had been reported, declaring that:

> raised ropes or chains were not always successful in achieving their purpose inasmuch as spectators often come close to and even on the field merely by stooping under them.

The court concluded that such ropes or other barricades constitute "hazards and nuisances to the students engaged in the other activities." It reversed the decision of the court of appeals and favored the school officials.

A 17-year-old girl, Donna Cadieux, stood on the sidelines of a football field although there were seats available in the stands.[18] She was aware that the participants often ran off the field into the sidelines. During a play toward the sideline where she was standing, a ball carrier and several tacklers crashed into her and injured her.

The New York Supreme Court, Schenectady County, granted the school district summary judgment and she

---

17. Turner v. Caddo Parish School Bd., 214 So. 2d 153 (La. 1968).
18. Cadieux v. Board of Educ. of City School Dist. of City of Schenectady, N. Y., 266 N.Y.S.2d 895 (N.Y. App. Div. 1966).

appealed. The supreme court, appellate division, referred to previous cases in baseball, ice hockey and even stickball to support the lower court's decision commenting that:

A spectator at a sporting event assumes the obvious and necessary risks incidental to the game, especially where he chooses to sit at an unsafe place despite the availability of protected seating.[19]

It reasoned that the same principle applied to a person standing on the sidelines of a football game. The court, therefore, affirmed the lower court's judgment for the school district.

C. Ice Hockey

A woman spectator was struck in the eye with a hockey puck and she sued the Providence, Rhode Island Hockey Club. She claimed that the hockey club was negligent for failing to warn her of the danger she was in, or providing another seat in a safe location.[20]

The defendant argued that the plaintiff assumed the risk of injury when she bought a ticket and took her seat in the arena. The plaintiff testified that she had attended ice hockey games for over 30 years at the arena and had seen many games on television, and that she customarily sat at the end of the arena because the seats were not as expensive as others in the arena. However, she had to purchase tickets in the section in which she was hit by the puck because they were the only remaining seats.

---

19. *Id.*
20. Kennedy v. Providence Hockey Club, Inc., 376 A.2d 329 (R.I. 1977).

The court felt that the plaintiff was well versed in the rudiments of ice hockey and the accompanying danger of a flying puck. Accordingly, the court denied her appeal because she was aware of the location of the seat and knowingly accepted it.

D. Basketball

It is unusual for a spectator at a basketball game to be injured by a basketball, but it happened in New Mexico in a game involving the Harlem Globe Trotters.[21] The Globe Trotters played a basketball game in a high school in Tucumcari, New Mexico and a member of the team threw a basketball into the crowd and hit a spectator in the face.

The injured woman complained that the player was negligent when he threw the ball into the stands and the defendant responded that the woman assumed the risk when she bought a ticket to the game. The defendant asserted that the accident was unforeseeable and could not be avoided.

The jury awarded the woman $18,700 and the defendant appealed to the Supreme Court of New Mexico. Since there is a lack of cases involving basketball, the defendant cited some baseball cases to prove that the player was not negligent. The Harlem Globe Trotters argued that the rule of assumption of risk should apply to basketball as well as to baseball for a defense.

The Supreme Court of New Mexico did not agree with the Globe Trotters and upheld the district court's decision in favor of the woman. It held that the member

---

21. McFatridge v. Harlem Globe Trotters, 365 P.2d 918 (N.M. 1961).

of the team who threw the ball into the stands was acting in the employment of the defendant when he injured the plaintiff and awarded the woman damages.

E. Wrestling

Manuel Silvia bought a front row ticket to a wrestling match at the Woodhouse Arenatorium in Dartmouth, Massachusetts.[22] During the first match a wrestler lifted his opponent, who weighed 290 lbs., and tossed him out of the ring. The wrestler attempted to get back into the ring but his opponent struck him and he fell back on the plaintiff's leg. The plaintiff asserted that no one warned him, either by a sign or announcement, that there was a danger of wrestlers falling out of the ring. He testified that he had attended previous matches and had never witnessed an action like the one he experienced the night he was hurt.

The president of Santos Wrestling Enterprises, and Woodhouse, the owner and operator of the arena, stated that they had seen similar incidents when wrestlers were thrown forcibly from a ring into spectators. Woodhouse's request for a directed verdict was denied.

The court explained that:

> A person maintaining a place of amusement, to which the public is invited, is bound to exercise reasonable care to keep the premises in a reasonably safe condition for the use of the patrons and to warn them of the dangers which he knew or ought to have known they might encounter there and of which they could not reasonably be expected to know.

---

22. Silvia v. Woodhouse, 248 N.E.2d 260 (Mass. 1969).

The court qualified the statement by adding that an operator of a sports facility did not have to issue a warning about a danger that was obvious to any person of normal intelligence. It found Woodhouse guilty of negligence because the seats were too close to the ring and he failed to warn the spectators that wrestlers could be thrown out of the ring. It held that Santos was not liable since he was the matchmaker and, unlike Woodhouse, had nothing to do with the condition of the arena or the seating arrangement.

F. Roller Derby

Ellsworth Brand attended a roller derby exhibition in a school gymnasium, which was sponsored by a service club that rented the facility for $80.[23] The service club provided "two firemen and twenty-five uniformed auxiliary policemen to control the crowd" while the school board furnished janitors to set up and remove the seats and clean up the area.

The plaintiff remained in his seat four or five minutes after the roller derby ended and then started toward the exit. A large woman pushed against the plaintiff and he fell over the rail sustaining injuries to his shoulder. No evidence was produced during the trial to indicate that the bleachers were defective or that the crowd was unruly. Brand charged the school board with assuming a "landlord-tenant" relationship which made it subject to liability.

The trial court granted the school board summary judgment and the plaintiff appealed. The Appellate

---

23. Brand v. Sertoma Club of Springfield, 349 N.E.2d 502 (Ill. App. 1976).

Court of Illinois favored the school board also, declaring that it did not assume a "lessor-lessee relationship" nor was it responsible for liability because it rented the building.

Disruptive Spectator Behavior

A. Throwing Objects

A group of fans threw objects that hit some spectators and landed on the basketball court prior to the game between New Mexico University and Brigham Young University.[24] It took over 40 minutes to restore the playing court to playing conditions.

William Orzen and Allen Cooper were charged with creating a disturbance and "unlawful assembly." Orzen reportedly threw a cup containing ice while Cooper tossed a liquid-filled balloon. New Mexico has a statute that prohibits unlawful assembly, but Orzen and Cooper argued that a sports event does not constitute a meeting.

The Court of Appeals of New Mexico referred to *Webster's Dictionary* to define a meeting. The dictionary interpreted a meeting of people as: "a gathering for business, social or other purposes." It reasoned that the definition covered the crowd at the basketball game as a meeting and decided that the "players were a meeting of people assembled for a lawful object." The court considered a 40-minute delay of game a disturbance. It therefore affirmed the lower court's judgment against the two men.

---

24. State v. Orzen, 493 P.2d 768 (N.M. App. 1972).

B. Abusive Language

A spectator, at a high school basketball game, expecting a confrontation between a group of black students and the school administrators, planned to take pictures and tape record the events as they happened.[25] An announcement was made prior to the game that anyone who refused to stand during the playing of the national anthem would not be allowed to attend future sports events and would be put out of the gymnasium.

The defendant was irritated by the announcement and shouted that such action was illegal and immediately got into a dispute with some spectators who told him to get quiet. He then gestured in an obscene way and shouted a lewd chant. A detective arrested him and led him from the gymnasium. He appealed his conviction to the Superior Court of New Jersey.

The defendant contended that his right of free speech under the First Amendment was violated by his arrest. The court responded that while the Constitution protects an individual's personal freedom, it equally protects others from "riotous or potentially dangerous disturbances."

It went on to comment:

> Defendant's conviction does not rest so much on what he said or on when he chose to say it, but rather on the allegedly abusive and disruptive character of his.

The New Jersey court referred to an earlier case which said:

> Surely, it cannot be contended, merely because a basketball game is more noisy in nature than

---

25. State v. Morgulis, 266 A.2d 136 (N.J. Super. App. Div. 1970).

a legislative assembly, that spectators at the former may engage in unbridled behavior regardless of its effect on other persons in attendance.[26]

In upholding the Union County Court's decision against the defendant, the superior court concluded:

As to defendants' free speech argument, it has been held that obscenity is not protected by the First Amendment and that the statute of prohibition is a valid condition of the police power.[27]

C. Fighting

A group of spectators were injured during a fight in a stadium parking lot following a high school football game between Harrisburg High School and Cedar Cliff High School. An announcement was made at the stadium over the public address system to try to restore order, but it had the opposite effect and more fighting erupted.

After several meetings were held to determine the cause of the disturbance, the responsibility was attributed to the Harrisburg school and it was placed on a two-year probation. One condition of the probation was that the school could not conduct any practice or game later than 4:00 p.m. The school sought to turn the decision aside.

The court made reference to Article IX of the Pennsylvania Interscholastic Athletic Association's

---

26. State v. Smith, 218 A.2d 147 (N.J. 1966).
27. *Supra* note 24.

(PIAA) Constitution defining a principal's responsibility regarding athletics:

> The principal of each school, in all matters pertaining to the interscholastic relations of his school, is responsible to the Association. He may delegate some of these powers but such delegation shall not relieve him of responsibility for any infraction by his school of the constitution and By Laws of this Association.

The Harrisburg principal admitted that his spectators did have dangerous objects in their possession such as:

> the razor blades, the ice picks, the broken bottles, the chains, the deadly weapons that can kill.

The court reasoned that the PIAA comes under state action since dues from gate receipts from state-owned facilities support it. It noted that the Harrisburg school was still a member of the PIAA and allowed to conduct its athletic programs with the single restraint of a 4:00 p.m. practice or game restriction. Since the association did not violate constitutional rights in this instance, it ruled that judicial interference was unwarranted. It upheld the decision of the Court of Common Pleas in favor of the PIAA.

A woman sought $90,000 in damages from the Louisiana High School Athletic Association because it prohibited her from attending any athletic contest involving Fenton High School for one year.[29] She claimed that her right of "free speech and assembly" was violated in addition to the "invasion of her privacy

---

28. School Dist. of City of Harrisburg v. Pennsylvania Interscholastic Athletic Ass'n, 309 A.2d 353 (Pa. 1973).
29. Watkins v. Louisiana High School Athletic Ass'n, 301 So. 2d 695 (La. App. 1974).

and damage to her reputation." She also contended that the association's action had degraded her in the community and with her own children.

The unusual penalty was the result of her post-game altercation with a referee. According to the principal of the opposing high school and the other basketball official, the woman charged onto the floor and argued with the referee about his officiating and "grabbed him by the arm."

The sportsmanship committee reviewed the incident with the plaintiff in attendance and devised the following penalty:

1. Fenton High School was fined $75 and placed on probation for one calendar year.

2. Fenton High School was forbidden from participation in any interscholastic athletic contest for one calendar year with the plaintiff in attendance.

The plaintiff complained that it was embarrassing and humiliating to have the principals of opposing schools check the crowd to see if she was present before starting a game. She also contended that her right of due process was denied since there was no sign in the gymnasium, or statement on the admission ticket, warning spectators not to touch or talk to officials.

The association responded that its schools have the responsibility of crowd control, not the association. It pointed out that Fenton High School had the option to let her attend athletic events and not participate in league games.

The Court of Appeals of Louisiana made an interesting observation regarding the athletic association's action in such matters when it declared:

The general rule in Louisiana is that the courts will not interfere with the internal affairs of a private association except in cases where the affairs and proceedings have not been conducted fairly and honestly, or in cases of fraud, lack of jurisdiction, the invasion of property or pecuniary rights, or when the action complained of is capricious, arbitrary or unjustly discriminatory.

The court favored the association because it found that it did not violate any of the conditions listed above.

IN MY OPINION

The United States is becoming a nation of spectators as evidenced by the record breaking crowds at almost every type of sports event. It seems logical that increased attendance will lead to situations that result in litigation.

Several things are apparent from the courts' opinions and decisions regarding spectators at sports events. Spectators usually accept the risks inherent in the sport they attend much like the participant. The exception seems to occur when the operator of a facility fails to provide protection in areas where there is the danger of injury. There are several such areas in most baseball parks that require protective screens. If the spectator chooses to sit elsewhere, he or she assumes the risk of injury rather than the owner or operator of the facility.

For some reason people like to get as close to the sidelines during collision sports such as football, soccer and lacrosse. Many times they take young children with them. Earl Edwards, a former coach at North Carolina State University, related how angry parents used to get when he requested them to move back into the stands with their children. He declared that a 230 pound football player wearing 23 pounds of football gear and running at full speed would hit with the same force as a speeding automobile.

The courts have denied recovery to adults who received injuries on the sidelines during football games, but I predict that the courts will rule differently if a very young child is injured because the sidelines were not supervised. The court does not require a warning if a danger exists if it is, or should be, obvious to a person of normal intelligence. Owners and operators should warn spectators of unknown dangers or dangers that they are not expected to know.

Spectators do not assume the risk of a sudden, unexpected act by a participant, nor do they assume the risk when a frustrated or angry participant throws a ball or other object into the stands.

The prudent administrator, owner or operator of a facility, should provide periodic inspection, duly recorded, of all equipment and facilities. A detailed record could prove helpful in the event litigation follows an injury and the cause is alleged to be some defect or unsafe condition of the equipment or facility.

Spectators often sue when they are unwillingly ejected from a sports event. In such instances they usually claim that their abusive language or disorderly conduct is protected by the guarantees of the First Amendment of the Federal Constitution. In these instances the courts are very consistent in ruling that such behavior is not protected or tolerated by the Constitution.

CHAPTER 10
The Team Physician

Perhaps no group has felt the whiplash of the impulse to sue more keenly than the medical profession.[1]

The medical profession has added a new dimension to its already important role in society — sports medicine. Dr. James A. Nicholas, who received national attention as Joe Namath's orthopedic surgeon, commented that if sports medicine had been a reality in 1964, Namath would probably have been turned down for professional football. Nicholas declared:

> Today, sports medicine is one of the fastest growing areas of interest among orthopedic surgeons and the team physician is one of medicine's newest sub-specialties.[2]

Physicians influence sports participants by regulating diets, exercise, conditioning, examinations, equipment, weight and treatment.

Although progress has been made, serious problems in sports medicine plague many communities throughout the United States. There is an acute shortage of team physicians while the number of sports participants increases each year. The problem may remain unless something can be done to alleviate the fear among physicians of malpractice suits that continue to threaten the medical profession.

---

1. *Why Everybody Is Suing Everybody,* U.S. NEWS AND WORLD REPORT, Dec. 4, 1978.
2. AMERICAN MEDICAL NEWS, Mar. 23, 1979.

This chapter will review the problems relating to sports medicine and the legal status of the team physician in amateur sports.

Sports-Related Medical Problems

A. Shortage of Team Physicians

Many schools are unable to obtain the services of physicians to administer pre-season physical examinations or supervise sports contests. The number of schools without the services of a team physician is alarming. John O'Neill, commenting on a survey of athletic directors for the *Kendall Sports Trail,* deplores the fact that six out of every ten athletes who participate in high school football suffer injuries.[3] O'Neill decries the lack of physicians available to the schools when he remarks:

> Another reason for the high ratio of athletic injuries at the high school level is that less than half of the schools surveyed have a team physician who attends all their home games, and only 29 percent have one on call during home games.[4]

In a report entitled "Athletic Injuries and Deaths in Secondary Schools and Colleges" the shortage of medical personnel was described as follows:

> Lack of available health personnel has led to modification of rules requiring specified medical or health services at athletic events. In a midwestern city, for example, a requirement that a doctor had to attend every interscholastic

---

3. KENDALL SPORTS TRAIL, Sept.-Oct., 1972.
4. *Id.*

football game was repealed when doctors could not be found to attend the games.[5]

Dr. Allan Ryan, editor-in-chief of *The Physician and Sportsmedicine,* recognizes the problem, but explains that:

> It can never be possible to have a physician in attendance at every sports competition, even in so-called contact sports. The important thing is to have the medical advisor or consultant who is available or accessible when needed and who has sufficient interest in the program to know what is needed.[6]

The need for medical protection becomes apparent when the shortage of medical personnel is placed alongside the statistic that over 22.5 million men and women participated in sports activities in secondary schools and colleges in 1975-1976. Added to this is the alarming statistic that over one million injuries occurred during the same reporting period.[7]

B. Legal Status of the Team Physician

Since there is a lack of case law governing the conduct of the team physician, he or she is bound by the "general principles of law relating to a doctor's

---

5. *Athletic Injuries and Deaths in Secondary Schools and Colleges, 1975-76, A Report on the Survey Mandated by Section 826 of Public Law 93-380,* Dept. of HEW, Washington, D.C., Feb. 1979.
6. Allan Ryan, *The Prevention of Injuries in Sports and Physical Education,* SPORTS SAFETY II, Chicago, Ill., Oct. 1976.
7. *Id.*

responsibilities and liabilities." [8] While the athlete may assume the risk of a sport, he or she is not responsible for the negligence of a physician. For example, the athlete would not be held responsible:

> If he were examined by a doctor, and the doctor, through negligence, erroneously found no medical condition making it inadvisable for him to participate in the sport.[9]

John C. Weistart and Cym H. Lowell, in *The Law of Sports,* foresee athletes suing their physicians when they believe that an improper medical examination caused their injury.[10] They comment:

> For example, if a football player died as a result of a heart attack it might be alleged that a doctor who gave the player a physical exam before the season began was negligent since death was the result of a defect or injury that should have been discovered in the examination.[11]

It may be difficult to prove that the alleged lack of a reasonable medical examination was the cause of an injury. The issue was raised in New York when, a boxer, George Flores, died from several "hard blows to the head." [12] Flores had received a severe beating in the two fights prior to the one in which he died of "cerebral hemorrhage and cerebral edema." The court of claims awarded the administrator of Flores' estate $80,000 in

---

8. Michael Gallagher, *Rights and Responsibilities of Team Physicians,* CURRENT SPORTS MEDICINE ISSUES, AAHPER, Washington, D.C., 1974.
9. *Id.*
10. JOHN C. WEISTART AND CYM H. LOWELL, THE LAW OF SPORTS, Bobbs-Merrill Co., Inc., Indianapolis, Ind., 1979.
11. *Id.*
12. Rosensweig v. State, 158 N.E.2d 229 (N.Y. 1959).

damages. The case was appealed. The attending physician testified that a physician examined Flores after each of the two fights in which he was "knocked out." In addition, he pointed out that he suspended Flores from further action until he could administer an encephalogram (EEG). He permitted Flores to fight as scheduled when the results of the EEG were "normal" and "generally good" and he was convinced that the boxer was in excellent physical condition. The supreme court, appellate division, reversed the previous decision and favored the physician and state of New York. The administrator appealed the case, but the court of appeals affirmed the decision in favor of the physician.

It is interesting to observe, however, that several justices dissented and while the decision stood, their opinion is noteworthy. They strongly opposed the decision that favored the physician and state of New York and said:

> Good medical practice demands a layoff for boxers who have suffered a knockout or severe beating about the head from six weeks to two months — This was not an error in judgment as the appellate division has indicated, but was a failure to give proper heed and consideration to obvious medical facts and practices.[13]

(Flores was examined after he was knocked out on July 24 and August 14 and permitted to fight on August 29.)

Weistart and Lowell discuss the liability of the average physician who endeavors to assist a sports program when they comment:

> When a doctor in general practice undertakes to treat a sports injury, he or she will have a duty

---

13. *Id.*

to perform with the degree of reasonable skill
and knowledge that would be utilized by the
members of the profession in good standing.[14]

In summary Weistart and Lowell conclude that the
physician will be judged on the basis of what is
reasonable in the medical profession. They believe,
however, that a physician who specializes in some area
of sports medicine may be held to a higher standard in
his or her area of expertise than the general
practitioner. It is possible, therefore, for the sports
medicine specialist to be held liable when the general
practitioner is not.[15]

C. Informed Consent

Many school officials and coaches are put in a
precarious position when they are unable to secure the
services of a physician at games away from home. As
a rule the host physician usually volunteers his services
to the opposing team. Michael Gallagher, an Ohio
attorney, advises the physician, in this instance, to
consider the fact that he may be risking legal action if
he is found negligent. He cautions that a physician who
treats in the absence of consent, either expressed or
informed, might face assault and battery charges. He
explains the perils inherent in such a situation when he
points out that:

> The doctrine of informed consent is one upon
> which many suits are currently based. Its real
> value to a plaintiff's attorney is that it obviates
> the need to establish negligence on the part of
> the doctor, more particularly, it avoids the

14. *Supra* note 10.
15. *Supra* note 10.

necessity of producing competent medical
testimony that the offending doctor has
deviated from the appropriate standard of
care.[16]

Gallagher adds that this doctrine applies to athletes
and recommends that physicians obtain written
permission for the authorization of care and treatment
for injuries sustained in a sports practice or game. He
warns that any treatment beyond emergency first aid
should be sanctioned by parental consent or the consent
of the participant who is informed of the risks
associated with the treatment.[17]

In some instances it may not be possible to locate a
parent or guardian to give permission for treatment
that goes beyond emergency care although the nature
of the injury requires additional and immediate medical
attention. The Supreme Court of Kansas decided a case
in which a 17-year-old girl gave her consent for surgery
on her finger.[18] The girl caught her finger in a door and
faced the loss of her finger unless she received
immediate surgery. The girl's parents were divorced
and her father lived 200 miles from the hospital. The
authorities could not locate him. Her mother had un-
dergone surgery and, at the time consent was sought,
was unconscious. The court held that the girl was close
to majority and knowingly consented to the operation.
It acknowledged that her action constituted an
exception to the rule of informed consent.

In Pennsylvania a physician was sued when his
patient died during surgery. The question was raised of

---

16. *Supra* note 8.
17. *Supra* note 8.
18. Younts v. St. Francis Hosp. and School of Nursing, Inc., 469
    P.2d 330 (Kan. 1970).

whether an emergency existed and, if in fact, the woman gave her consent to the operation.[19] The court favored the physician and, in so doing, made several comments that help set guidelines regarding informed consent. The court said:

> A physician must obtain consent of a patient before performing surgery unless need for consent is obviated by emergency which places patient in immediate danger and makes it impractical to secure such consent.

It also declared that:

> Consent is informed only if the patient knows what is apt to happen to him and the possible adverse results and dangers of the operation.[20]

William Herbert, professor of physical education at Virginia Polytechnic Institute, and David Herbert, an Ohio attorney, consider the liability of the people who administer exercise tests for adults. They suggest the following procedure in stress testing and also help clarify the guidelines of informed consent such as:

1. After informing the test participant of all the risks and dangers inherent in the GXT (graded exercise testing), ask the participant to execute a consent form.

2. The participant to give consent must:
   a. be legally capable of giving consent (he cannot be legally or mentally incapacitated);
   b. know and fully understand the risks he is consenting to;

---

19. Dunham v. Wright, 423 F.2d 940 (3d Cir. 1970).
20. *Id.*

      c. give his consent voluntarily and not
         under any mistake of fact or some
         duress.

3. Obtain additional legal protection by getting
   written consent from the participant's
   spouse and family physician.[21]

Dr. Allan Ryan recognizes the liability problems facing the physician and agrees that the physician takes many risks, but he gives physicians reassurance when he concludes:

> It is hard to see, however, how a system of procedure which has due regard for the individual, which includes careful record-keeping, and which backs every critical decision with good reasoning can get into serious disability barring some completely unpredictable happening.[22]

Dr. James C. Brewer has the athletes under his medical care, if they are of majority age, or their parents, if minors, sign a permission form for emergency medical treatment. A list of the athletes who have signed statements, and a copy of the permission form, is put in the medical kit for each sports team. In the event of an emergency, when the team physician is not available, the attending physician is reassured by the presence of a permission form. This enables any physician to treat the athlete with confidence that informed consent has been given.

---

21. William G. Herbert and David L. Herbert, Exercise Testing of Adults, Legal and Procedural Considerations for the Physical Educator and Exercise Specialist, (unpublished paper), Blacksburg, Va., 1974.
22. MEDICINE IN SPORTS NEWSLETTER, Vol. 10, No. 4, July, 1970.

The form reads as follows:

CONSENT FORM

PHYSICAL EXAMINATION FOR VARSITY ATHLETES [23]

NAME OF STUDENT-ATHLETE . . . .
                          (Last)   (First)   (Middle Initial)
Parent or Guardian Permission

As parent or legal guardian, I authorize Dr. . . . . acting
as team physician to examine the above named student and in the
event of injury to administer emergency care and to arrange for
any consultation by specialist, including surgeons he deems
necessary to insure proper care of any injury. Every effort will be
made to contact parents or guardians to explain the nature of the
problem prior to any involved treatment.

In the absence of the team or authorized physician, I grant
permission to a qualified physician to furnish emergency care
using the guidelines above.

NAME . . . . Date   . . . .
           (Parent or Guardian)

D. The Physical Examination

Controversy exists over the value of the annual
physical. While some state high school athletic
associations require a physical examination before a
student can participate in sports, others fail even to
mention it. Still others, like Pennsylvania, go beyond the
traditional annual physical and require separate
physical examinations for participation in each sport. It
is possible for a participant in Pennsylvania who plays
three sports to have three separate examinations in one
year. On the other hand, some colleges report that the
physical examination is so expensive they do not require
it for participation in sports.

---

23. *Dr. James C. Brewer,* Physical Examination for Varsity
    Athletes, Consent Form, Greensboro, N.C., June, 1979.

An article in *Time* magazine has raised the question of whether it might be called the "annual ripoff." [24] Dr. Anne Somers, a professor of community medicine at New Jersey Rutgers Medical School, and Dr. Leslie Breslow, a professor of public health at the University of California at Los Angeles, also question the value of an annual physical examination.[25] These two medical authorities recommend eleven thorough physical examinations beginning at age six and going through age sixty. They suggest "top to toe" physicals at ages six, nine, thirteen, once between eighteen and twenty-four, again at thirty, then every five years until sixty. After sixty they feel that healthy people should be examined every two years. They explain that the annual physical examination is "too-expensive" considering the few treatable or preventable ills it usually finds." [26]

On the other hand, Dr. Allan Ryan, a sports medicine authority stresses that:

> Physical examinations, including the important laboratory tests, are a necessity for competitive sports today in order to eliminate the unfit and to identify physical problems which may be correctable to allow safer participation. There are many practical difficulties in the way of achieving such examinations en masse on an annual basis. The availability of physicians, the cost, the time necessary and the willingness of athletes and their parents to comply with such requirements are the principal obstacles.[27]

---

24. *The Annual Ripoff?*, TIME, July 26, 1978.
25. Greensboro Daily News, Mar. 18, 1977.
26. *Id.*
27. *Supra* note 6.

Dr. Robert L. McMillan, a nationally prominent heart specialist, emphasizes the urgency of an annual pre-participation examination for all athletes.[28] He questions the practice of allowing sports regulatory organizations to dictate rules affecting the conduct of the athlete and institution, but neglecting to require a comprehensive physical examination to detect physical disabilities. Dr. McMillan illustrates his point in a startling article entitled "Sudden Death in Athletes and Marfans Syndrone," in which he discusses the tragic and unexpected death of four athletes in the Atlantic Coast Conference. He writes:

> At least four strong, expert, and apparently healthy young athletes have suddenly fallen dead in the past three years. Three of the athletes were nationally known basketball players and a fourth was a scholarship swimmer.[29]

Dr. McMillan stresses the importance of detecting suspicious medical problems among athletes, and points out that the advent of the black athlete into all areas of sports makes the annual examination even more important. He explains that blacks are particularly susceptible to some types of diseases, noting for example, that the occurrence of high blood pressure among young blacks is greater than among whites.[30]

---

28. Interview with Dr. Robert L. McMillan, Greensboro, N.C., June 9, 1979.
29. Robert L. McMillan, *Sudden Death in Athletes and Marfans Syndrone,* THE PHYSICIAN AND SPORTSMEDICINE, June, 1978.
30. *Id.*

A North Carolina case seems to support Dr. McMillan's observation regarding the black athlete and certain types of pre-existing physical conditions. Rodney Norman, a Lexington High School football player, sued his physician, the coaching staff and school board for $7.6 million for injuries he attributed to their negligence.[31] Norman claimed that he lost the use of the "function in his left hip because of a football injury he sustained during a pre-season summer football camp."

There was conflicting testimony during the trial from the players who were present at the time of the alleged incident. Five players testified that Norman was involved in a fight prior to practice, while other teammates reported that they did not see a fight.

Norman's mother sued the physician for $750,000, accusing him of negligence in treating her son. She claimed that the physician was unavailable to see her son for five days and refused to X-ray his hip. She admitted, however, that he did prescribe a mild painkilling drug for her son and referred him to Dr. George Rovere, a bone specialist in Winston-Salem, for further treatment.

At the trial, Dr. Rovere testified that there was no evidence of trauma in the area of the hip when he removed it. His tests indicated that the bone was still alive, supporting his opinion that the plaintiff's condition was not caused by a blow. The surgeon concluded:

> Norman's problem was caused by a condition which affects young blacks — a slipped capital epiphyses.

31. The Times, Thomasville, N.C., Oct. 26, 1978.

He added:

> Norman's disorder is caused by an imbalance of
> hormones, and that no blow to the leg was
> necessary to cause the slipped thigh cartilage.[32]

The superior court judge ruled that he could find no
evidence of negligence on the part of the physician or
other defendants and he dismissed the case.

E. The Physician's Assistant

Dr. McMillan recognizes the critical shortage of
physicians to administer the pre-season physical
examination. He believes that the physician can conduct
the examination in a more efficient manner and in a way
that will reduce costs. He recommends the use of
Physician's Assistants (P.A.'s) who are now regulated
by most states and are examined by certifying boards
and represented by the National Health Practitioner
Program in Arlington, Virginia.[33] Dr. McMillan points
out that:

> These professional "P.A.'s" are both male and
> female. In most states they work only under the
> supervision of a physician. Inquiry will reveal
> that their histories and physical examinations
> will be acceptable as bonafide testimony in
> court. These suggestions would surely help
> with physician shortages and expenses in all
> schools and colleges. These "P.A.'s" are, in the
> main, employed on salary to physicians and
> surgeons and they work under supervision and
> are more and more efficient as time goes on.[34]

32. The Times, Thomasville, N.C., Oct. 28, 1978.
33. *National Certification of Physician Assistants,* NATIONAL
    HEALTH PRACTITIONER PROGRAM, 4th ed., Arlington, Va.,
    1979-80.
34. *Supra* note 28.

He continues to explain the advantages of the "P.A.'s" by remarking that:

> They are trained in sub-specialties and it would seem to serve the examination best if limited to those trained in internal medicine and orthopedics. The bulk of state courts will not accept the examinations of any practitioner who does not have an M.D. These "P.A.'s" are well-trained to render first aid, but cannot prescribe any drugs. In practice they report directly to their supervising physician (M.D.).

Dr. McMillan concludes:

> With the compact physical examination forms, a quick check-off of findings, and easily filed records, the time and cost of annual examinations can be held to a simplified minimum.[35]

The National Health Practitioner Program agrees with the advantage of physicians utilizing the "P.A.'s" because:

> New health practitioners should allow physicians to concentrate on those biochemical problems that only they can manage, hopefully increasing patient, satisfaction, and perhaps reducing errors. In general, malpractice suits arise from patient-physicians interactions rather than negligence per se.[36]

Since the "P.A." works directly under the supervision of the physician and both share liability for negligence, it seems that:

> It is unlikely that a physician will authorize those health practitioners who share in his work

---

35. *Supra* note 28.
36. *Supra* note 33.

to function beyond the levels of their experience
and training.[37]

The outline below, compiled by Dr. James C. Brewer,
Team Physician at Guilford College, and Dr. Robert L.
McMillan, Emeritus Professor of Medicine (Cardiology)
Wake Forest University School of Medicine, is an
example of accurate, condensed and easily available
records. The two physicians suggest that the individual
athletic director should have the discretion to change
the outline if needed. They recommend that several
factors are important in the examination process,
including that:

> All examinations should be conducted in quiet,
> comfortable surroundings — portable tables
> with a soft mat are not expensive. Generally it
> is best to have only one examiner at a time in a
> given room to promote quiet for use of
> stethoscope on heart and lungs.[38]

---

37. *Supra* note 33.
38. *Supra* note 28.

HEALTH FORMS

Student Health Examination Card

The form listed below can be used on a card 5″ x 8″ or 12.6 cm x 20 cm. It can be filled out quickly and kept in a convenient card file.

Student Health Examination Record

Date		YEAR			YEAR			YEAR		YEAR	
Eyes-Vision											
Ears-Hearing											
Teeth											
Tonsils											
Neck											
Goiter											
Heart											
Lungs											
Hernia											
Breasts											
Spine											
Posture											
Feet											
Menses											
Abnormalities											
Nutrition											
Gen. Phy. Con.											
Height											
Weight											
Normal Weight											
Blood Pressure											
Doctor											

YEAR   PHYSICIANS REMARKS   GYMNASIUM

Absence of Litigation Involving the Team Physician in Amateur Sports

In a day when lawsuits dominate many areas of sports, the team physician at the amateur sports level enjoys a rare immunity. Gallagher, writing in *Current Sports Medicine Issues,* explains:

> I think it is because a competitive sports team physician holds a unique position in the eyes, and if you will, the hearts of our athletes to whom he ministers and, indeed, of their parents as well. Team physicians are not rewarded economically, their primary interest is in helping youngsters. This awareness on the part of athletes and their parents plays a large part in protecting the physician from litigation.[39]

Gallagher, who describes the absence of litigation against the team physician in amateur sports, may have foreseen a changing attitude toward the medical profession as early as 1972. He predicted at that time that some litigants may become dissatisfied with a school district's insurance coverage and seek other sources of revenue. He envisioned litigants suing physicians and hospitals for large sums of money and cautioned that "once they are successful, the flood gates will be open." [40]

Gallagher's prophecy came true in a case that same year when a 13-year-old boy was injured in a playground fight by another boy who struck him with a baseball bat. A physician and medical crew at the hospital examined and released him, only to readmit him several hours later for extensive emergency surgery. While the

---

39. *Supra* note 28.
40. *Supra* note 28.

boy collected $25,000 from the school district for its failure to supervise the playground, he received a record $4 million from the hospital.[41]

In like manner, a high school senior in New Jersey was seriously injured in a gymnastics class. His injury was compounded by what he attributed to negligence by the medical team at the hospital. The school district readily settled out of court for $75,000, while the insurance company representing the medical personnel at the hospital settled for $300,000.[42]

Dr. Frank Clippinger, President of the Committee on the Medical Aspects of Sports, North Carolina Medical Society, attributes the shortage of physicians who volunteer their services to amateur sports to a lack of time and fear of malpractice suits.[43] The state of California has recognized the need for the services of volunteer physicians to high schools and community colleges. The California Legislature enacted two statutes to meet this problem. The statutes protect volunteer physicians who serve the secondary school and community college students by providing immunity to the physician. The statute regarding the secondary school and the physician reads as follows:

> Notwithstanding any provision of any law, no physician and surgeon who in good faith and without compensation renders voluntary emergency assistance to a participant in a school athletic event or contest at the site

---

41. New York Daily News, Feb. 7, 1973.
42. New Jersey case settled in 1975 with the agreement that the name of the defendants would not be discussed with the amount of the award paid the plaintiff.
43. Report to Sports Medicine Committee, Raleigh, N.C., May 22, 1979.

thereof, or during transportation to a health care facility, for an injury suffered in the course of the event or contest, shall be liable for any civil damages as a result of any acts or omissions by the physician and surgeon in rendering the emergency medical care. The immunity granted by this paragraph shall not apply in the event of an act or omission constituting gross negligence.[44]

(The other statute is identical in its content except it refers to community colleges rather than to secondary schools.)

Litigation Involving the Team Physician in Professional Sports

Litigation involving professional sports adversely focuses attention on the controversy that often exists between the athlete, the team physician and the owner of a sports team.

Dick Butkus played his final football game for the Chicago Bears and then sued the team's owners for $1.6 million.[45] Butkus claimed that the Chicago Bears forced him to play when he was physically unfit. He contended that a team physician in professional sports is engaged in a conflict of interest situation that poses problems for the players. Butkus declared:

I don't see how you can have a physician hired by management, reporting to management, and treating the players and not reporting to them. It is a physician's duty to inform the patient of

---

44. Section 49409 of the Education Code, State of California, Chapter 547, Assembly Bill No. 3685, Session of the Legislature, 1977-78.
45. Philadelphia Inquirer, Sept. 28, 1976.

his condition. His prime obligation is to the patient.[46]

Butkus settled out of court for $600,000. The argument made by Butkus that the team physician in professional sports often fails to inform the player of his condition was the basis of a lawsuit against the Philadelphia Phillies baseball team.

Gerald Gemignani signed a baseball contract with the Philadelphia Phillies.[47] The team physician examined him before spring practice and discovered a symptomatic blood condition, but failed to treat it or report it to Gemignani. He was released from the team the following year and soon after he was hospitalized with a kidney disorder. He died several months later from uremic kidneys.

The parents of the deceased ballplayer sued the owners of the Philadelphia Phillies because their son's physician told them he learned from the defendants that they had detected a blood condition in the earlier examination. The parents believed that the team physician's failure to treat or report the condition led directly to the death of their son.

The defendants based their defense on the statute of limitation, but the court reasoned that the plaintiff had no way of knowing about his condition and therefore the statute of limitation should not begin to run until he had time to know that such a condition existed.[48]

A superior court in Alameda, California awarded Bill Enyart, a member of the Oakland Raiders football

---

46. *Id.*
47. Gemignani v. Philadelphia Phillies Nat'l League Baseball Club, Inc., 287 F. Supp. 465 (E.D. Pa. 1967).
48. *Id.*

team, $777,000 in a judgment against the team's orthopedic specialist.[49] Enyart sustained a knee injury during a pre-season exhibition game. He was cut from the Oakland team and attempted to get a try-out with the Green Bay Packers. He failed the physical at Green Bay and sued the Oakland team physician for failing to operate on his knee when he was first injured. The court found the physician guilty of malpractice and he appealed the decision declaring that awards of this type would open the door to future lawsuits and he predicted:

> Any disgruntled athlete not making the team will turn around and sue the team doctor for something he did not do.[50]

The Oakland team physician has appealed the case and it is pending at this time.

Don Chuy, a lineman for the Philadelphia Eagles, injured his shoulder against the New York Giants and was out of action for the rest of the season.[51] Chuy was advised by both his personal physician and the team physician for the Eagles to retire from football and off-season wrestling. The team physician found that Chuy was suffering from "an abnormal red blood cell condition, stress polycythemia."

A sports reporter heard that Chuy was retiring from football and called the team physician to verify the report. The physician allegedly told the reporter that Chuy was suffering from Polycythemia Vera (a

---

49. *Team Doctor to Appeal Malpractice Verdict,* THE PHYSICIAN AND SPORTSMEDICINE, June, 1977.

50. *Id.*

51. Chuy v. Philadelphia Eagles Football Team and The National Football League Nos. 77-1411, 77-1412, U.S. Court of Appeals (3d Cir. 1977).

potentially fatal blood condition.) The article appeared in the Philadelphia paper and was featured in the *Los Angeles Times* where Chuy was living. Chuy reportedly "panicked" and "his mind just snapped" when he read the article. He claimed that the article made him a "mental wreck" and caused him marital problems. Chuy sued the Philadelphia Eagles for causing him serious emotional stress. A district court held the Eagles liable for $10,000 in compensatory damages and $50,590.96 in punitive damages. The court explained its reasoning when it said:

> If you intentionally make a statement the natural and probable consequences of which it will be known to the person and cause him or her emotional distress and if the making of that statement is shocking and outrageous and exceeds the bounds of decency with respect to its natural and probable impact, then a case of intentional infliction of emotional distress is made out.[52]

The district court, however denied Chuy recovery on the defamation claim. Both the Philadelphia Eagles and Chuy appealed the decision. The United States Court of Appeals for the Third Circuit affirmed the lower court's decision to deny the Eagles a new trial and reversed the decision to deny Chuy's motion for a new trial regarding the defamation claim. It remanded the case back for a new trial on Chuy's contention of defamation.

---

52. *Id.*

IN MY OPINION

An unusual bumper sticker recently got my attention. It read as follows:

Support Your American Trial Lawyers Association, Send Your Son To Medical School.

It is unfortunate that the increase in lawsuits against the medical profession often causes some physicians to view their patients and the legal profession as potential adversaries. There is clearly less litigation on record against the team physician in amateur sports than the team physician in professional sports. Gallagher's prediction that the virtual immunity enjoyed by team physicians in amateur sports might begin to change seems to be coming true. It appears that many injured athletes do not want to sue, but, when crippling injuries occur, are forced by necessity to sue. The medical profession has been the target for many suits because it has the ability to pay large damage awards. The cases recorded in the chapter against the professional's team physician may be a harbinger of things to come for the amateur sports physician.

The professional athlete, unlike the amateur athlete, views the team physician with mistrust because they feel that the professional team's physician is accountable to management and not the athlete. Dick Butkus poses an interesting solution to the problem when he suggests that the professional athlete rely on a group of physicians separate from management which has an interest in the athlete. He believes that athletes could go to these physicians for consultation and feel that their best interests were being served.

An outstanding professional athlete in the National Basketball Association recently related a situation that refutes Butkus' claim that the professional team physician presents a conflict of interest situation that is detrimental to the athlete. One of the superstars on his team refused to practice or play because of a painful injury. The team's owner and coach were adamant and insisted that he play no matter how painful the injury might be. They ordered the team physician to release a statement to the press blasting the player and disclaiming his injury by declaring that he just would not play. The team physician refused to comply with their directive and submitted his resignation instead.

Dr. Don O'Donaghue, the orthopedic physician for the Oklahoma University football team admits that some team physicians feel obligated to management, but he believes they are in the minority. He declares that there is not conflict at all since:

> The player's health must always come first. I have always had an understanding with the Oklahoma football coaches. If I say a player should not play, he doesn't play — The team physician represents the player. Period.[53]

It seems that Dr. O'Donaghue's contention that the player's welfare comes first does extend to professional sports also. It is obvious, however, that whether it is in amateur or professional sports, a spirit of trust and mutual cooperation is needed between the player, the coach, and the team physician if the participant is to receive the maximum protection. This cooperative relationship will go a long way toward eliminating litigation.

In light of the shortage of physicians for sports programs, Dr. McMillan's suggestion that the physician

---

53. *Supra* note 2.

use the physician's assistant seems a valid one. While controversy still exists over the value of the annual physical examination for the average person, there is little doubt that medical sports authorities will continue to insist on a thorough pre-season physical examination for the athlete.

A well known authority in sports administration recently warned administrators and coaches not to conduct practices for contact sports unless a physician is in attendance. This is the ideal, but really not very practical. With many schools sponsoring four, five or more contact sports at the same time, the requirement of a physician at each one is obviously impossible.

In situations in which the physician is not available, the school administrator and coach should have a plan. This plan should be prepared before the season ever begins and include the following:

1. Keep a chart or card file with the telephone numbers of the players' family physicians or the nearest physician available to the school.

2. Have the telephone number of the local hospital and ambulance service.

3. Appoint a staff member to administer first aid in an emergency and transport the injured person to the physician or hospital.

4. Have a mode of transportation available in the event a person must be taken to the physician or hospital.

5. Have the exact change needed for an emergency telephone call.

CHAPTER 11

The Athletic Trainer

You can have the best team doctors in the
world, but if you have a poor trainer,
you will have a poor program.[1]

Along with the shortage of team physicians for sports programs, there is a critical need for qualified athletic trainers. The athletic trainer can compensate for the lack of physicians at practice sessions and fill the void that so often characterizes medical care at practice sessions for contact sports.

During the 93rd Congress, a bill was introduced that would require all schools and colleges sponsoring sports programs to furnish the services of a certified trainer. The bill was known as the "Athletic Care Act." [2] The bill was intended to reduce the number of injuries in sports that are approaching an all-time high.

Instead of considering the bill, Congress mandated, instead, that the Secretary of Health, Education, and Welfare (HEW) conduct a study for a 12-month period to determine the number of injuries and deaths that occur in sports and physical education programs and whether a qualified "health person was in attendance when they occurred." [3]

---

1. Sam Kegerreis, *Health Care for Student Athletes,* JOURNAL OF PHYSICAL EDUCATION AND RECREATION, Vol. 50, No. 6, June, 1979.
2. Athletic Care Act, HR 11304, 93rd Congress, Nov. 7, 1973.
3. Athletic Injuries and Deaths in Secondary Schools and Colleges, 1975-76, A Report on the Survey Mandated by

For purposes of the study, a trainer was determined to be, "all persons designated by their school as a trainer." This broad interpretation included the athletic trainer approved for certification by the National Association of Athletic Trainers (NATA), coaches who assume emergency care in addition to coaching duties, teachers who serve as trainers and student trainers. (For NATA Certification Procedures, see Appendix E.)

The HEW report was issued in February, 1979 and revealed many problems confronting schools such as:

1. Faced with financial pressures, many institutions feel that they are unable to afford hiring a qualified athletic trainer and, where such a trainer is available, the number of sports events in different locations creates coverage problems. Financial problems in athletics furthermore have been compounded by requirements for more equitable support of women's activities.
2. The relatively low pay for trainers may be discouraging some persons from entering the field. In Northern Virginia, for example, part-time athletic trainers reported that they were paid only $1,300 a year for their services.
3. School health facilities, run by a nurse, often close at the end of the school day, but long before the close of the athletic day.[5]

Several prominent health authorities criticized the HEW report as being inadequate and vague. Kenneth Clarke, Dean of Applied Life Studies at the University

---

Section 826 of Public Law 93-380, Department of Health, Education, and Welfare, Washington, D.C., Feb. 1979.

4. Washington Post, Sept. 25, 1976.
5. *Supra* note 3.

of Illinois, believes the report fails to accomplish several important things because:

> It does not show whether the number of athletic injuries is going up or down. Separate studies by his N.A.I.R.S. group and by individual colleges indicate that because of improvements in sports equipment and training techniques, the frequency of athletic injuries has gone down slightly over the past five years, despite increased participation by high school and college students.[6]

Dr. Bob Murphy, the head team physician at Ohio State University agrees with Clarke and observes that:

> I really think that college football is a safe sport. Given the proper coaching, the proper equipment, and the proper training, I think a kid is safer playing football than he would be if he were doing something else on his own.[7]

Murphy's response was in answer to the statistic that there were nine football injuries for every ten players at four-year colleges. In addition to the statistic on football, the report lists the following for 1975-1976:

1. College and high school athletes suffered more than one million injuries in sports programs.
2. There were 14 sports-related fatalities and 100,000 "major" injuries.
3. Injuries in varsity football were four times as numerous as injuries in non-contact sports.

---

6. THE CHRONICLE OF HIGHER EDUCATION, Vol. XVIII, No. 2, Mar. 5, 1979.
7. *Id.*

4. While 30 percent of the varsity athletes were women, they sustained only 16 percent of the injuries.[8]

The HEW report focused on the lack of qualified trainers in schools at all levels that offer sports programs. It made an interesting observation regarding the number of certified trainers that includes the following:

	Percentage of Trainers	Percentage of NATA Approved Trainers
Public Secondary Schools	10.9%	5.0%
Private Secondary Schools	15.4%	5.0%
Two-Year Colleges	16.1%	7.0%
Four-Year Colleges	40.2%	28.0%

Many of the people designated as "athletic trainers" in the schools are teachers, coaches, and, in some instances, students. While these trainers do much good for the sports program, they often operate outside the law in many states. Lan Barnes, a staff writer for *The Physician and Sportsmedicine,* discusses the non-certified trainer's dilemma in "Beloved Outlaws: Trainers Look at Liability." Barnes reports that only Georgia, Kentucky and Texas offer licensure for athletic trainers.[9]

Legal Implications for the Non-Certified Trainer

Boyd Baker, a school law authority at the University of Arizona, and Clifford Rode, a physical therapist at the University of Arizona, in an unpublished article, discuss the status of non-certified trainers and the legal

---

8. *Supra* note 3.
9. Lan Barnes, *Beloved Outlaws: Trainers Look at Liability,* THE PHYSICIAN AND SPORTSMEDICINE, Sept. 1978.

implications facing them.[10] Baker and Rode explain that
the physical therapist has been licensed since the early
1960's by many states. They note that the definition of
the physical therapist is similar in most states. They cite
Oklahoma's definition as being typical; it describes the
physical therapist's practice as:

> The treatment of human beings by the use of
> exercise, heat, cold, water, radiant energy,
> electricity, or sound for the purpose of
> correcting or alleviating any physical or mental
> disability, or the performance of
> neuromuscular-skeletal measurements to
> determine the existence and extent of body
> malfunction, provided, however, that physical
> therapy shall not include radiology,
> electrosurgery, orthopedics or the practice of
> optometry.[11]

Baker and Rode observe that athletic trainers have
been using the modalities as "unlicensed paramedicals"
although such treatments are usually reserved for the
physical therapist and medical doctor. They list four
categories of statutes regarding the legal limits of the
athletic trainers in the various states. The list of states
in the four categories are as follows:

1. States limiting the practice of physical
   therapy to those licensed to do so in that
   particular state: Alabama, California,
   Connecticut, Delaware, Hawaii, Indiana,
   Nevada, Maine, New Mexico, North

---

10. Boyd Baker and Clifford Rode, Legal Implications
Concerning the Use of Physical Therapy Modalities by
Athletic Trainers, (unpublished paper), University of
Arizona, 1975.

11. *Id.*

Carolina, North Dakota, Ohio, Oregon, Rhode Island, South Dakota, Tennessee, Vermont and Wisconsin.

2. States which require licensure to practice physical therapy or hold oneself out as a physical therapist but do not limit any person licensed under the law from engaging in the practice of which he or she is licensed or registered: Kentucky, Nebraska, New Hampshire, Oklahoma, Texas, Utah, West Virginia and Wyoming.[12]

Athletic trainers in categories one or two who are not licensed, are, in all probability, working outside the law. As most statutes read, the trainer in these states is not legally able to use physical therapy modalities such as heat, light, water and sound.

3. States which require licensure to practice physical therapy or hold oneself out as a physical therapist, which do not limit any person licensed or registered in the state under the law from engaging in the practice for which he or she is licensed or registered, and which permit the use of physical therapy as previously defined, by unlicensed personnel under the supervision of someone who is licensed: Arizona, Illinois, Louisiana, Massachusetts, New Jersey and Virginia.

An athletic trainer in category three can work legally under the direction of a licensed therapist or physician.

4. States placing no licensure requirements as to practice of physical therapy as defined,

---

12. *Supra* note 10.

so long as one does not hold oneself out to be a licensed physical therapist: Florida, Georgia, Idaho, Iowa, Kansas, Maryland, Minnesota, Mississippi, Missouri, Montana and South Carolina.[13]

In category four, athletic trainers can work with the modalities mentioned above as long as they do not represent themselves as licensed therapists.

Paraprofessionals

An interesting case was decided by the New York Commissioner of Education regarding paraprofessionals who are employed as health aides. (This could include athletic trainers.) [14]

The petitioners contended that the Brentwood School District utilized paraprofessionals to do the job reserved for "school nurse-teachers or to registered professional or licensed practical nurses." They also argued that the health aides were not adequately supervised. The Brentwood School District responded that the so-called paraprofessionals were supervised and that they administered first aid only wherever necessary, which is not against the law.

The New York Commissioner of Education ruled that the use of paraprofessionals did not constitute a violation of the law, and he subsequently dismissed the appeal.

In some states coaches receive salary supplements, but athletic trainers do not get financial remuneration. Some schools attempt to meet the situation by giving

---

13. *Supra* note 10.
14. In the Matter of Appeal of Zuckerman with respect to employment of health aides (No. 8628, April, 1973).

the trainer the title of coach so he or she can receive a supplement. The trainer may or may not assist in the actual coaching duties.

A New Jersey case illustrates a problem that came before that state's Commissioner of Education regarding a part-time coach who was used as an athletic trainer.[15]

The Education Association of Brick Township brought the complaint against the school board. The education association claimed that the school board violated the New Jersey statutes when it employed a part-time person as an athletic coach in the school district. During the hearing several facts were revealed, including:

1. The person assisted the athletic department as a "trainer" for the last ten years. He received no salary from the Board of Education.

2. The Board of Education has never taken any official action designating him as a trainer.

3. His services were performed on a voluntary basis.

The New Jersey statutes require a person to be certified by the State Department of Education to teach or coach in the public schools. They also require a person who works with students in athletics to be certified to teach and be employed on a full-time basis. An exception can be made in an emergency if the Superintendent of Schools approves the hiring of a part-time person.

---

15. Brick Township Educ. Ass'n v. Board of Educ. of Brick Ocean County (Decision of the Commissioner of Educ. of N.J., 1975).

The reasons given for the regulations were:

1. To avoid the evil of having school boards of education employ professional athletes or other uniquely qualified persons on a minimal part-time basis as a guise for securing their coaching talents.
2. To insure that boys and girls in the public schools will be coached and trained by teachers who have been trained to foster the development of the mind, body, and character of each pupil as the foremost goal.

The New Jersey Commissioner of Education directed the school board to adhere to the regulations if the person was to continue as trainer in the athletic program.

Sam Kegerreis, a contributing editor for athletic training for the *Journal of Physical Education and Recreation,* makes a timely comment when he says:

The American Medical Association identifies the following components as being vital to the success of all athletic programs: good coaching, good officiating, good equipment and facilities, and good health supervision. Unfortunately, the latter of these components is glaringly absent from today's secondary schools.[16]

He concludes with a statement that applies to most athletic programs when he declares:

An athletic department that takes for granted the health of your sons and daughters requires a serious re-examination of priorities.[17]

---

16. *Supra* note 1.
17. *Supra* note 1.

IN MY OPINION

In the HEW survey referred to in this chapter, it was reported that 80% of the injuries to the men and 77% of the injuries to the women took place when a person designated to administer health care was present. However, it must be noted that in most instances, assistance was provided by someone other than a certified trainer.[18]

Most coaches will tell you that one of their biggest worries is the lack of qualified medical personnel at their practices and contests. Many feel frustrated and threatened because they are unprepared to administer first aid and constantly fear that a serious injury will happen when medical help is not available.

A New Jersey baseball coach told me that he was coaching at a school some distance from town. One of his players was hit in the head with a baseball and died before medical help arrived. He confessed that he knew nothing about first aid and felt guilty because one of his players died and he could not help him.

Many states and national organizations are attempting to meet the crisis in various ways. Maryland is trying to pass legislation that will require all bus drivers, coaches and physical education teachers to be certified in emergency first aid. This is a step in the right direction and, if passed, could serve as a model for other states to follow.

North Carolina received funds from the General Assembly to promote programs for sports medicine. The legislation provides each North Carolina public secondary school with $500 to provide paramedical life

---

18. *Supra* note 3.

saving services and $10,000 for in-service programs to develop emergency paramedical skills for the school personnel.

North Carolina, a pioneer in sports medicine, has developed a Sports Medicine Department that is attempting to meet the medical needs of the sports participants throughout the state. The North Carolina Sports Medicine Department has been training teacher-trainers in the state. Dr. Al Proctor, the Director of the Sports Medicine Program issued data that supported his conclusion that teacher-trainers in North Carolina were reducing injuries in football. Proctor listed the results of a 1978 study that compared to one taken in 1972.[19]

1972	1978
Coaches were responsible for the prevention and management of injuries.	Teacher-Athletic-Trainers were responsible for the prevention and management of injuries.
Injury Rate: 50%	Injury Rate: 22%
Reinjury Rate: 71%	Reinjury Rate: 11%
Injuries in practice: 78%	Injuries in practice: 62%
Game Injuries: 32%	Game Injuries: 38%

In addition to certifying teachers as athletic trainers, the Sports Medicine Department is attempting to:

1. Modify the state's statutes to permit non-licensed athletic trainers to work under the direction of licensed physical therapists or medical doctors.
2. Develop a program of licensure for athletic trainers.

---

19. Report to Sports Medical Committee, Raleigh, N.C., May 22, 1979.

3. Secure adequate insurance coverage to protect trainers.

In 1979, the North Carolina Legislature enacted a law "to provide sports medicine and emergency life saving skills to students in the public schools." This legislation should serve as a model to other states and represents a boost to the prevention and care of injuries. (See Appendix F for the General Assembly of North Carolina Session 1979 Ratified Bill and the proposed plan to implement it in North Carolina.)

The Indiana County Chapter of the American Red Cross has proposed a unique program to train coaches, teachers and others who work as trainers in a program of emergency first aid and the prevention of sports injuries. It suggests a course named "American Red Cross Basic Instruction in the Prevention of and First Aid to Athletic Injuries."

The need for qualified athletic trainers is critical and essential to the well-being of our participants. We have vastly improved the quality of our coaching, sports equipment and facilities during the past decade. It is time we provide quality health care if we are to meet our obligation and responsibility to our participants.

CHAPTER 12
Sports Facilities

Important in each sport is the environment in which it is practiced, whether it takes place on land, on the water, under the water or in the air. Each medium poses its own particular problems.[1]

The playing field, stadium, gymnasium, ski slope and golf course are popular sports facilities and all pose unique problems for the sports administrator and participant. The sports administrator may be faced with a request to lease a facility to a group his constituents consider to be controversial. While the use of a sports facility may not be considered a sporting event, the constitutional questions its use raises may be of great significance to the sports administrator.

Since the safety of the sports facility is essential to the participants well-being, injuries attributed to unsafe conditions often result in litigation.

This chapter will review several court cases involving the use of sports facilities by various groups and litigation in which injuries are ascribed to the unsafe condition of the facility.

Use of Sports Facilities

Many institutions rent or lease their sports facilities to outside groups for various reasons. For most the intent is to gain extra revenue to support the institution. Some communities share their facilities to save money or to develop a spirit of civic cooperation. In some

---

1. Allan Ryan, *The Prevention of Injuries in Sports and Physical Education,* SPORTS SAFETY II, Chicago, Ill., 1976.

instances, outside groups are denied the use of the facilities and as a result seek redress in court.

A. Religious Groups

Institutions often permit religious groups to use their facilities. People who oppose such a practice frequently sue and base their objection on constitutional questions. An Arizona case illustrates such opposition to the use of public facilities by a religious group.

The Reverend Billy Graham rented Sun Devil Stadium on the campus of Arizona State University in Tempe, Arizona.[2] Graham agreed to pay $39,995.00 for seven days use of the sports facility. The Board of Regents defended their action by a provision that stipulated that the board had the authority to:

> Purchase, receive, hold, make and take leases of, and sell real and personal property, for the benefit of the state and for the use of the institutions under its jurisdictions.

A citizen in Arizona challenged the board's right to lease the stadium to a religious group. He contended that such a lease violated the First Amendment to the United States Constitution's provision for separation of church and state. He also pointed to the Arizona Constitution which read as follows:

> No public money or property shall be appropriated for or applied to any religious worship, exercise, or instruction, or to the support of any religious establishment.

The petitioner claimed that the Arizona Constitution intended to prevent state government from supporting "one religion over another or of religion over

---

2. Pratt v. Arizona Bd. of Regents, 520 P.2d 514 (Ariz. 1974).

nonreligion." The court responded that it was a common practice for communities, in the days of the one-room schoolhouse, to use school facilities for religious worship as long as they did not interfere with the school's educational programs.

It reasoned that Graham's use of the stadium was business-like and the rental price fair. It declared in

> Leasing a forum for Reverend Graham's worship services, a forum available to all others — that Board of Regents has not sought to favor or handicap Evangelist Graham. Reverend Graham will flourish or flounder, not because of the appeal or lack of thereof, of his dogma. The State neutrality in this matter extends to all religions or worship, as it involved a mere business transaction and nothing more.

The Supreme Court of Arizona denied the petitioner's request and permitted Graham to lease the stadium.

The New Jersey Supreme Court also allowed a religious group to use a school facility on a temporary basis when school was not in session.[3] It held that the use of the public school facility did not violate either New Jersey's State Constitution or the Establishment Clause of the United States Constitution.

B. Political Groups

Thirteen students, members of a Bicentennial Commission at Lawrence University in Wisconsin, requested permission from the Board of Education to rent the Appleton High School gymnasium for a public

---

3. Resnick v. East Brunswick Bd. of Educ., 389 A.2d 944 (N.J. 1978).

lecture by Angela Davis.[4] Davis, a professor at California's Claremont College and a well-known member of the Communist Party, was prohibited from using the facility.

The students sought injunctive relief from the court, claiming that the board's refusal violated certain rights guaranteed by the First, Fifth, and Fourteenth Amendments to the United States Constitution. They also contended that the denial of their application stated a cause of action based on 42 U.S.C. Section 1983, and the Wisconsin court agreed.

Davis, a black woman with a doctorate in philosophy, frequently lectured on womens' rights, the rights of black people and the condition of political prisoners all over the world. Her topic for the proposed meeting in Appleton was "200 Years of Social Change in the United States."

The court recognized that the statutes permitted the Board of Education to rent all school facilities on a "break even basis." They specified, however, that the facilities could not be rented to religious or political groups unless the activities were "non-partisan or non-denominational."

The students assured the board that Davis would comply with the provisions of the statutes and not appear as a "political speaker" or a representative for any political party. They asked the board to reconsider the decision. The board answered that it was troubled over the possibility of violence or disruption if Davis appeared at the school. The attorney for the students reported that no disruptive behavior had taken place at

---

4. Lawrence Univ. Bicentennial Comm'n v. City of Appleton, Wis., 409 F. Supp. 1319 (E.D. Wis. 1976).

previous lectures by Davis, but the board refused, once
again, to grant permission for the use of the facility by
Davis.

The plaintiffs continued to plead their case by
pointing out that the board frequently rented the
gymnasium to candidates for political office and others
who lectured on political and social topics. The court
responded:

> If the First Amendment means anything, it
> means that Government shall not look to
> subject matter in regulating expression.

It commented, however, that:

> To be sure, reasonable regulation of the time,
> place, and manner of speaking is permissible.

The plaintiffs stated that the lecture would be held at
night and not interfere with any school program. They
declared that the board had excluded their speaker
because they anticipated the topic she might present.

The problem confronts school officials in many parts
of the United States and is a highly emotional and
controversial issue. The Wisconsin court made several
key points that could be important considerations in
future situations when it said:

> The state is under no duty to make school
> buildings available for school meetings. . . . If
> it elects to do so, however, it cannot arbitrarily
> prevent any member of the public from holding
> meetings.[5]

It then declared:

> The ancient right to free speech in public parks
> and streets cannot be made conditional upon the

---

5. *Id.*

permission of a public official, if that permission is used as an "instrument of arbitrary, suppression of free expression." [6]

It then issued an injunction that required the Board of Education to rent the gymnasium to the students for the Angela Davis lecture. It concluded:

It is not for the state to control the influence of a public forum by censoring the ideas, the proponents, or the audience; if it could, that freedom which is the life of democratic assembly would be stilled.[7]

C. Commercial Groups

It has become a common practice for professional sports teams to play exhibitions, and occasionally regular season contests, in private and public sports facilities. But permission to use such facilities is not automatic, as Northwestern University found out.

The City of Evanston, Illinois passed an ordinance prohibiting the university from using its property for commercial endeavors.[8] The ordinance included Dyche Stadium, a 55,000 seat football arena and McGaw Hall, an 11,226 seat field house. The university argued that the restrictive ordinance was unconstitutional.

The Chicago Bears agreed to play the Philadelphia Eagles in Dyche Stadium and when permission was refused, sought a court order granting permission to play. The circuit court agreed that it was "unreasonable, arbitrary and discriminatory" to deny the Bears the use of the university's sports facility.

------

6. *Supra* note 4.
7. *Supra* note 4.
8. Northwestern Univ. v. City of Evanston, 370 N.E.2d 1073 (Ill. App. 1977).

While the city was appealing the court order, the game was played and the case dismissed because the issue was *moot.*

The city then amended its ordinance to allow the use of university facilities for all "professional athletics, sports or games, or other commercial purposes." The city then attempted to prevent the university from sponsoring professional tennis in McGaw Hall and professional basketball and soccer in their facilities.

The university petitioned to amend the zoning ordinance to permit the following:

> professional or amateur athletic contests, Fourth of July shows, circuses, carnivals, home shows, horse shows, speeches by notable persons, meetings, convocations, commencements, entertainments, expositions, and exhibitions.

The city argued that the university failed to "exhaust its local and administrative remedies" before going to court, but the university responded that it had complied with such procedures.

The Appellate Court of Illinois conceded that the City of Evanston had a long history of denying the university permission to sponsor professional sports in its facilities and that the university had exhausted its remedies. It therefore reversed the trial court's order which had dismissed the university's petition and sent it back, instead, to the circuit court to determine the constitutionality of the ordinance.

D. Private Groups

The question is frequently posed regarding the use of public, municipal facilities by private schools that are racially segregated. An Alabama decision may serve as a guide for future litigation.

Four private schools in Montgomery, Alabama, with all-white enrollments, used the city's municipal stadium.[9] During the fall of 1971 approximately 14 games were played between public schools and one football game was conducted involving a Roman Catholic school which was racially desegregated.

The district court directed the Department of Health, Education and Welfare to devise a plan that would insure the elimination of a dual system of education since the schools in Montgomery in 1965 were operating racially segregated schools.

The district court reasoned that the use of the public stadium aided the private schools in the following manner:

1. The opportunity to play athletic contests in public facilities contributes considerably to the attractiveness of the all-white private schools and draws white students from public schools thus increasing the difficulty of desegregating public education.

2. The use of public facilities saves the capital outlay required to build similar facilities, and

3. The City's action in granting the schools exclusive possession of city property for the duration of the contest provides a means by which the school can raise extra revenue through the sale of tickets and refreshments.

The district court decided that the use of the football stadium and other recreational facilities such as "baseball diamonds, basketball courts and tennis courts

---

9. Gilmore v. City of Montgomery, 473 F.2d 832 (5th Cir. 1973).

for official athletic contests and similar functions sponsored by racially segregated private schools" aided these schools and impaired the cause of the public school.

The U. S. Court of Appeals, Fifth Circuit, supported the attitude of the district court by ruling that it was within its jurisdiction to enjoin the officials of the City of Montgomery from providing the facilities of the city for use by the private schools.

The court of appeals made a distinction, however, between the use of the stadium for a football game and the use of the public facilities for individuals or groups of children who happened to be enrolled in private schools. It emphatically stated that "the children enrolled in private schools have an unquestioned right as citizens to make use of municipal recreational facilities." The court of appeals then made an interesting observation when it commented that:

> permitting private school groups to enjoy such recreational facilities as zoos, museums, and parks or to attend, along with other citizens, civic and cultural events conducted in city recreational facilities does not involve the same degree of affirmative state action as granting exclusive control of public facilities for private school functions.

It distinguished between the various uses of public facilities by adding that:

> nonexclusive use of governmental facilities and services does not provide a means by which schools may raise revenue. No schools, public or private, were shown to have constructed or maintained facilities such as zoos, parks, and the like.

It concluded, therefore, that the nonexclusive use of facilities by private school children did not pose a threat to the desegregation of public education. It concluded that while the district court could enjoin the City of Montgomery from letting private all-white schools use its public facilities it should make a distinction and not deny nonexclusive use of its recreational facilities to private school children or other groups.

Injuries Attributed to Unsafe Facilities

With the increasing number of sports participants and the diversity of sports facilities, it is apparent that injuries often will be followed by lawsuits. The following cases illustrate the type of situations that involve the owners and operators of sports facilities when injured participants charge them with negligence and sue for damages.

A. Ski Slopes

James Sunday, a 20-year-old beginning skier, was seriously injured when his ski became entangled with either a small bush or brush on a novice ski trail in Stratton, Vermont.[10] Sunday, a permanent quadriplegic since the injury, sued the ski resort for negligence in trail maintenance. The Vermont Superior Court, Crittenden County, awarded him $1,500,000 in damages and the defendant appealed the verdict.

The defendant argued that it was not responsible for Sunday's injury since he voluntarily assumed the risk of injury when he entered the premises to ski. The defendant also claimed that the award of $1,500,000 was excessive.

---

10. Sunday v. Stratton Corp., 390 A.2d 398 (Vt. 1978).

The Supreme Court of Vermont observed that the ski resort took special care to maintain the slopes in a "top quality" manner. The ski resort also employed over 52 patrolmen and a crew of workers to inspect the trails for hazards. It reportedly enjoyed an excellent reputation for keeping its slopes in good condition.

The defendant pointed to *Wright v. Mt. Mansfield Lift, Inc.* in which the court found that a hidden tree stump, concealed by loose snow, constituted a danger that was inherent in the sport of skiing. The court refused to award damages to an injured skier.[11] The Supreme Court of Vermont, however, did not agree that a hidden tree stump could be a danger that is inherent in skiing or one that is assumed by a skier. It noted that ski resorts, today, attempt to attract participants to its slopes with advertisements and other inducements. In addition, the modern ski slope may be held liable for a hidden tree stump since improved techniques for grooming slopes prevail.[12]

The Supreme Court of Vermont then cited a Vermont case in which a softball player was injured when he stepped in a hole on a softball field.[13] It referred to a statement by Justice Kerper:

> By also urging that the plaintiff assumed the risks inherent with the sport, the defendant has mistakenly associated the injury with the playing of the sport itself whereas it is not. Rather it is the condition of the recreation field

---

11. Wright v. Mt. Mansfield Lift, Inc., 96 F. Supp. 786 (D. Vt. 1951).
12. *Supra* note 10.
13. Garafano v. Neshobe Beach Club, Inc., 238 A.2d 70 (Vt. 1968).

provided for the game that was the cause of the injury.[14]

It concluded that skiers often fall when skiing but "this does not make every fall a danger inherent in the sport." [15] The Supreme Court of Vermont affirmed the trial court's refusal to grant the defendant ski resort a new trial.

The court then considered the charge that the award of $1,500,000 was excessive. It described the plaintiff's condition as follows:

> Ignoring any compensation whatever for pain and suffering, the amounts involved as far in excess of the verdict returned. We do not propose to evaluate a course of treatment involving eight operations, coma, intensive care, and severe drug reaction. The degree of physical care involved, by others, takes 3½ hours each morning. There are problems of urinary and bloodstream infection, and spasmodic pain. There is a propensity to bladder stones, and a need for all kinds of special equipment to perform the few limited bodily functions remaining to the plaintiff in his quadriplegia.[16]

The court then commented that the plaintiff's effort to finish his education was filled with unbelievable problems. It then described the plaintiff's financial burden by stating:

> In round figures, required daily care by visiting and registered nurses projects to more than $875,000. Future hospitalization, even at

---

14. *Id.*
15. *Supra* note 10.
16. *Supra* note 10.

present rates, approximates $1,500,000. Loss of future earnings is more than $300,000. One medication alone has a projected cost of $94,500. A required daytime attendant at $3.00 per hour, comes to over $500,000. Medical bills to date approximate $70,000 — Without any projected inflation, arguably offsetting reduction to present worth, financial loss to the plaintiff, standing alone, is almost twice the verdict returned.[17]

The court ruled that the verdict was not excessive and thereby affirmed the decision of the trial court.

The major insurance companies that insured the Vermont ski resorts thereafter threatened to cancel all liability policies of the State of Vermont failed to take action to relieve the operators of the ski resorts from the full responsibility for the participants safety. Vermont depends heavily on revenue from the ski industry and estimates place the yearly ski revenue at $80 million. As a result of the crisis, the Vermont legislature took immediate action by enacting a law known as an "assumption of risk" statute. The statute's intent is to:

Relieve the ski slope operator of total responsibility and place the burden of safe skiing on the participant.[18]

Howard J. Bruns, president of the Sporting Goods Manufacturing Association, praised the Vermont statute commenting that:

It would mark the return to sanity in the area of defining and assigning responsibility. We've seen automobile insurance rates skyrocket.

---

17. *Supra* note 10.
18. NATIONAL COACH, Vol. 1, No. 17, Spring, 1978.

We've seen medical malpractice insurance double, triple and even quadruple the cost of health care.

Bruns added:

But the sports and recreation-field has been especially vulnerable. School athletic programs have been curtailed, even completely eliminated in one wealthy Maryland county, because the liability insurance cost has contributed significantly to a financial burden that has become intolerable.[19]

In North Carolina, the General Assembly in its 1979 Session, introduced legislation regarding ski injuries and subsequent actions. It proposed to amend its General Statutes to read as follows:

99B-1 *Assumption of Risks* — It is recognized that the sport of downhill or alpine skiing and the use of associated tramways and facilities may be hazardous to skiers and other persons attending a ski area, regardless of all feasible safety measures that may be taken. Consequently, each voluntary participant shall accept and assume the risks of and legal responsibility for any injury to his person or property arising out of natural and foreseeable dangers inherent in the sport of skiing and the use of associated ski area facilities. For [the] purpose of this chapter, ski area means all passenger tramways, trails, slopes, areas and facilities open to the general public for the purpose of participating in the sport of skiing.[20]

---

19. *Id.*
20. Senate Bill 450, Ski Injury Actions, General Assembly of North Carolina, Session 1979, Mar. 12, 1979.

It is clear that states, in which skiing is a profitable industry, similar statutes may be enacted to protect the economy of the ski industry.

Several other ski cases illustrate the type of litigation before the court.

In Colorado, an expert skier sued an experienced ski instructor for an injury she received when the instructor collided with her on the ski slope.[21] At the time of the accident, the plaintiff was skiing on Nix Nox, a graded slope that was rated "more difficult." She was attempting a traverse in which she was skiing across rather than straight down when the instructor hit her. He claimed that she was skiing very slowly and as he attempted to pass her, she suddenly stopped. The defendant admitted that he did not attempt to slow down or change directions or even yell at her which could have avoided the accident.

The U. S. District Court for the District of Colorado favored the defendant ski instructor and the plaintiff appealed to the Court of Appeals. The plaintiff argued that the lower court failed to consider the safety guidelines used by skiers which require the trailing skier to yield the slope to the person below who had the right-of-way.

The Court of Appeals felt that the ski instructor could not avoid the plaintiff because she stopped unexpectedly in front of him. It made a timely comment regarding the attitude of many jurors in situations involving high risk sports such as skiing, when it said:

> It is true that the jury in a ski slope case tends to view the entire skiing scene as one involving

---

21. LaVine v. Clear Creek Skiing Corp., 557 F.2d 730 (10th Cir. 1977).

a high degree of risk by merely taking to the slopes. This is an attitude which tends to be pervasive in injuries which involve participation in sports.

It refused to change the jury's verdict and favored the ski instructor.

Joy Fischer was on a ski outing in Colorado with several friends.[22] She paid for a ticket to the ski facility and it included the use of the ski lift. The lift at the ski slope did not use a safety bar but a stud on the left was designed so that a bar could be attached if desired. As Fischer was attempting to get off the lift she realized that her sleeve had been caught on the chair's stud. She could not free herself from the chair and was "carried through mid-air for a few feet." She was aided by two ski patrolmen as soon as the lift stopped. A bone in her left arm was broken by the accident.

The operator of the ski facility claimed that Fischer had "assumed the risk" of injury when she got on the ski lift and that the accident could not have been avoided. The Colorado Court of Appeals did not agree with the operator of the ski slope, but held that the injury was caused by the negligence of the operator and favored the skier.

B. Golf Courses

Robert A. Scalf, Professor of Law at Cleveland Marshall Law School, and Robert E. Robinson, editor for the Allen Smith Company and former special counsel to the Indiana State Board of Health, observed that the golf-related lawsuits are so numerous that one

---

22. Arapahoe Basin, Inc. v. Fischer, 475 P.2d 631 (Colo. 1970).

might think golf is the "most hazardous sport played in this nation." [23] Regarding golf injuries they remarked:

> It is apparent that the "hazards" faced by a golfer are not limited to sand traps and water. A well hit golf ball travels, at impact, 250 feet per second, or about 170 miles per hour. It is, in brief, a projectile, and a very dangerous one. Predictably, there are many injuries.[24]

Frank Curran purchased a home next to the Green Hills County Club in Melbrae, California with the promise that a fence would be built to protect him from stray golf balls.[25] The club's board of directors failed to erect the fence, and an accident took place.

Curran testified during the trial that he normally would not let the members of his family use the family swimming pool or even sit in the backyard until six or seven in the evening. On the day of the accident, however, he reported that he and his daughter were in the pool although it was only 5:30 p.m. He explained that it was Saturday, when most golfers started play early, and that the course was usually empty by 4:00 p.m. In addition he testified that, as was his custom, he checked the golf course to see if any golfers were approaching.

With all the precautions, however, a golfer hit a ball and Curran was struck by it.

---

23. R. A. Scalf and R. E. Robinson, *Injuries Arising out of Amateur and Professional Sports: Viability of the Assumption of Risk Defense,* DEFENSE LAW JOURNAL, Vol. 27, No. 5, 1978.
24. *Id.*
25. Curran v. Green Hills Country Club, 101 Cal. Rptr. 158 (Cal. App. 1972).

The court considered the doctrine of assumption of risk and made several points that apply in general to all sports participants. It observed:

1. To warrant the doctrine of assumption of risk, the evidence must show that the injured party appreciated the specific danger involved.

2. He must have not only general knowledge of a danger, but also knowledge and appreciation of the particular danger and the magnitude of the risk involved.

3. The doctrine of assumption of risk should not be applied with liberality, if it be applicable at all, where the injury takes place on plaintiff's own property, which is safe and rendered dangerous only by invasion of missiles from adjacent land.

4. In general, the plaintiff is not required to surrender a valuable legal right, such as the use of his own property as he sees fit, merely because the defendant's conduct has threatened him with harm if the right is exercised.

The appellate court reversed the lower court's decision and chose to favor the homeowner instead. It commented that the plaintiff would otherwise be a virtual prisoner in his own home if he was "vulnerable to assumption of risk" if he went outside his home unless he was absolutely certain that all the golfers had left the course. It would render the plaintiff defenseless and give him no opportunity to remedy a situation in which the defendant was totally protected by the doctrine.

Arvilla Beauchamp was walking on a cement veranda from the parking lot to the starting area of the Los

Gatos Golf Course in California.[26] She wore golf shoes with spikes that were badly worn and needed replacing. Beauchamp slipped and fell injuring her "back, legs and an arm." She sued the golf course operators for negligence in causing her injury.

The defendants, representing the golf course, stated that over 4,000 people used this area each month and pointed to the worn out condition of the plaintiff's shoes as the reason she fell. The Superior Court of Santa Clara County entered a judgment of nonsuit and the plaintiff appealed.

The Court of Appeals, First District, considered the case and made a number of comments that are important to those who own or operate sports facilities. The court declared:

1. In exercise of ordinary care, the possessor of land owes a duty to an invitee to make the property reasonably safe for the intended use by the intended user, and to warn of latent or concealed dangers and to guard against possible dangers by reasonable inspection of the premises.

2. Possessor of land is not liable for injury to an invitee from a danger which is obvious, or should have been observed in exercise of reasonable care.

3. Invitation to use premises is to use them in condition in which they are openly and plainly visible.

4. Possessor of land is not an insurer of the safety of its users.

---

26. Beauchamp v. Los Gatos Golf Course, 77 Cal. Rptr. 914 (Cal. App. 1969).

5. Absence of other accidents is not proof per
se that no dangerous condition exists.[27]

The court of appeals held that the lower court's
decision in favor of the golf course operators should be
reversed and the issue determined by a jury.

Scalf and Robinson, writing about the vast number of
golf cases that go to court, predict that the "courts
rarely impose liability as a result of those injuries." [28]
Many golfers likewise assume that any injury
associated with golf is the fault of the person who is
injured. The popular belief is that a golfer automatically
assumes all risk of injury when playing. However,
several cases illustrate that the plaintiff can and does
win occasionally in court when an injury, due to
another's negligence, is sustained.

One such case took place in Louisiana at the Pinewood
Country Club when a golfer was hit by a member of his
foursome and suffered severe facial injuries.[29] Leo
Allen walked ahead of another member of his group,
who had topped his ball, and hit a weak 75 yard drive.

The golfer testified that he yelled "fore" and then hit
his ball. When he saw it proceeding toward the plaintiff,
whose back was turned, he shouted "fore" again. This
time, the plaintiff turned and was struck on the face
with the ball. The District Court of St. Tammany Parish
held that the plaintiff had violated the established rules
of golf when he went ahead of a golfer who, as a
member of the foursome, was supposed to hit his ball
before any of his companions left the tee area. The
plaintiff appealed the decision.

_____

27. *Id.*
28. *Supra* note 23.
29. Allen v. Pinewood Country Club, Inc., 292 So. 2d 786 (La.
   App. 1974).

The Court of Appeals of Louisiana viewed the circumstances of the case in a different manner. The court commented on several practices that golfers recognize as rules of the facility and game, such as:

1. A golfer must give warning to those who may be near the line of flight of the ball by shouting "fore," and then affording sufficient time for them to step aside far enough to avoid danger.

2. A golfer is not required to give warning to players on contiguous holes or fairways to whom danger is not reasonably foreseeable or to another player whom he knows already has him in view and is aware of his intention to drive.

3. A golfer owes to a companion player the duty of warning the other of his intent to drive when he knows, or should know, the companion is in the intended line of flight.

The court held that the defendants failed to give the plaintiff time to move before he hit his ball. Therefore it awarded the plaintiff $3,500 in damages for his painful injury. In so doing, it reversed the previous decision of the district court.

The court in the previous case emphasized the importance of the warning of "fore" before the ball is hit and stressed the need for the golfer to wait until his warning has been observed and the people move before proceeding to hit his ball. In like manner, a court in Pennsylvania seriously questions the use of the warning "fore" after the ball has been hit. It made its opinion clear in *Boynton v. Ryan* when it disputed the use of the warning by declaring:

We do not see any connection between a duty to shout "fore" after the shot and the prevention of the plaintiff's injury. Golf balls travel at great speeds and can change directions suddenly — In the reported cases where the belated call has been given, the target has only had more time to turn a vital organ toward the flight of the ball.[30]

C. Gymnasiums and Adjacent Areas

Martin Numez III was a member of the St. Bernard basketball team participating in a Christmas tournament played and sponsored by Isidore Newman High School.[31] The proceeds of the tournament were to go to the Isidore Newman High School. On the day of the game there was an unusual amount of humidity, which caused water to condense on the floor of the Newman Gym. During the day, in preparation for the first game, the school's janitors wiped water off the floor and turned the heat fans on to dry the floor out. During the game, in which Numez was playing, the janitors continued to mop the floor. In the third quarter of the game, Numez attempted a jump shot and slipped, injuring his back.

The boy's father insisted that since the host school charged admission to the game his son was a "business invitee" and that the school breached its duty to provide a safe place for him to participate. He cited the specific duty the school owed his son when he declared:

> An owner or occupier of lands and buildings must take reasonable and ordinary care to protect invitees from any dangerous conditions on the premises. He must also warn them of any

---

30. Boynton v. Ryan, 257 F.2d 70 (3d Cir. 1958).
31. Nunez v. Isidore Newman High School, 306 So. 2d 457 (La. App. 1975).

latent dangerous defects in the premises and
inspect the premises for any possible
dangerous conditions of which he does not
know.[32]

Over nineteen witnesses testified during the trial in
support of Numez and his father, stating that the
basketball floor was slippery and dangerous. The
referees, however, differed from this testimony,
commenting that they had experienced no problem with
their footing during the game and that no one
complained to them about the condition of the floor until
the game was over. They observed, however, that the
second game was cancelled. The plaintiff's coach
remarked that he did not notice anything wrong with
the gymnasium floor and never thought of stopping the
play during the game.

The court considered the referees' and coach's
testimony to be important since all of them had years of
experience in high school athletics and none of them
questioned the conditions of the gymnasium.

The Commissioner of the Louisiana High School
Athletic Association testified that an official has:

Complete control of a basketball game from 30
minutes before a game starts until the final
score is recorded in the scorebook. The referees
had the responsibility of approving all playing
conditions. The coaches have the obligation to
control the players conduct and must "look out
for their welfare." [33]

The Louisiana Court of Appeals held that the fact
that the referees and coach did not feel that a danger

---

32. WILLIAM L. PROSSER, LAW OF TORTS, 4th Ed., at 61.
33. *Supra* note 31.

existed was sufficient for it to rule in favor of the defendant, Isidore Newman School.

The father of two sons who attended Addison Trail High School in Illinois accepted an invitation to attend a wrestling program at the school.[34] He parked his car in the school's parking lot and walked toward the school. No one was present at the entrance of the building to show the spectators which door was open. He passed by the front doors and went to other doors nearer the gym, but they were locked. The plaintiff then walked around the school building to a grassy slope which led to a lower level of doors. The area was poorly lighted and the plaintiff reported that he could not tell that the slope was muddy and slippery. He slipped on the mud, fell and broke his wrist. During the trial he declared that:

1. There was no sign to warn him of the muddy condition of the slope.

2. The muddy condition existed for some time according to the statements of a student and coach.

3. The football team used the slope regularly and it was common to slide down rather than walk down since it was so slippery.

The plaintiff admitted that he was familiar with the area and that he could have avoided the slope by taking a safer, but longer, route to the gymnasium.

The appellate court referred to an earlier Illinois court to answer the question of the plaintiff's liability based on contributory negligence. The court remarked:

If a plaintiff has available to him two different methods or ways of doing a job, performing a

34. Shannon v. Addison Trail School, Dist. No. 88, 339 N.E.2d 372 (Ill. App. 1975).

task, or proceeding, one previously tried and
known to be safe, — the other either unknown
or unexplored or known to involve certain
possible hazards, — and he chooses the method
or way which is unknown or unexplored or
known to involve certain possible hazards, and
is injured in the process, he is contributorily
negligent in the matter of law.[35]

Although this decision was reversed and did not favor
the plaintiff, the standard involved in the case has been
applied in subsequent litigation. The Illinois Appellate
Court realized that the plaintiff was familiar with both
routes, but chose the one down a hill in a dimly lit area,
while he could have taken the paved path in safety. The
court felt that a reasonable man would have taken the
safe path and ruled that it could find no evidence of
negligence by the school. It affirmed the trial court's
decision in favor of the school.

Roger Clary, a 17-year-old senior at Stony Point High
School in North Carolina, sued the Alexander County
Board of Education for serious injuries he received in
the school's gymnasium.[36] Roger had participated on
the school's basketball team for three years and was
familiar with the glass windows which were located
three feet from the end of the basketball court. On the
day he was injured, he testified, he was running wind
sprints directed by his coach. He indicated during the
trial that:

I didn't have any trouble seeing the window,
and I knew it was there — I knew I had to stop
or run into something.

---

35. Geraghty v. Burr Oak Lanes, Inc., 118 N.E.2d 63 (Ill. App.
    1954).
36. Clary v. Alexander County Bd. of Educ., 199 S.E.2d 738 (N.C.
    App. 1973).

He failed to stop or slow down and crashed into the glass window, shattering the glass and cutting himself severely. He sued the school for maintaining a negligent and unsafe facility. The school district, in rebuttal, argued that it could not be responsible for the player's liability when he was contributorily negligent. During the trial, it was determined that the school had waived its immunity when it purchased liability insurance and therefore the rules of liability applied to the school just as they do to any landlord.

The plaintiff insisted that he was not guilty of contributory negligence since his coach had commanded him to run wind sprints. The Court of Appeals of North Carolina disagreed however and declared:

> The rule with respect to acting in obedience to the orders of a person in authority requires that such orders be disregarded when a reasonable man under similar circumstances would know that his compliance with such orders would result in his injury.

The court was of the opinion that the athlete was guilty of contributory negligence since he was familiar with the conditions of the gymnasium, but ignored his own safety by refusing to use reasonable care. It held that while the injuries he suffered were regrettable, the trial court did not err in favoring the school board.

D. Stadiums and Playing Fields

Robert K. Epstein, a staff writer for the Players Association of the National Football League, discusses the controversy over synthetic turf in *Trial* Magazine.[37]

---

37. Robert K. Epstein, *The Case Against Artificial Turf,* TRIAL, Vol. 13, No. 1, Jan. 1977.

Epstein quotes a Baltimore Colt official who observed, after six Colts were hurt on polyturf at the New England Patriot's stadium, that:

> The only good thing about artificial turf is that it keeps uniforms clean.

Epstein cites a study compiled by the Stanford Research Institute on artificial turf that reveals that:

> the five stadiums with the highest major injury rates and ten of the twelve most dangerous, each have synthetic turf surfaces, as compared to the four lowest and ten of the eleven least dangerous, all of which are natural grass.[38]

He then points to the same study which concludes:

> The significantly higher injury rates consistently obtained in the NFL over the past three years from playing on synthetic surfaces, in such categories as "lost time injuries," "punishment" beyond the reported, injuries and even "playable injuries" all point to the conclusion that synthetic surfaces for football cannot be justified on the injury prevention basis; in general, natural turfs are safer.[39]

On the other hand, F. E. Troy, the Director of Markets, Recreational Products for the Monsanto Company, answers the criticism of synthetic turf in *Trial*.[40] Troy defends synthetic turf in sports facilities and refers to the Stanford Research Institute's 1973 study that declares:

> Injuries occur more frequently on synthetic turf than on natural turf when minor injuries

---

38. *Id.*
39. *Supra* note 37.
40. F. E. Troy, *In Defense of Synthetic Turf,* TRIAL, Vol. 13, No. 1, Jan. 1977.

are included, but no difference between the two is observed when gradients of injury severity are analyzed.[41]

A June 1975 report of the SRI adds support to Troy's argument by adding:

When several gradients of severe injuries were analyzed, (e.g. reinjuries, injuries causing two or more missed games, injuries requiring hospitalizations, surgeries, third degree injuries and season-ending injuries) no consistent statistical differences between synthetic and natural surfaces were observed.[42]

Kyle Thomas, a high school player in Chicago, was involved in a lawsuit involving the maintenance of synthetic turf.[43] Thomas was injured during a football game played in Hanson Park Stadium. The stadium was owned by the Chicago Board of Education. He accused his coaches and the school district of requiring him to play on synthetic turf that was "constructed, installed and maintained improperly."

Illinois had a provision in its School Code that protected teachers and coaches from liability when they were conducting an activity in which discipline of the students under their direction was involved. The coaches then assumed *in loco parentis* status. The plaintiff, however, contended that the coaches should not receive immunity because:

---

41. Stanford Research Institute, National Football League Injury Study: 1969-1972, Apr., 1973.
42. Stanford Research Institute, National Football League Injury Study, June, 1975.
43. Thomas v. Chicago Bd. of Educ., 377 N.E.2d 55 (Ill. App. 1978).

the football game was not part of the regular educational program. It was a non-credit, extracurricular activity conducted after school hours away from the school premises.

The Appellate Court of Illinois, First District, Third Division, did not agree with the plaintiff and remarked:

The determination of when liability will attach for negligent supervision does not depend upon whether the teacher is employed by a school which has sports facilities located on school grounds or by a school which must conduct its athletic program away from the premises.

It also defined the varsity football program and commented:

Although participation in the program is voluntary and not for credit, it does not follow that the program itself is unconnected with the school curriculum. Athletics are an integral part of virtually all school programs at every level.

The court reversed the circuit court's dismissal against the school board and the coaches and remanded it back for determination.

Justice J. Simon concurred in part by saying:

The defendants should be equally responsible when the defect that gives rise to injury results from the defendant's failure to inspect and test the playing field surface. A playing field is just as much a part of the equipment used by a football team as is a helmet, especially as far as its potential for causing injury and the need for proper inspection of it is concerned.[44]

---

44. *Id.*

The school board accepted the decision but the coaches appealed. The question before the court was whether the coaches could claim immunity under the School Code and Tort Immunity Act for allegedly issuing defective equipment. While the court felt that a school district could not relax its duty to furnish safe equipment for its students, it did not extend this obligation to its coaches. It said:

> First, the school district has the authority to purchase and *furnish* equipment to students. This authority is not shared with teachers and coaches, who have instead the distinct competence or authority to *supervise* the students and their use of that equipment. A coach's duty to inspect the equipment is subsumed within his or her duty to supervise but does not fall under the school district's authority to furnish.

The court made an interesting comment when it stated:

> In the interest of student-teacher harmony, litigation between them should not be encouraged — absent wilful and wanton conduct.

It continued:

> If we were to place the duty of ordinary care (while furnishing equipment) on teachers, we would burden them to the extent that a teacher might become immobile in the performance of his obligations. They would 'not be free and unhampered in the discharge of their duties, since they would live in fear that each judgment they made would bring a lawsuit.'

The court then ruled that the coaches were immune from liability for negligence attributed to defective athletic equipment. It concluded with a statement that has significance for teachers and coaches:

> Moreover, a proliferation of such actions for negligence would drain teachers' time, encourage second guessing teachers' judgment by courts, and quite possibly discourage persons from the career of teaching.[45]

E. Responsibility Releases

Sports participants frequently sign so-called responsibility releases when they engage in high risk activities or use facilities in which the owner or operator wants the promise that liability will be waived in the event of injury. A New York court case is important because it illustrates that a responsibility release does not automatically eliminate the possibility of liability.

Bruce Gross enrolled in the Stormville Parachute Training School so that he could learn to parachute jump.[46] He was "requested to sign a 'responsibility release' before he could receive instructions." Gross did so, and after training that amounted to just one hour on land, he jumped from an airplane 2800 feet in the air. He suffered a broken leg when he landed.

The plaintiff sued the parachute school and based his claim on the following:

1. the defendants were negligent in not complying with Federal Aviation Administration Regulations and failing to instruct properly.
2. defendants expressly and impliedly warranted that they were qualified instructors.

---

45. Thomas v. Chicago Bd. of Educ., No. 50964, Agenda 17 (Mar. 1979).
46. Gross v. Sweet, 407 N.Y.S.2d 254 (N.Y. App. Div. 1978).

3. the negligence was gross, wanton and reckless.

The defendants charged that the plaintiff's "responsibility release" barred any recovery against them. The Special Term of the Supreme Court, Ulster County, granted the defendants summary judgment and the plaintiff appealed.

The issue of the "responsibility release" became the controlling question in the appeal. The "release" stated:

> I, the undersigned, hereby, and by these covenants, do waive any and all claims that I, my heirs, and/or assignees may have against Nathanial Sweet, the master and the pilot who shall operate the aircraft when used for the purpose of parachute jumping for any personal injuries or property damage that I may sustain or which may arise out of my learning, practicing or actually jumping from an aircraft. I also assume full responsibility for any damage that I may do or cause while participating in this sport.
> I have read the above and agree and request permission to participate in sport parachuting.

The plaintiff admitted that he signed the waiver, but contended that he could institute a lawsuit because it did not release the defendants "from liability for injuries caused by their negligence." He listed the reasons he was suing the defendants as:

1. failure by the defendants to comply with the Federal Aviation Administration Requirements that he obtain a medical certificate of his physical condition prior to jumping,

2. failure to provide him with safe, adequate and necessary pre-jump training instructions required by the FAA.

3. allowing him to jump with a parachute that
was not proper for a student parachutist.

The Supreme Court, Appellate Division, decided that
the "release" did not cover the omissions pointed out by
the plaintiff. It therefore reversed the lower court's
decision in favor of the defendants stating that:

> The release does not relieve defendants from
> negligence in the performance of their
> instructions or from injuries arising out of
> improper and incorrect instructions.

IN MY OPINION

For years we have been impressed by the beautiful
snow-covered ski slopes, from Vermont to Squaw
Valley, featured in promotional advertisements.
Suddenly, *Sunday v. Stratton* changed all that. Today,
ski slopes are warning in advertisements that skiing
may be hazardous to your health and selling tickets
proclaiming that skiing is a hazardous sport. In states
that thrive on the ski industry legislatures are
considering bills, similar to the one enacted in Vermont,
that will shift the responsibility for ski injuries from the
ski slope operators to the skier.

It is evident that lawsuits are changing the operation
of sports facilities and the standard of care is becoming
an issue. It is clear that the participant deserves
facilities that are as safe as possible. To provide less is
an invitation to disaster — both for the participant as
well as the owner or operator of the facility.

After reading this chapter, I hope the reader will
realize that automatic immunity is not extended, for
example, to all activity that takes place on the golf
course. Too many people, including my attorney friends,
believe that golf participation is synonymous with the

assumption of risk doctrine and any injury is really the injured person's own responsibility. The message in this chapter is simple — negligent conduct results in liability no matter where it takes place.

One thing that is interesting is generally overlooked by many people. A large number of golfers feel that the warning "fore" is shouted after a ball is hit toward another golfer. In this chapter, the court describes the need for the warning before the ball is hit to alert the golfers ahead that a ball is about to be hit. The Pennsylvania judge in *Boynton* said it well when he commented that once you hit the ball, the cry of "fore" merely causes the golfer to turn in time to expose some organ to danger.

Another trend is gradually becoming accepted policy regarding the use of facilities. School authorities realize that it is poor policy and worse economics to let a facility stand idle after limited use. For this reason, school facilities are being leased or rented to outside groups. This promotes community good will and generates important revenue. We seem to have gone full circle and returned to the past when school buildings were used by the total community.

Such use of the facilities by outside religious, political and other groups will often lead to litigation based on constitutional guarantees. This is perhaps the wrong basis of a suit, however, since the court has been specific in its ruling that if any *group* is allowed the use of a facility *all* groups are so privileged. The guideline, for purposes of administration, seems to be that a fee must be charged, that educational programs should not be interfered with and that no damage should be done to the facility.

The administrator should delegate the responsibility for inspection and repair of the facilities to a specific individual or group. Periodic inspection and care to correct defects will protect the institution but more important it will safeguard the most important person, the participant.

CHAPTER 13

Sports Equipment

*Sports are of more interest to Americans than
weather or politics. And next year may well
be the last game for the Super Bowl; and
the likes of Olga Korbut may be never
seen in this country again — if
the product liability crisis
is not abated.*[1]

Sports equipment is the basis of much controversy, and product liability litigation continues to escalate. Howard Bruns, president of the Sporting Goods Manufacturing Association, deplores the rising costs of insurance and huge damage awards confronting the manufacturer of sports equipment. He foresees a drastic change in sports if the trend is not turned around. Bruns blames the rising cost of product liability on:

1. The "sue syndrome."
2. The source of wealth to the plaintiff bar.
3. The filing of frivolous suits that never get to court but cost the system millions of dollars in defense attorney fees.
4. Settling out of court to avoid lengthy defense costs or a possible unfriendly or sub-educated jury.[2]

---

1. Howard Bruns, *Testimony before the U.S. Senate's Select Committee on Small Business,* Sporting Goods Manufacturing Association, July, 1977.
2. *Id.*

The Multi-Association Action Committee for Product Liability Reform regrets the increase in lawsuits against manufacturers of sports equipment. The committee attributes the rise in litigation to a prevailing attitude that every injury should be compensated for and that both the manufacturers and their insurance companies have unlimited financial resources. The committee condemns the contingency fee basis that enables attorneys to litigate cases for a percentage of the amount of damages awarded (usually one third). It also opposes the number of cases involving manufacturers that are settled before they ever get to court.[3]

Out-of-Court Settlements

School authorities and sports participants involved in sports-related lawsuits are becoming increasingly aware of the problem that out-of-court settlements pose. Many are beginning to join manufacturers and owners of businesses in expressing their concern over the atmosphere in which these judgments are rendered.

A school supervisor disclosed that his school district was preparing to settle a case in which a high school student was injured on a trampoline. He admitted that no one was negligent, but quickly added that the school authorities preferred to settle for $100,000 rather than go through the ordeal of a trial. He reasoned that the insurance company would pay the bill.

A New York case, while not dealing specifically with sports equipment, nevertheless, illustrates the problem that exists with settlements. An injured athlete named

---

3. *Multi-Association Action Committee: For Product Liability Reform,* Vol. 1, No. 1, Jan., 1978.

the school superintendent and high school football coach as defendants in a personal injury suit. The defendants reported that their attorney settled the case before they could answer the boy's erroneous statements against them. Their attorney explained that he did not believe he could win the suit after he saw the horrified look on the faces of the jurors when they saw the boy's knee, mutilated by repeated operations.

When dealing with juries, attorneys, for both plaintiff and defendant, consider many factors that ultimately determine their decision on a settlement. Juries frequently are influenced by the type of accident, the defendant's ability to pay, the plaintiff's need for money, the plaintiff's age, race, creed, color and personal style, and the reputation of the respective attorneys.[4] Melvin Belli, an outstanding trial lawyer, reports that juries in metropolitan areas grant higher awards than in rural areas. In like manner Belli declares:

> Juries tend to give higher verdicts against corporations, trucking companies, railroads, bus companies, or drivers of Cadillacs than where the defendant is a private individual or of apparent limited means, such as a school teacher, clerk, or laborer driving a 1938 Ford.[5]

Since judicial decisions often are based on precedent, a dilemma may be created by cases being settled indiscriminately out of court. For this reason many manufacturers oppose settlements and want

---

4. MELVIN BELLI, MODERN TRIALS, Bobbs-Merrill Co., Inc., Indianapolis, Ind., at 749.
5. *Id.*

safeguards built into their insurance policies. They suggest that:

> Some companies would even like to see liability policies written in such a fashion as to force insurance companies to take more cases to court, where businesses win 70% of the time. Firms claim that the large number of out-of-court settlements simply increases settlement costs and enhances the expectations of consumer victories.[6]

With such opposition to settlements, Belli states that 14 out of every 15 cases are settled without a trial, explaining that the courts would be forty years behind schedule if all cases had to go through a jury trial.[7]

Besides crowded calendars, however, settlements often are made for convenience. The average lawyer cannot spend needless hours in court when he can save time for himself and his client by a settlement. Some legal writers claim that settlements actually advance the judicial process when appropriate cases are settled and even encourage lawyers to consider the following:

> A lawyer, no matter what side he is on, should not be closeminded about the possibility of a settlement. In fact, if he is defending a matter in which liability is clear or the possibility exists that the court will so find, he has an ethical duty to seek a reasonable settlement and not risk the fortunes of his client.[8]

---

6. *Product Liability: Is There a Cure?*, INDUSTRY WEEK, Vol. 193, No. 5, June 6, 1977.
7. *Supra* note 4.
8. North Carolina Bar Association Foundation, Institute on Civil Trial Strategy and Advocacy, at 319.

National Injury Report

The National Injury Report Clearinghouse reports that three of the top four categories of equipment that produce injuries are sports related: bicycles rank first, with football equipment third and baseball gear fourth. The report is based on an index which is derived from the number of injuries reported to hospital emergency rooms plus the severity of the injuries. It lists the top four as:

Bicycles	40.608
Stairs	23.506
Football	13.682
Baseball	12.908 [9]

The report also notes that skateboards, which were 18th on the list in 1976, moved to 7th place in 1977 with 140,070 injuries reported. From such figures as these it is evident that there is a wide variety of sports equipment that presents hazards to the participants of a particular activity.

Cases Involving Protective Headgears

Protective headgears for various sports are involved in many product liability suits against the manufacturers of sports equipment.

A. Football Helmets

The football helmet has received criticism in recent years and has been the target of numerous lawsuits. As a result, a crisis may be threatening the existence of football in our high schools and colleges. For years opponents of football have pointed to the high cost of

---

9. Greensboro Record, July 5, 1978.

football as a basis for urging its discontinuance. Today the same critics believe they have legitimate ammunition to compel administrators and school boards to consider the elimination of football. This does not come from a lack of interest or participation in the sport, since both are at an all-time high. The crisis results from the excessive courtroom awards against school districts and sports equipment manufacturers.

There are over 100 helmet-related injury cases alone pending in the court today, with total claims estimated to be over $300 million. The huge awards made by juries in the last five years have caused six manufacturers of helmets to discontinue production. Although some of the remaining companies still manufacture protective headgears, the logical question is, "How long will they continue?" These helmet companies are a part of corporate conglomerates that have a "bottom-line" philosophy that demands profits. These companies report that the combined total profit of eight companies that manufactured football helmets in 1976 amounted to less than $1 million.[10] Richard Black, an Arizona attorney, predicts that the number of helmet-producing companies will drop to six in the near future.[11]

If juries continue to make astronomical awards to injured athletes, soccer may replace football as the sport of the future in the United States. The problem is two-fold: first, companies may refuse to gamble on expensive lawsuits and stop producing helmets; second, for those who manufacture helmets, skyrocketing insurance costs for product liability may result in

---

10. NATIONAL COACH, Vol. 1, No. 12, Fall, 1976.
11. Richard Black, Remarks made at AAHPER Convention, New Orleans, La., Mar. 17, 1979.

helmets that cost more than high schools or colleges can afford.

The seriousness of this problem is demonstrated by examination of several recent court cases involving helmet-related injuries.

Gary Stead, a 16-year-old football player at Miami Edison High School, broke his neck in a game played in Miami's Orange Bowl when he attempted to tackle an opponent.[12] As a result of the injury, Gary is a permanent quadriplegic. He accused the Riddell Company of producing a defective helmet. The trial court agreed, awarding Gary a staggering $5.3 million and his father an additional $73,312.19 for medical expenses.

At the trial, Jake Gaither, Florida A & M's veteran coach, testified that the faceguard on the helmet was too long for safety and stated that one of his players died as a result of an injury inflicted by the same type of helmet in 1959. Yet, during the emotional trial, no evidence was produced that proved that Gary was even wearing a Riddell helmet when he was injured. The Riddell Company appealed the decision and it is reported that the case was finally settled out of court for over $3 million.[13]

Kevin Byrns attempted to field an "on-side" kick during a high school game in Arizona.[14] He sustained a serious injury when an opposing player met him head-on. Bryns sued the school district and helmet company for designing a defective helmet and failing to warn the participants of its dangers.

---

12. Sentinel, Winston-Salem, N.C., July 21, 1977.
13. U. S. NEWS AND WORLD REPORT, Dec. 4, 1978.
14. Byrns v. Riddell, Inc., 550 P.2d 1065 (Ariz. 1976).

Several experts testified in the boys' behalf by contending that the shape of the top of the helmet caused the injury. The Riddell Company showed the game film and the accident to the jury, and the high school coach testified that the injury was not caused by the helmet. The trial court favored the defendants, but the Arizona Supreme Court reversed the decision and sent it back for a new trial. The Superior Court of Arizona then heard testimony from over 30 witnesses and viewed 200 exhibits along with a film of the game and several tests. It decided in favor of the manufacturer.[15] Helmet manufacturers reportedly pooled their financial resources together in an attempt to win the case. It is estimated that it cost $250,000 to litigate the case. Prior to this decision, many helmet cases had been settled out of court in favor of the plaintiff. The manufacturers believe the decision may set a precedent that will enable them to win future helmet-related cases.[16]

Matthew Gerrity, a 15-year-old football player in Illinois, received serious injuries when he made a tackle during a junior varsity game.[17] Gerrity sued the attending physician, the hospital, the school district, and the helmet manufacturer. He contended that the school negligently furnished him with a football helmet that did not fit properly even though they knew that the ill-fitting helmet might cause him to be injured.

The State of Illinois has a general policy prohibiting children from suing their parents for negligence unless it constitutes "willful and wanton misconduct." The

15. *Supra* note 3.
16. *Supra* note 11.
17. Gerrity v. Beatty, 373 N.E.2d 1323 (Ill. 1978).

Illinois General Assembly extended this immunity to teachers in 1965 and applied it to:

> all activities connected with the school program and may be exercised at any time for the safety and supervision of the pupils in the absence of their parents and guardians.

The Supreme Court of Illinois noted that the statute did not apply in this case since equipment, not supervision, was the issue. It felt that selecting proper equipment and making certain that it fit the athlete properly did not impose a burden on the coach. It therefore reversed the circuit court's earlier decision favoring the defendants, and remanded it back with directions. The supreme court held that the school district was not immune from suit since Gerrity did not have to prove "willful and wanton conduct." It felt that a school district could not ignore its duty to provide its students with equipment that fit safely. The case is still pending.

John Horgan was seriously crippled from a hard blow to the top of his football helmet during a high school game.[18] He is now a permanent quadriplegic. Horgan sued the Rawlings Company for allegedly failing to warn him of the risk associated with the helmet and the sport of football. A jury in Boston, Massachusetts, favored the Rawlings Company in a decision that its attorney called "the first such case that has been tried to a conclusion before a jury."

While the attorneys for the Rawlings Company did not see the victory as a "swinging of the pendulum,"

---

18. *Jury Finds for Helmet Makers,* THE PHYSICIAN AND SPORTSMEDICINE, Vol. 7, No. 2, Feb. 1979.

they did believe that similar cases could be won if "sound medical and biochemical testing" could be presented. One attorney made an interesting observation when he remarked:

> If I made equipment, I'd want to stop selling helmets, but then football would cease to exist and there would go the profits on shoulder pads and hip pads.[19]

Richard Ball, an attorney for the Riddell Company and the American Baseball Cap Company, feels that the criticism of sports equipment is unfounded. He writes that:

> Claims against manufacturers universally involve a charge that the equipment was improperly designed. They do not arise from instances where the equipment failed as a result of some manufacturing defect.[20]

Ball feels that the criticism of protective athletic equipment comes from people who are "outside of both manufacturing and athletics." [21] He believes that the opposition to sports equipment is based on theory and experiments conducted in the laboratory rather than from experience on the playing field, where the actual competition takes place. He declares:

> Most often the person attacking a football helmet does so by way of comparing it to a different helmet, which in laboratory experiment produces results which are allegedly better.[22]

---

19. *Id.*
20. Richard T. Ball, *Litigation: Will it Destroy Athletics?*, THE FIRST AIDER, Vol. 48, No. 1, Sept. 1978.
21. *Id.*
22. *Supra* note 20.

To meet the crisis, the National Operating Commission on Standards for Athletic Equipment (NOCSAE) has formulated safety standards for football helmets that became mandatory for colleges in 1978 and will take effect in high schools by 1980. The NOCSAE-approved helmet is intended to decrease the number of head injuries in football and, hopefully, reduce the number of helmet-related lawsuits.[23]

Other sports authorities believe the problem can be reduced if coaches teach blocking and tackling using the shoulders instead of the head. These authorities encourage officials to enforce the rule on "spearing" to protect the players. Dr. Allan Ryan, editor-in-chief of *Physician and Sportsmedicine,* however, still urges coaches to be careful to select durable and proper fitting equipment which will not present a hazard to the player or opponent.[24]

B. Hockey Helmets

Hockey helmets, like other protective headgear, are often involved in litigation. An interesting case occurred in Boston in which an ice hockey player was injured. William Everett, Jr. threw himself on the ice to block an opponent's shot and was struck by the puck.[25] He was a 19-year-old ice hockey defenseman playing for New Preparatory School against the Brown University freshmen. The puck penetrated the gap of the three-sided helmet, causing him a fractured skull. The

---

23. V. R. Hodgson, *NOCSAE: A Program to Reduce Serious Injuries in Athletics,* SPORTS SAFETY II, The American Alliance for Health, Physical Education and Recreation, Washington, D.C., 1977.
24. *Id.* at 60.
25. Everett v. Buckey Warren, Inc., 380 N.E.2d 653 (Mass. 1978).

injury necessitated the insertion of a plate in his skull
and medical authorities predict he will continue to
suffer from headaches indefinitely.

The player sued the manufacturer of the helmet, the
sporting goods company who sold it to the school, and
the school he attended. He charged all three defendants
with negligence that attributed to his injury. The
defendants claimed he was guilty of contributory
negligence and assumption of risk.

The Superior Court of Suffolk County,
Massachusetts jury found all the defendants guilty and
awarded the athlete $85,000. The judge disallowed the
verdict holding the plaintiff was assuming the risk of
injury.

The plaintiff appealed to the Supreme Judicial Court
of Massachusetts. The court reviewed the evidence and
made several observations. It reasoned that the
three-piece helmet was not designed as much for safety
as it was for accommodation. It felt the helmet was
designed to facilitate adjustment. The court also found
that the coach was well versed in the sport of ice hockey
and as such was responsible for a "higher standard of
care and knowledge than would the average person."
The coach had previously testified that the one-piece
helmet was admittedly safer than the three-piece one he
purchased for the team. The court also gave weight to
the statement of a neurosurgeon who treated the
plaintiff. The surgeon had experience in sports medicine
and was familiar with sports equipment. He supported
the coach's testimony stating that the one-piece helmet
was safer than the one the plaintiff used.

The court also reasoned that while the athlete played
a high risk sport such as ice hockey, he did not
automatically assumed the risks inherent in the sport.

The athlete trusted his coach's judgment when he
issued the helmet and did not question its safety when
he wore it. The court affirmed the earlier decision of the
jury and reinstated its decision of $85,000 in damages to
the injured player.

Cases Involving Additional Sports Equipment

A. Fencing Mask and Sabre

Jose Domingo Garcia injured his eye during a college
fencing match when his opponent's sabre penetrated his
fencing mask.[26] He sued the manufacturer of the blade
and the manufacturer of the fencing mask because he
attributed his injury to the defective condition of their
products.

During the trial there was no specific evidence to
prove which of two companies supplied the blade that
was involved in the accident. Both coaches had
examined the blade after the injury but it got mixed up
in the confusion following the injury.

In the football helmet case in Florida, it was reported
that there was no conclusive evidence that the injured
athlete was wearing a Riddell helmet, yet the jury
awarded the athlete $5.3 million.[27] In the present
fencing case, however, the court took a different
approach when it declared:

> Regardless of the theory which liability is
> predicated upon, whether negligence, breach of
> warranty, strict liability in tort, or other
> grounds, it is obvious that to hold a producer,
> manufacturer, or seller liable for injury caused

---

26. Garcia v. Joseph Vince Co., 148 Cal. Rptr. 843 (Cal. App.
    1978).
27. *Supra* note 10.

by a particular product, there must first be proof that the defendant produced, manufactured, sold, or was in some way responsible for the product.[28]

It realized that the evidence as to which company produced the sabre was merely speculative. The court considered the allegation against the fencing mask and was able to determine its manufacturer. However, it felt that the mask exceeded acceptable standards and no liability was warranted.

The California court considered the evidence and found that the manufacturer of the fencing mask was not guilty of producing a defective product and the producer of the sabre was undetermined; hence, no liability could be determined. In ruling in favor of the defendants the court stated:

> Fencing is a form of combat, a dangerous sport. The fencing rules provide that the fencers assume the risk of injury during a bout.[29]

It concluded:

> An injured plaintiff has always had the burden to prove the existence of the defect. The reasonableness of alternative designs, where a design defect is claimed, is part of that burden. . . .[30]

B. Baseball Pitching Machine

Danville High School in Indiana bought a baseball pitching machine from the Dudley Sports Company.[31]

---

28. 51 A.L.R.3d 1344, 1349.
29. *Supra* note 26.
30. *Supra* note 26.
31. Dudley Sports Co. v. Schmitt, 279 N.E.2d 266 (Ind. App. 1972).

The machine was manufactured by another company, however, and the Dudley Company was only the distributor. There was nothing on the machine or in the advertisement of the machine to indicate that any company other than Dudley manufactured it.

The vice principal and baseball coach opened the crate and found a general warning tag but no operating instructions. They stored the machine in a locked locker room, set the arm of the machine at six o'clock, and unplugged the machine.

Lawrence Schmitt, a student, entered the locker room in which the machine was stored, to sweep the room as was his custom. The arm of the pitching machine hit him in the face causing severe injuries that required four operations and left his face permanently scarred. The Marion Superior Court found the Dudley Company liable for Schmitt's injuries and awarded him $35,000. The company appealed the decision.

During the trial the Court of Appeals of Indiana considered several issues relating to product liability. It ruled that a vendor is liable for injuries caused by a product it represents as its own just as a manufacturer must maintain a standard of care for the safe use of a product. It reasoned that the public purchases a product, in many instances, because it relies on a particular company's reputation. The purchaser does not have the knowledge as to the true manufacturer and the vendor therefore "vouches for the product and assumes the manufacturer's responsibility as his own."

The court of appeals reasoned that a manufacturer may not be held liable for dangers that are obvious in a product, but is liable for hidden or latent dangers. In the instant case, the court held that a 16-year-old student was not aware of the danger of the pitching machine. It agreed with the Dudley Company's contention that the pitching machine was as advanced in technology as any pitching machine manufactured in the industry. The court concluded that the "standards set by an entire industry can be found negligently low if they fail to meet the test of reasonableness."

The court of appeals, therefore, held the Dudley Company negligent for Schmitt's injury because the pitching machine's design and manufacture did conceal latent defects which were not known to the student. It affirmed the award of $35,000 by the lower court.

C. Trampolines

The American Academy of Pediatrics shocked trampoline participants when it recommended the elimination of these devices in physical education and competitive sports programs.[32] The academy based its edict on the fact that while the number of injuries is not unusually large, the number of crippling types of injuries is significant. It noted that nine cases of permanent paralysis and 25 more involving temporary paralysis occurred from 1973-1975.

In trampoline cases the issue usually is not the defective condition of the trampoline, but other factors. The most common complaints involve the competency of the instructors and spotters and the lack of adequate instruction or supervision. Four cases indicate the issues involving the trampoline currently before the courts.

Bruno Garzolini, Jr., a 13-year-old boy, was swimming at the beach. He attempted to jump from the platform of an Aqua Diver onto the bed of a trampoline from

32. *Sports Illustrated,* Oct. 17, 1977.

which he intended to spring into the water.[33] Garzolini landed on the bed of the trampoline and one of his feet became entangled in the elastic cables of the trampoline. He fell from the trampoline, but one of his legs remained entangled in the cables. His leg was broken and was later amputated above the knee.

During the trial, testimony was produced that revealed that an individual's foot could go through the cables that connected the bed to the frame of the trampoline. The court also noted that the manufacturer of the trampoline failed to issue a warning that such an occurrence was possible.

The Indiana Circuit Court, Sullivan County, granted the plaintiff a new trial; although the jury's verdict favored the manufacturer and the manufacturer appealed. The Court of Appeals of Indiana found that the evidence pointed to a defective product that posed a danger to the participant when it was not accompanied by a warning or instruction. It ordered a new trial. It was reported that the court reinstated the jury's verdict. There were, however, two settlements made by the defendants and the plaintiff received a substantial amount of money for his injury.

David Chapman, a pre-engineering freshman student at Washington State University, was an outstanding student-athlete.[34] He was proficient on the trampoline before he entered the university. Chapman elected to enroll in a gymnastics course to satisfy the physical education requirement. Students met in class twice a week for one hour and occasionally remained after class

---

33. Nissen Trampoline Co. v. Terre Haute First Nat'l Bank, 332 N.E.2d 820 (Ind. App. 1975).
34. Chapman v. State, 492 P.2d 607 (Wash. App. 1972).

to practice various stunts and exercises. On the day of
the accident, Chapman stayed after class to work on the
trampoline. While four spotters were required during
the class, he had only one spotter to help him. The
instructor was working with a student on the horizontal
bar, which was 30 feet away. The instructor testified
that he realized that Chapman was on the trampoline,
but admitted that he paid little attention to what he was
practicing on the trampoline. Chapman lost his balance
during a "double-forward somersault," fell on the floor
and sustained serious injuries.

The plaintiff sued the university for negligence
because it allegedly failed to do the following:

1. properly supervise the activities of the
   plaintiff and others who were using the
   trampoline.

2. provide a sufficient number of safety
   spotters at the trampoline on which the
   plaintiff was working.

3. properly and fully instruct the members of
   the plaintiff's gym class in the proper
   method of safety spotting for those using
   the trampoline.

4. provide safety padding on the floor area
   around the trampoline on which the
   plaintiff was working.

5. exercise that degree of care and caution in
   supervising this activity in the gym at the
   time as a reasonably cautious and prudent
   instructor employed by the University
   should have exercised under the same or
   similar circumstances.

The Washington Superior Court, Douglas County,
instructed the jury that it was not necessary for it to

prove each act of negligence against the defendants, but only:

A fair preponderance of the evidence there is established one or more acts of negligence which was a proximate cause of the injuries and damages.

The superior court found that the defendants were not guilty of negligence and the plaintiff appealed to the court of appeals.

The court of appeals considered the plaintiff's claim that the instructor had the last clear chance to prevent the accident and, since he failed to do so, was guilty of negligence. Instead, it held that the plaintiff, not the instructor, had the opportunity to avoid the injury. The plaintiff, it ruled, should have gotten off the trampoline when he realized he had only one spotter. It upheld the lower court's decision by favoring the defendants.

Michael Berg, a senior at Crossland Senior High School in Maryland, fractured his neck during a gymnastic exercise on the trampoline.[35] As a result of the injury, Michael is a paraplegic and permanently disabled.

Michael and his mother sued the instructor, the principal and superintendent, and the school board for negligence. The plaintiffs charged the defendants with negligence for failing to furnish adequate and competent supervision, failing to use a trampoline frame to insure safe performance by the students, and failing to keep records of each student's progress.

The jury was satisfied that the instructor was qualified in gymnastics, both as a performer and

---

35. Berg v. Merricks, 318 A.2d 220 (Md. Spec. App. 1974).

teacher of trampolining. It discussed the inherent risks of such activities as gymnastics when it said:

> The nature of physical education activities comprehends physical hazards. The instructor must avoid as many of these hazards as he is humanly able considering the limitations, under which he instructs, but the system cannot be made childproof.

The Maryland court found no evidence of negligence and upheld the decision of the lower court favoring the defendants. It made an interesting comment that should encourage instructors or coaches of high risk activities by emphasizing that:

> The courts are just as much a shield to a teacher who has acted prudently as they are a weapon against him if he has neglected his duty.[36]

Thomas Cardamone was injured when he fell from a trampoline while practicing with the gymnasts at the University of Pittsburgh.[37] The plaintiff is "paralyzed from the neck down and will require extensive medical care throughout his lifetime." The university paid all his medical bills for three years and then notified him that it was terminating the payments. The plaintiff claimed that the medical costs were prohibitive and that he could not possibly meet the financial costs. He sued the university to honor its commitment to pay all bills connected with the accident. The university contended that they had agreed to pay the medical bills "for all time or such period as the University may determine

---

36. *Id.*
37. Cardamone v. University of Pittsburgh, 384 A.2d 1228 (Pa. Super. 1978).

feasible." The university contended that the terms of its agreement with the plaintiff were as follows:

1. To pay no more than $2,000 per month of those of appellee's medical expenses that are not subject to state or federal monetary grants or programs.

2. These payments are to continue until a verdict is reached.

3. The University does not:
   a. in any manner legally obligate itself to continue payments for all time
   b. waive any legal rights or defenses which it may have pursuant to any legal action

The university declared that it had willingly paid bills beyond what it agreed to do. At the time of the appeal, it had already paid approximately $100,000.

The plaintiff sought a mandatory injunction to compel the university to continue the medical payments. The Superior Court of Pennsylvania viewed the plaintiff's request for mandatory injunction to be a harsh remedy. It disagreed with his contention that the university was obligated to pay the bills and favored the university.

In spite of the litigation involving the trampoline, it is expected to return to most sports programs that temporarily eliminated it because of the American Academy of Pediatrics' suggested ban. The American Alliance for Health, Physical Education and Recreation (AAHPER) recognizes the risks the trampoline presents, but feels that the benefits outweigh the dangers if safety standards are met. AAHPER has recommended safety guidelines for the instructor and

---

38. *Supra* note 23.

participant that, if followed, should greatly reduce the possibility of injury. (See Appendix G for the AAHPER Guidelines.)

IN MY OPINION

It seems that unsafe and defective equipment has always concerned us. As early as 161 A.D., the upper tier of the Roman Coliseum collapsed killing many spectators. The use of shoddy building material in apartment houses in Rome caused so many structures to collapse that the Emperor Augustus was forced to issue a law limiting the number of floors in an apartment house. This may have been the first zoning law on record. While the problem of defective equipment seems to be an age-old problem, today's generation appears to be the first to demand compensation through the courts for equipment-related injuries.

Manufacturers deplore the willingness of people to sue for any and all reasons and characterize this as the "sue syndrome." William Knepper, an adjunct professor of law at Ohio State University, quotes the American Bar Association president who describes the liability crisis as follows:

> Juries hand down large judgments seemingly regardless of blame. Insurance companies pay the judgments, then raise the premiums on the insured. Finally the insureds pass along the premiums to the rest of us in the prices of their products and services.[39]

---

39. William Knepper, *Review of Recent Tort Trends,* DEFENSE LAW JOURNAL, Vol. 28, No. 1, 1979.

Granted, there are a number of frivolous suits that plague the manufacturer but the "sue syndrome" and its accompanying threat of lawsuits may well be the reason that manufacturers and sports administrators are providing better equipment than ever before and enforcing rules of safety that will enable sports activities to be conducted in a safer environment.

The number of football helmet-related lawsuits is staggering yet experts in the field of sports equipment argue that the present helmet is the safest ever. If anyone remembers the football helmets of our former athletes of years gone by, it is clear that the helmets were paper-thin and could be folded and carried in one's pocket. These helmets were not designed to protect the athlete; rather, they were supposed to prevent an athlete from grabbing a player's hair while making a tackle. Dr. Stephen Rundio describes the situation that existed then in a book on the history of Guilford College athletics:

> No padding of any kind, no shinguards, nothing to wear on heads except heavy growths of football hair, which was in style, eased the force of a blow a good deal, when a fellow hit the earth with his head.

It is ironic that while the modern helmet is described as the finest ever, it faces elimination because of the enormous awards against it and the spiraling cost of insurance to protect the manufacturers from suit. One prominent New York attorney reports that he has settled three helmet-related injury suits out of court for substantial amounts. In the three cases in which the athletes were permanently crippled, the issue was not the construction or design of the helmet, but the technique of tackling taught by the coach.

Richard Black, a Phoenix attorney, urges coaches to warn their athletes not to use their helmets to butt, ram or spear an opponent. He suggests that the helmet companies put a warning inside the helmets to caution the athletes to be careful in the use of the headgear. Black advises coaches to xerox the rules of acceptable conduct and put it on the first page of the playbook.

Kenneth Clarke, of the University of Illinois and a sports safety expert, echoes the sentiments of Black, and cautions coaches to teach safe blocking and tackling techniques or expect to lose lawsuits in court. Clarke predicts that helmet-related lawsuits will be predicated on the technique of blocking and tackling rather than the helmet itself. Caution by coaches clearly is indicated.

The safety of the sports participant should be the primary concern of the administrator and instructor and if wise selection of equipment is observed and rules are followed, warnings given and accepted standards followed, the sports participant will be protected as never before.

Epilogue

Sports and the Courts completes a series of four books pertaining to the law and sports. When the series began ten years ago, sports law was practically nonexistent as we now know it. Today, every type of sports litigation comes before the court and cases that raise constitutional questions are increasing faster than the usual injury lawsuits. Although the athlete is involved in the vast majority of cases, the courtroom is now shared with various sport participants such as the coach, official, team physician, owner of a sports facility and manufacturer of sports equipment. It seems that no one associated with sports is immune from the possibility of litigation.

There is an unprecedented interest in sports at this time, accompanied by a record number of sports-related lawsuits. An attitude prevails among many people that every injury should receive compensation. Society on the whole expects the courts to settle any issue and there is a belief that an attorney can solve any problem. Lawsuits that would have been laughed out of court ten years ago are now a serious cause for concern. For example: A student sued his German instructor and the University of Michigan for $850,000 because he received a D grade when he thought he earned an A. A woman breast feeding her baby at a municipal pool was asked to leave. She sued the owners of the pool for damages. These types of lawsuits so common in today's society have spread to the sports field. A Chicago softball team sought judicial permission to use baseball gloves in competition. Washington Redskins fans tried to get an injunction to overturn a St. Louis touchdown in an important professional game. Cases of this type are becoming common in the courts today.

A Yale law graduate credits the increase in litigation to the fact that people today have an amazing awareness of the law. He points out that the people in his community know more law than the average attorney and comments that his school district leads the nation in the number of school-related lawsuits.

Malpractice has become a key word that gets immediate attention from the various professions. No longer are malpractice suits limited to the medical profession, but now extend to most professions. Even the legal and education professions have been included in recent malpractice suits. As a result of the threat of malpractice litigation, the cost of liability insurance has escalated to unbelievable proportions. It is the consumer who eventually bears the brunt of the high cost of insurance. The price of sports equipment, facilities, and other included costs of sports are at an all-time high.

The cost of insurance is enormous because juries are awarding record amounts of money to plaintiffs all over the United States. About 14 years ago, a $350,000 award to an injured student in a gymnastics class electrified the state of New Jersey and sent immediate shock waves throughout the nation. As a result of the award, many schools outlawed the springboard and doubled their insurance protection. Today, such an award would be hardly noticed since athletes sue for millions and huge awards are accepted by our present-day society.

There is widespread disagreement among many sports authorities over the effect of sports litigation. Many predict the demise of sports because of the litigation. However, it may well be that the opposite is true — sports may actually benefit from the increased litigation. During the past ten years since the series of books began, very little has been done to correct or eliminate the ills that often characterize sports. It took 58 years for the court to reverse the *Plessy v. Ferguson,* "separate but equal" doctrine with the *Brown* decision of 1954 that ended segregation. Racial discrimination did not end because of the church, school or other social agencies; it ended as a result of judicial action. In like manner, the court has begun to speak out, and has become the dominant force to end discrimination, negligence, and violence in sports. If this trend continues, the court will affect the changes that have been needed for years.

Stephen Horn, President of California State University at Long Beach, in an address before the American Alliance of Health, Physical Education and Recreation, challenged the leaders of sports to remember that:

> We live in an age where bigness is sometimes confused with goodness, where life experiences are reduced to substance of too often dulling television shows. We cannot, certainly not in the name of amateurism and supposedly health producing sportsmanship — simply allow student athletes to be perceived as products in an assembly line factory. They are all human beings, not just meat on the hoof. Some may, indeed, end up in the brilliant glare of the winner's circle. But we must be concerned with the fate of the rest.

From the decisions of the courts during these past ten years, it appears that Horn's concerns are being answered by the courts. It is the courts that accentuate the importance and welfare of the individual; it is the courts that attempt to end discrimination of every sort in sports; and, it is the courts that curb the rising violence that too often takes place in the sports arena. The courts are making sports participation the best ever as the participant now enjoys the safest equipment, finest facilities, medical care, and coaching ever. Truly, sports law is here to stay.

APPENDIX A

Disqualifying Conditions for Sports Participation (AMA Revised 1976)

Conditions	Collision[1]	Contact[2]	Noncontact[3]	Other[4]
GENERAL				
Acute infections:				
Respiratory, genitourinary, infectious mononucleosis, hepatitis, active rheumatic fever, active tuberculosis	X	X	X	X
Obvious physical immaturity in comparison with other competitors	X	X		
Hemorrhagic disease:				
Hemophilia, purpura, and other serious bleeding tendencies	X	X	X	
Diabetes, inadequately controlled	X	X	X	X
Diabetes, controlled				
Jaundice	X	X	X	X
EYES				
Absence or loss of function of one eye	X	X		
RESPIRATORY				
Tuberculosis (active or symptomatic)	X	X	X	X
Severe pulmonary insufficiency	X	X	X	X

Conditions	Collision[1]	Contact[2]	Noncontact[3]	Other[4]
CARDIOVASCULAR				
Mitral stenosis, aortic stenosis, aortic insufficiency, coarctation of aorta, cyanotic heart disease, recent carditis of any etiology	X	X	X	X
Hypertension on organic basis	X	X	X	X
Previous heart surgery for congenital or acquired heart disease*				
LIVER				
Enlarged liver	X	X		
SKIN				
Boils, impetigo, and herpes simplex gladiatorum	X	X		
SPLEEN				
Enlarged spleen	X	X		
HERNIA				
Inguinal or femoral hernia	X	X	X	
MUSCULOSKELETAL				
Symptomatic abnormalities or inflammations	X	X	X	X
Functional inadequacy of the musculoskeletal system, congenital or acquired, incompatible with the contact or skill demands of the sport	X	X	X	

Conditions	Collision[1]	Contact[2]	Noncontact[3]	Other[4]
NEUROLOGICAL				
History or symptoms of previous serious head trauma, or repeated concussions	X			
Controlled convulsive disorder**				
Convulsive disorder not completely controlled by medication	X	X	X	
Previous surgery on head	X	X		
RENAL				
Absence of one kidney	X	X		
Renal disease	X	X	X	X
GENITALIA*				
Absence of one testicle				
Undescended testicle				

---

[1] Football, rugby, hockey, lacrosse, etc.

[2] Baseball, soccer, basketball, wrestling, etc.

[3] Cross country, track, tennis, crew, swimming, etc.

[4] Bowling, golf, archery, field events, etc.

* Each patient should be judged on an individual basis in conjunction with his cardiologist and operating surgeon.

** Each patient should be judged on an individual basis. All things being equal, it is probably better to encourage a young boy or girl to participate in a non-contact sport rather than a contact sport. However, if a particular patient has a great desire to play a contact sport, and this is deemed a major ameliorating factor in his/her adjustment to school, associates and the seizure disorder, serious consideration should be given to letting him/her participate if the seizures are controlled.

*** The Committee approves the concept of contact sports participation for youths with only one testicle or with an undescended testicle(s), except in specific cases such as an inguinal canal undescended testicle(s), following appropriate medical evaluation to rule out unusual injury risk. However, the athlete, parents and school authorities should be fully informed that participation in contact sports for such youths with only one testicle does carry a slight injury risk to the remaining healthy testicle. Following such an injury, fertility may be adversely affected. But the chances of an injury to a descended testicle are rare, and the injury risk can be further substantially minimized with an athletic supporter and protective device.

APPENDIX B

Amendments to the Constitution Involving Sports

AMENDMENT (I)

Congress shall make no law respecting an establishment of religion, or prohibiting the free exercise thereof; or abridging the freedom of speech, or of the press; or the right of the people peaceably to assemble, and to petition the Government for a redress of grievances.

AMENDMENT (IV)

The right of the people to be secure in their persons, houses, papers, and effects, against unreasonable searches and seizures, shall not be violated, and no Warrants shall issue, but upon probable cause, supported by Oath or affirmation, and particularly describing the place to be searched, and the persons or things to be seized.

AMENDMENT (V)

No person shall be held to answer for a capital, or otherwise infamous crime, unless on a presentment or indictment of a Grand Jury, except in cases arising in the land or naval forces, or in Militia, when in actual service in time of War or public danger; nor shall any person be subject for the same offence to be twice put in jeopardy of life or limb; nor shall be compelled in any criminal case to be a witness against himself, nor be deprived of life, liberty, or property, without due process of law; nor shall private property be taken for public use, without just compensation.

AMENDMENT (IX)

The enumeration in the Constitution, of certain rights, shall not be construed to deny or disparage others retained by the people.

AMENDMENT XIV

Section 1. All persons born or naturalized in the United States, and subject to the jurisdiction thereof, are citizens of the United States and of the State wherein they reside. No State shall make or enforce any law which shall abridge the privileges or immunities of citizens of the United States; or shall any State deprive any person of life, liberty, or property, without due process of law; nor deny to any person within its jurisdiction the equal protection of the laws.

APPENDIX C

Alternative for Title IX Compliance

Duke University
Durham
North Carolina 27706

Office of the President

May 22, 1979

Mr. F. Peter Libassi
General Counsel
Department of Health, Education
   and Welfare
The Office of the Secretary
Washington, D. C. 20201

Dear Peter:

As you requested, we are enclosing our proposal for an alternative for Title IX compliance. We hope that you and the Secretary will give it serious consideration.

University officials whose names are listed at the end of the letter have authorized me to sign their names to indicate their strong support for this alternative.

We also believe it will have the strong support of a broad coalition of colleges and universities throughout the country. It has the endorsement *now* of the organizers and coordinators of the coalition of universities formed to try to achieve a solution to the Title IX problem.

Let me assure you, personally and on behalf of my colleagues, of our support for the continued growth of

intercollegiate athletics for women. We fully support
Title IX and the principle of nondiscrimination. We
believe in and are encouraging increasing opportunities
for participation by women in athletics at Duke, and we
will continue to do so.

This proposal turns over the responsibility for
determining methods of complying to the individual
institution, which is where it should be. We trust you
agree.

The strength of our educational system lies in the
diversity of our institutions. Duke is not Boston College.
Holy Cross is not Notre Dame. Lincoln is not Texas.
New Mexico is not the University of the Pacific.

It seems apparent that there is no single approach nor
standard for measuring compliance that will insure an
environment of nondiscrimination on university
campuses through the country. And, there is no reason
to expect that there could be or should be.

There are, however, procedural safeguards that can
be followed by each institution to insure that goals and
objectives are established by which each institution can
achieve an environment substantially free of
discrimination.

We accept that HEW's Proposed Policy
Interpretation is a good faith attempt to allow diverse
approaches to compliance. However, we suggest that
the per capita spending standard suggested is an
anathema to the universities because it distorts the
purposes and will not adequately measure
opportunities. We know that such a dollar standard
would make it easier for the compliance officer, but that
is not the objective. We suggest that the compliance

officer will have less work to do under this plan, and that the law will be more effectively implemented, as well as administered.

The most important mission is to get on with the job of helping the colleges and universities comply with Title IX and, thereby, improve opportunities for women in intercollegiate athletics.

There has been too much confusion, too much debate, too much misunderstanding.

We stand ready to join with you, the Office of Civil Rights, with the NCAA and the AIAW to convert this energy to a creative and constructive solution.

We believe that HEW should withdraw its proposed policy interpretation.

We propose that you advise the colleges to develop their institutional plans for compliance with the law and the regulations, in accordance with the attached approach.

We look forward to hearing from you and working with you in an effort to resolve this problem, once and for all.

With best wishes always,

Sincerely,

Terry Sanford

A COUNTER PROPOSAL FOR COMPLIANCE
WITH TITLE IX

Plan Summary. Each institution shall develop a plan to insure an intercollegiate athletic program which will accommodate the interests and abilities of its students in a nondiscriminatory environment.

The institution will involve all interested parties in developing its program. Certain procedural standards must be met, and the approach adopted by the institution must be reasonable. HEW will use the institutional plan as the framework for evaluating complaints and assessing compliance.

Basic Principle. There shall be no sex-based discrimination in the manner in which an institution commits its resources or administers its program.

Rationale. Individual institutions can best determine the policies, plans and procedures by which they can assure nondiscrimination in athletic programs on their campus — an environment of equal opportunity.

1. *Plan based on realistic assessment.* Each institution will develop its plan to insure nondiscrimination only after conducting a realistic assessment of the state of athletic opportunities for men and women on its campus. Each plan shall include procedures for handling complaints from students or others in connection with Title IX.

2. *Representative planning group.* The plan and the assessment shall provide for representative participation by all affected parties on campus (women, men, students, faculty, appropriate administrators, alumni, and institutional supporters). Recommendations of the planning group shall go to the institution's governing board, as appropriate, and its appointed officials, who

are finally responsible for the conduct of a nondiscriminatory athletic program.

3. *Plan elements.*

a. Elements to be considered would include the following:

(1) Goals and timetables as appropriate for completion and execution of the plan.

(2) Participation levels.

(3) Number of sports to be offered, for men, for women, coed.

(4) A mechanism to assess the financial resources required by the plan and how they are to be used.

(5) Levels of expenditure for each sport, which may vary, based on sex neutral factors, and in keeping with the institution's plan.

(6) Provisions for publicizing the plan, and the opportunities for women and men in athletics at the institution.

(7) Procedures for continuing review of the plan as it relates to student needs.

b. Other elements which may be considered would include:

(1) Scope and levels of competition to be maintained or achieved for each sport. For instance, some sports may be fully developed, with national competition. Others may be local, state or regional.

(2) Spectator, community, alumni interest and support of various programs.

(3) Goals and traditions of the institution.

Relevant sex neutral factors to be considered in a plan, some of which are outlined above, will be determined by participants in the development of an institution's plan and approved by the institution's governing board. These factors may vary from institution to institution.

4. *Compliance.* The principal standard for determining whether or not an institution is providing a nondiscriminatory environment for intercollegiate athletics will be the extent to which its plan satisfies, in an even-handed fashion, the legitimate interests of the involved constituencies of the institution, men and women, and its performance in fulfilling the objectives of the plan. Some measures of this may include:

    a. Its actual performance in conforming to its plan.

    b. Its adherence to procedural standards.

    c. Its mechanism for evaluating the program's appeal and accommodation to the interests and abilities of its men and women constituents.

    d. Its resolution of justifiable complaints.

APPENDIX D

Survey of the States and Territories of the United States Regarding the Status of Coaches

State	Can coaches be granted tenure?	Number of years proba- tionary status	Can a teacher- coach give up coaching and still teach?	Can coaches have due process?
Alabama	No		Yes	Yes
Alaska	Yes	2	Yes	Yes
American-Samoa	Yes	1	Yes	No
Arizona	No		Yes	No
Arkansas	No		Yes	Yes
California	No		Yes	No
Canal Zone	Yes	2	Yes	Yes
Colorado	Yes	3	Yes	Varies by district
Connecticut	No		Yes	No reply
Delaware	No		Yes	Yes
Dist. of Columbia	No		Yes	Yes
Florida	Yes	5	Yes	Yes
Georgia	No		Yes	No—unless dis- trict agrees
Guam	No		Yes	No
Hawaii	No		Yes	Yes
Idaho	No		Varies by district	Yes
Illinois	No		Yes	No
Indiana	No		Yes	No
Iowa	No		No	Yes
Kansas	No		No	No
Kentucky	No		Yes	Subject to situ- ation
Louisiana	No		If a position is available	Yes
Maine	No		Yes	Yes
Maryland	No		Yes	Yes
Massachusetts	No		Yes	No
Michigan	No		Yes	No
Minnesota	Yes	3	Yes	Yes
Mississippi	No		Yes	Yes
Missouri	No		Not specified in statutes	No
Montana		All handled on a local basis		

State	Can coaches be granted tenure?	Number of years probationary status	Can a teacher-coach give up coaching and still teach?	Can coaches have due process?
Nebraska		No Reply		
Nevada	No		Yes	Yes
New Hampshire	No		Yes	No
New Jersey		No Reply		
New Mexico	Yes	3	Yes	No
New York	No		Yes	No unless district provides
North Carolina	No		Yes	Yes
North Dakota	No		Yes	Yes
Ohio	No		Yes	No
Oklahoma	No		Yes	No
Oregon	Yes	3	Yes	Yes
Pennsylvania	No		Yes	No
Puerto Rico	No		Yes	Yes
Rhode Island	No		Yes	Yes
South Carolina	No		Yes	No unless district provides
South Dakota	Yes	2	Yes	Yes
Tennessee		No Reply		
Texas	No		Varies with school district	No—unless it involves firing
Utah	Yes	3	Yes	No
Vermont	No			
Virginia	No		Yes	No
Virgin Islands	No		Yes	Optional
Washington	No		Yes	Yes
West Virginia	No		Yes	Yes
Wisconsin	No		Yes	Yes
Wyoming	Yes	3	Depends on contract	Yes (if tenured)

APPENDIX E

National Athletic Trainers Association Procedure For Certification

(Revised: January, 1973)

TO BECOME CERTIFIED AS AN ATHLETIC TRAINER BY THE NATIONAL ATHLETIC TRAINERS ASSOCIATION, AN INDIVIDUAL MUST MEET THE REQUIREMENTS IN ONE OF THE FOLLOWING SECTIONS I, II, III or IV. *QUALIFICATION IN MORE THAN ONE SECTION IS NOT REQUIRED.*

SECTION I. ATHLETIC TRAINERS ACTIVELY ENGAGED WITHIN THE PROFESSION — This section deals with athletic trainers actively engaged within the profession *but* not yet certified.

The N.A.T.A. definition of "actively engaged" is as follows:

A person who is on a salary basis (no fee) employed by an educational institution, professional athletic organization, or other bona fide athletic organization for the duration of the institution's school year or for the length of the athletic organization season and who performs the duties of athletic trainer as a major responsibility of his employment; or whose responsibility is the teaching in an N.A.T.A. approved athletic training curriculum is actively engaged in athletic training.

A Staff person may become certified by:

1. Proof of five years of athletic training experience, beyond that as a student athletic

trainer on an undergraduate level (effective July 1, 1975).

2. Passing an examination which includes the basic principles of athletic training.

3. Proof of graduation from an accredited four year college or university.

4. By presentation of a letter of recommendation from an N.A.T.A. certified athletic trainer.

5. By presentation of a letter of recommendation by his acting team physician.

6. Proof of two (2) years of continuous Active membership in N.A.T.A. immediately prior to application for certification.

Athletic Trainers actively engaged in the profession should *be encouraged* to continue their education toward an advanced degree and/or certificate in an AMA approved Allied Health Profession. (Programs leading to certification as a Physical Therapist, Orthopedic Assistant, Medical Assistant, etc.) These individuals should attend workshops in advanced techniques of athletic medicine approved and/or sponsored by the AMA, APTA, ACSM, NATA, and other accredited organizations.

SECTION II. STUDENTS WHO HAVE GRADUATED FROM AN APPROVED UNDERGRADUATE OR GRADUATE PROGRAM, who have met the following criteria:

1. *Completion of the N.A.T.A. approved athletic training curriculum requirements,* and proof of a Bachelor's degree from an accredited college or university.

2. Have spent a minimum of two (2) years under the direct supervision of N.A.T.A. approved supervisors.

3. Passed an examination which includes basic principles of athletic training.

4. Proof of two (2) years of continuous Active or Student membership in N.A.T.A. immediately prior to application for certification.

Athletic Trainers certified in Section II should also *be encouraged* to continue their education toward an advanced degree and/or certificate in an AMA Allied Health Profession and other activities mentioned in Section No. I.

SECTION III. PHYSICAL THERAPY DEGREE GRADUATE — Physical Therapy graduates may be awarded certification provided they meet the following requirements.

1. A minimum of two (2) years experience in Athletic Training, beyond that as a student athletic trainer on a secondary school level, under direct N.A.T.A. approved supervision.

2. Proof of a Bachelor's degree from an accredited college or university.

3. By the passing of a required examination which includes basic principles of Athletic Training.

4. Proof of two (2) years of continuous Active or Student membership in N.A.T.A. immediately prior to application for certification.

Athletic Trainers certified under Section III should *be encouraged* to continue their education toward an advanced degree and other activities mentioned in Section No. I.

SECTION IV. APPRENTICESHIP — Students of Athletic Training may qualify for certification by:

1. On the job training (minimum 1800 hours) under direct supervision of a certified N.A.T.A. member.
2. Passed an examination which includes basic principles of athletic training.
3. Proof of a Bachelor's degree from an accredited college or university.
4. By presentation of a letter of recommendation by his N.A.T.A. immediate supervisor.
5. By presentation of a letter of recommendation by his acting Team Physician.
6. Proof of two (2) years of continuous Active or Student membership in N.A.T.A. immediately prior to application for certification.

Students who complete the apprenticeship program should *be encouraged* to continue their education toward an advanced degree and/or certificate in an AMA Allied Health Profession and other activities mentioned in Section I.

SECTION V. SPECIAL CONSIDERATION — Any member who has passed an Athletic Training Course (See Appendix A — Section II-K), or presents evidence of successful completion of an N.A.T.A. approved workshop for credit and has satisfied the requirements for a State Teaching License with at least a minor in Physical Education and/or Health Education may *be endorsed* as a secondary school athletic trainer.

All N.A.T.A. Athletic Trainers should be encouraged to continue their education toward an advanced degree and/or certificate of an AMA approved Allied Health

Profession and other activities mentioned in Section I. Endorsement may be extended to full certification when requirements of any other section are met. Application for full certification must be initiated within five (5) years of initial endorsement or endorsement shall be terminated.

In the N.A.T.A. approved program of education, the athletic trainer should be encouraged to act as liaison with the departments of physical education and student health. The program includes a major study in physical education, and necessary courses required by the states for a teaching license. Also entered in the degree program are prerequisites for entry to schools of physical therapy as suggested by the American Physical Therapy Association. *The basic minimal requirements as recommended by N.A.T.A. are as follows:*

I. A major study including teaching license in physical education and/or health education variable by states.

A. Total of 24 semester hours in laboratory physical, biological, and social sciences.

1. Biology — zoology. (anatomy and Physiology)   . . . . .   8 hours
2. Physics and/or chemistry .   6 hours
3. Social sciences (at least 6 hours in psychology)   . . . . . .   10 hours

B. Electives strongly advised —

1. Additional biological and social sciences
2. Physical education such as group activities, dancing, etc.

3. Hygiene
4. Speech

II. Specific required courses (if not included in I, these must be added) —

A. Anatomy — one or more courses which will include human anatomy.
B. Physiology — circulation, respiration, digestion, excretion, nerve, brain and sense organs.
C. Physiology of exercise.
D. Applied Anatomy and Kinesiology — the muscles; emphasis on their function in and development for specific activities.
E. Laboratory Physical Science — six semester hours in physics and/or chemistry.
F. Psychology — one advanced course beyond the basic general psychology course.
G. First Aid and Safety — minimum Advanced Red Cross First-Aid Certification.
H. Nutrition and Foods.

1. Basic principles of nutrition.
2. Basic diet and special diet.

I. Remedial Exercise, Therapeutic Exercise, Adapted Exercise or Corrective Exercise — exercise for atypical and/or both temporary and permanent handicaps.
J. Personal, Community, and School Health.
K. Techniques of Athletic Training — basic general course (acceptable course for all coaches).
L. Advanced techniques of Athletic Training.

1. Special course for athletic training candidates with full academic background.
2. Laboratory practices (six [6] semester hours credit or two years equivalent work of six hundred [600] clock hours).

III. Recommended Courses

A. General Physics.
B. Pharmacology — specific side effects of drugs.
C. Histology — tissues and methods of studying them.
D. Pathology — laboratory study of tissues in pathological condition.
E. Organization and Administration of Health and Physical Education Programs.
F. Psychology of Coaching.
G. Coaching Techniques.

1. Highly recommended — football, basketball and track coaching technique courses.
2. Also recommended courses in baseball, soccer, wrestling and preferred sports by geographic areas.

APPENDIX F

North Carolina Plan for Prevention of Sports-Related Injuries and Deaths in Public Schools

GENERAL ASSEMBLY OF NORTH CAROLINA

SESSION 1979

RATIFIED BILL

CHAPTER 986

HOUSE BILL 618

AN ACT TO PROVIDE SPORTS MEDICINE AND EMERGENCY PARAMEDICAL SERVICES, AND EMERGENCY LIFE SAVING SKILLS TO STUDENTS IN THE PUBLIC SCHOOLS.

Whereas, most North Carolina schools provide interscholastic athletic activities for students in the high schools; and

Whereas, the majority of these schools do not have paramedical or medical personnel responsible for preventive measures against death or serious injury to students participating in school activities; and

Whereas, deaths and serious injuries do occur to students participating in school sports activities as well as in other school activities; and

Whereas, injuries have been significantly reduced through the part-time assignment of a teacher or other qualified employee to exercise preventive measures against injury and to provide sports medicine and emergency paramedical services for injuries that do occur; and

Whereas, Resolution 73 of the 1977 Session Laws recommends first aid and life saving instructional services be made available to public school students; and

Whereas, the State Board of Education provides for in-service training for teachers or other qualified employees to be responsible for such sports medicine and emergency paramedical services; Now, therefore, The General Assembly of North Carolina enacts:

Section 1. Chapter 115 of the General Statutes is amended by adding a new Section 115-142.4 to read as follows:

"The State Board of Education is authorized and directed to develop a comprehensive plan to train and make available to the public schools personnel who shall have major responsibility for exercising preventive measures against sports related deaths and injuries and for providing sports medicine and emergency paramedical services for injuries that occur in school related activities. The plan shall include, but is not limited to, the training, assignment of responsibilities, and appropriate additional reimbursement for individuals participating in the program.

The State Board of Education is authorized and directed to develop an implementation schedule and a program funding formula that will enable each high school to have a qualified sports medicine and emergency paramedic program by July 1, 1984.

The State Board of Education is authorized and directed to establish minimum educational standards necessary to enable individuals serving as sports medicine and emergency paramedical staff to provide such services, including first aid and emergency life saving skills, to students participating in school activities."

Sec. 2. There is hereby appropriated from the General Fund to the State Board of Education:

(a) for fiscal year 1979-80 the sum of fifty thousand dollars ($50,000) to be allocated to local education agencies at a rate not to exceed five hundred dollars ($500.00) per high school as supplemental funds to provide sports medicine and paramedical emergency life saving services as approved by the State Board of Education and ten thousand dollars ($10,000) to provide in-service educational training for the development of sports medicine and emergency paramedical skills for public school personnel as provided for in this act; and

(b) for fiscal year 1980-81 the sum of seventy-five thousand dollars ($75,000) to provide allocations to local education agencies at a rate not to exceed five hundred dollars ($500.00) per high school as supplemental funds to provide sports medicine and paramedical emergency life saving services as approved by the State Board of Education and twenty thousand dollars ($20,000) to provide in-service and continued educational programs for the development of sports medicine and emergency paramedical skills for public school personnel.

Sec. 3. This act shall become effective on July 1, 1979.

In the General Assembly read three times and ratified, this the 8th day of June, 1979.

JAMES C. GREEN

James C. Green
President of the Senate

CARL J. STEWART, JR.

Carl J. Stewart, Jr.
Speaker of the House of Representatives

PROPOSED PLAN FOR
IMPLEMENTATION OF HB 618
SPORTS MEDICINE DIVISION
NORTH CAROLINA DEPARTMENT OF PUBLIC
INSTRUCTION

September 1979

I. Introduction

This plan is designed to implement the directives of HB 618 ratified by the 1979 North Carolina General Assembly to train and make available to the public schools, personnel who shall have major responsibility for exercising preventive measures against sports related death and injuries and for providing sports medicine and emergency paramedical services for injuries that occur in school related activities. HB 618 appropriates $50,000 in FY 79-80 to be allocated to local education agencies at a rate not to exceed $500 per high school as supplemental funds to provide sports medicine and paramedical emergency life saving services as approved by the State Board of Education, and $10,000 to provide in-service educational training for the development of sports medicine and paramedical emergency life saving skills for public school personnel. Full implementation of this program making these services available in all high schools is projected by July 1, 1984.

The term "paramedical emergency life saving services" refers to the provision of first aid services and cardio-pulmonary resuscitation services to any student in the public school who presents the need for such emergency services. The term "sports medicine" refers to those services relevant to the prevention, treatment and reconditioning of injuries received by participants in sports activities.

II. Assignment of Responsibilities

It is proposed that the responsibilities of paramedical emergency life saving and sports medicine services identified in HB 618 be assigned to a designated athletic trainer who may be a teacher or other public school staff member. This person shall be referred to as a teacher athletic trainer.

III. In-service Training for Teacher Athletic Trainers

Successful completion of the following programs fulfills the minimum educational requirements for assuming the responsibilities identified in HB 618:

A. Minimum Education Requirements

1. Paramedical Emergency Life Saving Courses

a. Cardio-Pulmonary Resuscitation Certification

It shall be required that each person providing services identified in HB 618 qualify for cardio-pulmonary resuscitation certification at the basic rescue level through any of the following community service agencies:

The North Carolina Heart Association

The American Red Cross

The North Carolina Office of Emergency Medical Services, or an equivalent course approved by the Department of Public Instruction

b. First Aid Certification

It shall be required that each person providing services identified in HB 618 qualify for first aid certification at the basic rescue level through either of the following courses:

American Red Cross Standard First Aid and Personal Safety, or Multimedia Standard First Aid, or an equivalent course approved by the Department of Public Instruction.

2. Sports Medicine Courses

a. Basic Athletic Training Course

It shall be required that each person providing services identified in HB 618 shall satisfactorily complete the Basic Athletic Training Course developed by the Department of Public Instruction or an equivalent course approved by the Department of Public Instruction. This course is designed to introduce the teacher athletic trainer to the basic concepts of prevention, management and care of the injured athelte. Instructors for the course shall be selected by the Department of Public Instruction and approved according to State policies and procedures governing the provision of such instructional services.

b. Advanced Athletic Training Course

It shall be required that each person providing services identified in HB 618 shall satisfactorily complete the Advanced Athletic Training course developed by the Department of Public Instruction or an equivalent course approved by the Department of Public Instruction. The prerequisite for this course is the Basic Athletic Training Course or its equivalent. Instructors for the course shall be selected by the Department of Public Instruction and approved according to State policies and procedures governing the provision of such instructional services.

B. Alternative Education Programs for Training in Sports Medicine
   1. Teacher Athletic Trainer Instructional Program which is a program approved by the National Athletic Trainers Association.
   2. Athletic training curricula which are graduate and/or undergraduate programs approved by the National Athletic Trainers Association.

IV. Criteria for Local Education Agencies to Qualify for Funds
   A. To qualify for allocations appropriated in HB 618 the local superintendent shall designate one or more teachers or public school staff members to assume responsibilities for paramedical emergency life saving and sports medicine services.
   B. The person(s) designated the responsibilities identified in HB 618 must not have additional coaching responsibilities during the football season, or may not have head coaching responsibilities in any sport except when approved by the Department of Public Instruction for emergency reasons.
   C. The person assigned the responsibilities identified in HB 618 shall be in attendance at all football practices and games, except when excused for emergencies by the local administrator to whom he/she is responsible. If two or more persons are assigned the responsibilities it is only necessary to assign one of these persons to football coverage.
   D. The decision regarding coverage for all other sports shall be made at the discretion of the local education agency. However, it is advised that such coverage shall include those sports involving contact between players, or those sports which are considered to be most conducive to injury.

E. The person assigned the responsibilities identified in HB 618 shall keep accurate records on all injuries to student athletes. Injury is defined as that physical condition which causes a student athlete to miss practice, a game, or school or which causes a student to have his/her practice altered to prevent full participation in the sport. Any injury resulting in the permanent disability or death of a student shall be reported to the Department of Public Instruction as soon as the severity of the injury is determined by the attending physician(s) and reported to the family and the school administrators.

F. The person assigned the responsibilities identified in HB 618 shall be "on call" for any emergency resulting in physical injury to a student that occurs in the school to which he/she is assigned at the time of the injury.

V. Use of Funds

A. Funds appropriated by HB 618 to local education agencies may be used for the costs of attending workshops and courses sponsored or approved by the Department of Public Instruction for public or school personnel to become qualified to provide sports medicine and paramedical services as identified in HB 618. These costs may include per diem, mileage, tuition, registration fees, supplies and materials or appropriate additional reimbursement necessary for the designated person to become qualified to provide sports medicine and/or paramedical services or additional costs incurred in providing such services.

B. Funds appropriated by HB 618 for in-service training shall be available to the Department of

Public Instruction for the development of sports medicine and emergency paramedical skills for public school personnel.

VI. Application for Funds

Application for the funds appropriated by HB 618 shall be submitted by the local education agency on forms to be developed and made available by the Department of Public Instruction. Compliance with the requirements for funding shall be the responsibility of the local education agency in accordance with the criteria approved by the State Board of Education.

VII. Program Funding

Allocations shall not exceed $500 per high school. The Controller shall make allocations, upon recommendation from the State Superintendent, and provide forms for the reporting of expenditures. Any unused funds shall be refunded to the State Board of Education prior to June 30. The Controller shall provide information to the State Board of Education on the allocation and use of these funds.

APPENDIX G

The Use of Trampolines and Mini-tramps in Physical Education

(A POSITION STATEMENT APPROVED BY THE AMERICAN ALLIANCE FOR HEALTH, PHYSICAL EDUCATION, AND RECREATION)

Over the years, trampoline accidents have resulted in a significant number of cases of quadriplegia. The annual frequency appears to be low yet persistent. Late in 1977, the American Academy of Pediatrics took a public position that the trampoline was posing an undue risk of serious injury and therefore warned that it should not be utilized as a competitive sport nor as an activity within physical education.

Subsequently, further examination of injury patterns and the benefits justifying selective inclusion of the trampoline within a physical education program, whether in educational institutions or recreational settings, has permitted the American Alliance for Health, Physical Education and Recreation to formulate the following statement.

Risk of injury, including serious injury, accompanies many physical activities enjoyed by young persons, even under the best of conditions. The vast majority of known cases of quadriplegia resulting from trampoline accidents have stemmed from improper execution of a somersault. While there is little encouragement for trampolining as an interscholastic or intercollegiate event, the use of the trampoline in physical education classes does not apparently constitute an unreasonable risk of serious injury providing that the following controls are ensured:

1. That the program is offered as an elective. No student should be required to engage in trampolining. It follows that all new participants should be helped to appreciate the risks of this activity and the measures being taken to control those risks.

2. That the program is supervised by an instructor with professional preparation in teaching trampolining. This implies that the selection of skills being taught are commensurate with the readiness of the student in a proper progressive manner, and that reminders of injury control measures are incorporated in the teaching process. By supervision is meant direct observation of the activity plus intervention capabilities when warranted.

3. That spotters be in position whenever the trampoline is being used and that all students (and teaching aides, if used) be trained by the instructor in the principles and techniques of spotting.

4. That the somersault not be permitted to be attempted in regular classes. If special opportunities exist in the physical education program for advanced students with demonstrated proficiency, the foot-to-foot somersault may be taught if the safety harness is used and if the objective clearly is not to wean the student away from the harness to execute skills involving the somersault. The safety harness must be controlled by person trained by the instructor and capable for this task.

5. That the apparatus be locked, and otherwise secured as best the facilities provide, to prevent unauthorized and unsupervised use.

6. That the apparatus be erected, inspected, and maintained in accordance with the manufacturer's recommendations.

7. That policies for emergency care be preplanned and actively understood by all affected personnel. This includes first aid competence at hand, class supervision during the initial management of the injured student, communicative accessibility to appropriate medical assistance when needed, and transportation capability to appropriate medical facility when needed.

8. That participation and accident records be maintained for the trampoline and other gymnastic apparatuses and periodically be analyzed.

THE TRAMPOLETTE (MINI-TRAMP)

The mini-tramp, while different in nature and purpose from the trampoline, shares its association with risk of spinal cord injury from poorly executed somersaults. The best of mats do not provide substantial protection from the mini-tramp accident that leads to quadriplegia. As recommended for trampoline safety, the mini tramp should constitute an elective activity requiring competent instruction and supervision, spotters trained for that function, emphasis on the danger of somersaults and dive-rolls, security against unsupervised use, proper erection and maintenance of the apparatus, a plan for emergency care should an accident occur, and documentation of participation and of any accidents which occur.

In addition to that stipulated in the preceding paragraph, the following constitute the controlled conditions to be ensured.

1. No multiple somersault be attempted.
2. No single somersault be attempted unless:

   a. the intended result is a footlanding.

   b. the student has demonstrated reasonable ability for such on the trampoline with a safety harness, off the diving board of a swimming pool, or in tumbling.

   c. a competent spotter(s) is in position, knowing the skill which the student is attempting, and physically capable of handling an improper execution. If the safety harness is employed, the instructor must be satisfied that it is controlled competently.

   d. the mini-tramp is reasonably secured to help prevent slipping at the time of execution.

   e. a mat should be utilized, sufficiently wide and long to prevent a landing on the mat's edge and provide for proper footing of the spotter(s).

APPENDIX H

HEW Policy Interpretation Regarding Title IX and Intercollegiate Athletics

---

DEPARTMENT OF HEALTH, EDUCATION, AND WELFARE

Office for Civil Rights

Office of the Secretary

(45 CFR Part 86)

Title IX of the Education Amendments of 1972; a Policy Interpretation

Title IX and Intercollegiate Athletics

AGENCY: Office for Civil Rights, Office of the Secretary, HEW

ACTION: Policy Interpretation

EFFECTIVE DATE: (Date of publication in Federal Register).

SUMMARY: The following Policy Interpretation represents the Department of Health, Education, and Welfare's interpretation of the intercollegiate athletic provisions of Title IX of the Education Amendments of 1972 and its implementing regulation. Title IX prohibits educational programs and institutions funded or otherwise supported by the Department from discriminating on the basis of sex. The Department published a proposed Policy Interpretation for public comment on December 11, 1978. Over 700 comments reflecting a broad range of opinion were received. In addition, HEW staff visited eight universities during June and July, 1979, to see how the proposed policy and other suggested alternatives would apply in actual practice at individual campuses. The final Policy Interpretation reflects the many comments HEW received and the results of the individual campus visits.

FOR FURTHER INFORMATION CONTACT: Colleen O'Connor, 330 Independence Avenue, Washington, D. C. (202) 245-6671

SUPPLEMENTARY INFORMATION
I. *LEGAL BACKGROUND*
    A. *The Statute*
Section 901(a) of Title IX of the Education Amendments of 1972 provides:

> No person in the United States shall, on the basis of sex, be excluded from participation in, be denied the benefits of, or be subjected to discrimination under any education program or activity receiving Federal financial assistance.

Section 844 of the Education Amendments of 1974 further provides:

> The Secretary (of HEW) shall prepare and publish . . . proposed regulations implementing the provisions of Title IX of the Education Amendments of 1972 relating to the prohibition of sex discrimination in federally assisted education programs which shall include with respect to intercollegiate athletic activities reasonable provisions considering the nature of particular sports.

Congress passed Section 844 after the Conference Committee deleted a Senate floor amendment that would have exempted revenue-producing athletics from the jurisdiction of Title IX.

B. *The Regulation*

The regulation implementing Title IX is set forth, in pertinent part, in the Policy Interpretation below. It was signed by President Ford on May 27, 1975, and submitted to the Congress for review pursuant to Section 431(d)(1) of the General Education Provisions Act (GEPA).

During this review, the House Subcommittee on Postsecondary Education held hearings on a resolution disapproving the regulation. The Congress did not disapprove the regulation within the 45 days allowed under GEPA, and it therefore became effective on July 21, 1975.

Subsequent hearings were held in the Senate Subcommittee on Education on a bill to exclude revenues produced by sports to the extent they are used to pay the costs of those sports. The Committee, however, took no action on this bill.

The regulation established a three year transition period to give institutions time to comply with its equal athletic opportunity requirements. That transition period expired on July 21, 1978.

II. *PURPOSE OF POLICY INTERPRETATION*

By the end of July 1978, the Department had received nearly 100 complaints alleging discrimination in athletics against more than 50 institutions of higher education. In attempting to investigate these complaints, and to answer questions from the university community, the Department determined that it should provide further guidance on what constitutes compliance with the law. Accordingly, this Policy Interpretation explains the regulation so as to provide a framework within which the complaints can be resolved, and to provide institutions of higher education with additional guidance on the requirements for compliance with Title IX in intercollegiate athletic programs.

III. *SCOPE OF APPLICATION*

This Policy Interpretation is designed specifically for intercollegiate athletics. However, its general principles will often apply to club, intramural, and interscholastic athletic programs, which are also covered by regulation.* Accordingly, the Policy Interpretation may be used for guidance by the administrators of such programs when appropriate.

This Policy Interpretation applies to any public or private institution, person or other entity that operates an educational program or activity which receives or benefits from financial assistance authorized or extended under a law administered by the Department. This includes educational institutions whose students participate in HEW funded or guaranteed student loan or assistance programs. For further information see definition of "recipient" in Section 86.2 of the Title IX regulation.

IV. *SUMMARY OF FINAL POLICY INTERPRETATION*

The final Policy Interpretation clarifies the meaning of "equal opportunity" in intercollegiate athletics. It explains the factors and standards set out in the law and

---

* The regulation specifically refers to club sports separately from intercollegiate athletics. Accordingly, under this Policy Interpretation, club teams will not be considered to be intercollegiate teams except in those instances where they regularly participate in varsity competition.

regulation which the Department will consider in determining whether an institution's intercollegiate athletics program complies with the law and regulations. It also provides guidance to assist institutions in determining whether any disparities which may exist between men's and women's programs are justifiable and nondiscriminatory. The Policy Interpretation is divided into three sections:

• *Compliance in Financial Assistance (Scholarships) Based on Athletic Ability:* Pursuant to the regulation, the governing principle in this area is that all such assistance should be available on a substantially proportional basis to the number of male and female participants in the institution's athletic program.

• *Compliance in Other Program Areas (Equipment and supplies; games and practice times; travel and per diem; coaching and academic tutoring; assignment and compensation of coaches and tutors; locker rooms, and practice and competitive facilities; medical and training facilities; housing and dining facilities; publicity; recruitment; and support services):* Pursuant to the regulation, the governing principle is that male and female athletes should receive equivalent treatment, benefits, and opportunities.

• *Compliance in Meeting the Interests and Abilities of Male and Female Students:* Pursuant to the regulation, the governing principle in this area is that the athletic interests and abilities of male and female students must be equally effectively accommodated.

V. *MAJOR CHANGES TO PROPOSED POLICY INTERPRETATION*

The final Policy Interpretation has been revised from the one published in proposed form on December 11, 1978. The proposed Policy Interpretation was based on a two-part approach. Part I addressed equal opportunity for participants in athletic programs. It required the elimination of discrimination in financial support and other benefits and opportunities in an institution's existing athletic program. Institutions could establish a presumption of compliance if they could demonstrate that:

● "Average per capita" expenditures for male and female athletes were substantially equal in the area of "readily financially measurable" benefits and opportunities or, if not, that any disparities were the result of nondiscriminatory factors, and

● Benefits and opportunities for male and female athletes, in areas which are not financially measurable, "were comparable."

Part II of the proposed Policy Interpretation addressed an institution's obligation to accommodate effectively the athletic interests and abilities of women as well as men on a continuing basis. It required an institution either:

● To follow a policy of development of its women's athletic program to provide the participation and competition opportunities needed to accommodate the growing interests and abilities of women, or

● To demonstrate that it was effectively (and equally) accommodating the athletic interests and abilities of students, particularly as the interests and abilities of women students developed.

While the basic considerations of equal opportunity remain, the final Policy Interpretation sets forth the factors that will be examined to determine an institution's actual, as opposed to presumed, compliance with Title IX in the area of intercollegiate athletics.

The final Policy Interpretation does not contain a separate section on institutions' future responsibilities.

However, institutions remain obligated by the Title IX regulation to accommodate effectively the interests and abilities of male and female students with regard to the selection of sports and levels of competition available. In most cases, this will entail development of athletic programs that substantially expand opportunities for women to participate and compete at all levels.

The major reasons for the change in approach are as follows:

(1) Institutions and representatives of athletic program participants expressed a need for more definitive guidance on what constituted compliance than the discussion of a presumption of compliance provided. Consequently the final Policy Interpretation explains the meaning of "equal athletic opportunity" in such a way as to facilitate an assessment of compliance.

(2) Many comments reflected a serious misunderstanding of the presumption of compliance. Most institutions based objections to the proposed Policy Interpretation in part on the assumption that failure to provide compelling justifications for disparities in per capita expenditures would have automatically resulted in a finding of noncompliance. In fact, such a failure would only have deprived an institution of the benefit of the presumption that it was in compliance with the law. The Department would still have had the burden of demonstrating that the institution was actually engaged in unlawful discrimination. Since the purpose of issuing a policy interpretation was to clarify the regulation, the Department has determined that the approach of stating actual compliance factors would be more useful to all concerned.

(3) The Department has concluded that purely financial measures such as the per capita test do not in

themselves offer conclusive documentation of discrimination, except where the benefit or opportunity under review, like a scholarship, is itself financial in nature. Consequently, in the final Policy Interpretation, the Department has detailed the factors to be considered in assessing actual compliance. While per capita breakdowns and other devices to examine expenditures patterns will be used as tools of analysis in the Department's investigative process, it is achievement of "equal opportunity" for which recipients are responsible and to which the final Policy Interpretation is addressed.

A description of the comments received, and other information obtained through the comment/consultation process, with a description of Departmental action in response to the major points raised, is set forth at Appendix "B" to this document.*

VI. HISTORIC PATTERNS OF INTERCOLLEGIATE ATHLETICS PROGRAM DEVELOPMENT AND OPERATIONS

In its proposed Policy Interpretation of December 11, 1978, the Department published a summary of historic patterns affecting the relative status of men's and women's athletic programs. The Department has modified that summary to reflect additional information obtained during the comment and consultation process. The summary is set forth at Appendix A to this document.

---

* Editor's note. — Appendices A and B to this document are herein omitted; for information regarding them, contact Colleen O'Connor, 330 Independence Avenue, Washington, D.C. (202) 245-6671.

VII. *THE POLICY INTERPRETATION*

This Policy Interpretation clarifies the obligations which recipients of Federal aid have under Title IX to provide equal opportunities in athletic programs. In particular, this Policy Interpretation provides a means to assess an institution's compliance with the equal opportunity requirements of the regulation which are set forth at 45 CFR 86.37(c) and 86.41(c).

A. *Athletic Financial Assistance (Scholarships)*

1. *The Regulation*

Section 86.37(c) of the regulation provides:

[Institutions] must provide reasonable opportunities for such award [of financial assistance] for members of each sex in proportion to the number of students of each sex participating in ... intercollegiate athletics.*

2. *The Policy*

The Department will examine compliance with this provision of the regulation primarily by means of a financial comparison to determine whether proportionately equal amounts of financial assistance (scholarship aid) are available to men's and women's athletic programs. The Department will measure compliance with this standard by dividing the amounts of aid available for the members of each sex by the numbers of male or female participants in the athletic program and comparing the results. Institutions may be found in compliance if this comparison results in substantially equal amounts or if a resulting disparity can be explained by adjustments to take into account

---

* See also Section 86.37(a) of the regulation.

legitimate, nondiscriminatory factors. Two such factors are:

a. At public institutions, the higher costs of tuition for students from out-of-state may in some years be unevenly distributed between men's and women's programs. These differences will be considered nondiscriminatory if they are not the result of policies or practices which disproportionately limit the availability of out-of-state scholarships to either men or women.

b. An institution may make reasonable professional decisions concerning the awards most appropriate for program development. For example, team development initially may require spreading scholarships over as much as a full generation (four years) of student athletes. This may result in the award of fewer scholarships in the first few years than would be necessary to create proportionality between male and female athletes.

3. *Application of the Policy*

a. This section does not require a proportionate number of scholarships for men and women or individual scholarships of equal dollar value. It does mean that the total amount of scholarship aid made available to men and women must be substantially proportionate to their participation rates.

b. When financial assistance is provided in forms other than grants, the distribution of non-grant assistance will also be compared to determine whether equivalent benefits are proportionately available to male and female athletes. A disproportionate amount of work-related aid or loans in the assistance made available to the members of one sex, for example, could constitute a violation of Title IX.

4. *Definition*

For purposes of examining compliance with this Section, the participants will be defined as those athletes:

a. who are receiving the institutionally-sponsored support normally provided to athletes competing at the institution involved, e.g., coaching, equipment, medical and training room services, on a regular basis during a sport's season; and

b. who are participating in organized practice sessions and other team meetings and activities on a regular basis during a sport's season; and

c. who are listed on the eligibility or squad lists maintained for each sport, or

d. who, because of injury, cannot meet 'a', 'b', or 'c' above but continue to receive financial aid on the basis of athletic ability.

B. *Equivalence in Other Athletic Benefits and Opportunities*

1. *The Regulation*

The Regulation requires that recipients that operate or sponsor interscholastic, intercollegiate, club, or intramural athletics, "provide equal athletic opportunities for members of both sexes." In determining whether an institution is providing equal opportunity in intercollegiate athletics, the regulation requires the Department to consider, among others, the following factors:

(1) *

(2) provision and maintenance of equipment and supplies;

---

* 86.41(c)(1) on the accommodation of student interests and abilities, is covered in detail in the following Section C of this Policy Interpretation.

(3) scheduling of games and practice times;

(4) travel and per diem expenses;

(5) opportunity to receive coaching and academic tutoring;

(6) assignment and compensation of coaches and tutors;

(7) provision of locker rooms, practice and competitive facilities;

(8) provision of medical and training services and facilities;

(9) provision of housing and dining services and facilities; and

(10) publicity.

Section 86.41(c) also permits the Director of the Office for Civil Rights to consider other factors in the determination of equal opportunity. Accordingly, this Section also addresses recruitment of student athletes and provision of support services.

This list is not exhaustive. Under the regulation, it may be expanded as necessary at the discretion of the Director of the Office for Civil Rights.*

2. *The Policy*

The Department will assess compliance with both the recruitment and the general athletic program requirements of the regulation by comparing the availability, quality and kinds of benefits, opportunities, and treatment afforded members of both sexes. Institutions will be in compliance if the compared program components are equivalent, that is, equal or equal in effect. Under this standard, identical benefits, opportunities, or treatment are not required, provided the overall effect of any differences is negligible.

---

* See also Section 86.41(a) and (b) of the regulation.

If comparisons of program components reveal that treatment, benefits, or opportunities are not equivalent in kind, quality or availability, a finding of compliance may still be justified if the differences are the result of nondiscriminatory factors. Some of the factors that may justify these differences are as follows:

a. Some aspects of athletic programs may not be equivalent for men and women because of unique aspects of particular sports or athletic activities. This type of distinction was called for by the "Javits' Amendment" ** to Title IX, which instructed HEW to make "reasonable [regulatory] provisions considering the nature of particular sports" in intercollegiate athletics.

Generally, these differences will be the result of factors that are inherent to the basic operation of specific sports. Such factors may include rules of play, nature/replacement of equipment, rates of injury resulting from participation, nature of facilities required for competition, and the maintenance/upkeep requirements of those facilities. For the most part, differences involving such factors will occur in programs offering football, and consequently these differences will favor men. If sport-specific needs are met equivalently in both men's and women's programs, however, differences in particular program components will be found to be justifiable.

b. Some aspects of athletic programs may not be equivalent for men and women because of legitimately sex-neutral factors related to special circumstances of a temporary nature. For example, large disparities in

---

** Section 844 of the Education Amendments of 1974, Pub. L. 93-380, Title VIII, (August 21, 1974) 88 Stat. 612.

recruitment activity for any particular year may be the result of annual fluctuations in team needs for first-year athletes. Such differences are justifiable to the extent that they do not reduce overall equality of opportunity.

c. The activities directly associated with the operation of a competitive event in a single-sex sport may, under some circumstances, create unique demands or imbalances in particular program components. Provided any special demands associated with the activities of sports involving participants of the other sex are met to an equivalent degree, the resulting differences may be found nondiscriminatory. At many schools, for example, certain sports — notably football and men's basketball — traditionally draw large crowds. Since the costs of managing an athletic event increase with crowd size, the overall support made available for event management to men's and women's programs may differ in degree and kind. These differences would not violate Title IX if the recipient does not limit the potential for women's athletic events to rise in spectator appeal and if the levels of event management support available to both programs are based on sex-neutral criteria (e.g., facilities used, projected attendance, and staffing needs).

d. Some aspects of athletic programs may not be equivalent for men and women because institutions are undertaking voluntary affirmative actions to overcome effects of historical conditions that have limited participation in athletics by the members of one sex. This is authorized at Section 86.3(b) of the regulation.

    3. *Application of the Policy — General Athletic Program Components*

        a. *Equipment and Supplies [Section 86.41(c)(2)]*

Equipment and supplies include but are not limited to uniforms, other apparel, sport-specific equipment and supplies, general equipment and supplies, instructional devices, and conditioning and weight training equipment.

Compliance will be assessed by examining, among other factors, the equivalence for men and women of:

(1) the quality of equipment and supplies;

(2) the amount of equipment and supplies;

(3) the suitability of equipment and supplies;

(4) the maintenance and replacement of the equipment and supplies; and

(5) the availability of equipment and supplies.

b. *Scheduling of Games and Practice Times [Section 86.41(c)(3)]*

Compliance will be assessed by examining, among other factors, the equivalence for men and women of:

(1) the number of competitive events per sport;

(2) the number and length of practice opportunities;

(3) the time of day competitive events are scheduled;

(4) the time of day practice opportunities are scheduled; and

(5) the opportunities to engage in available pre-season and post-season competition.

c. *Travel and Per Diem Allowances [Section 86.41(c)(4)]*

Compliance will be assessed by examining, among other factors, the equivalence for men and women of:

(1) modes of transportation;

(2) housing furnished during travel;

(3) length of stay before and after competitive events;

(4) per diem allowances; and

(5) dining arrangements.

d. *Opportunity to Receive Coaching and Academic Tutoring [Section 86.41(c)(5)]*

(1) Coaching — Compliance will be assessed by examining, among other factors:

(a) relative availability of full-time coaches;

(b) relative availability of part-time and assistant coaches; and

(c) relative availability of graduate assistants.

(2) Academic tutoring — Compliance will be assessed by examining, among other factors, the equivalence for men and women of:

(a) the availability of tutoring; and

(b) procedures and criteria for obtaining tutorial assistance.

e. *Assignment and Compensation of Coaches and Tutors [Section 86.41(c)(6)]* *

In general, a violation of Section 86.41(c)(6) will be found only where compensation or assignment policies or practices deny male and female athletes coaching of equivalent quality, nature, or availability.

Nondiscriminatory factors can affect the compensation of coaches. In determining whether differences are caused by permissible factors, the range

---

* The Department's jurisdiction over the employment practices of recipients under Subpart E, Section 86.51-86.61 of the Title IX regulation has been successfully challenged in several court cases. Accordingly, the Department has suspended enforcement of Subpart E. Section 86.41(c)(6) of the regulation, however, authorizes the Department to consider the compensation of coaches of men and women in the determination of the equality of athletic opportunity provided to male and female athletes. It is on this section of the regulation that this Policy Interpretation is based.

and nature of duties, the experience of individual coaches, the number of participants for particular sports, the number of assistant coaches supervised, and the level of competition will be considered.

Where these or similar factors represent valid differences in skill, effort, responsibility or working conditions they may, in specific circumstances, justify differences in compensation. Similarly, there may be unique situations in which a particular person may possess such an outstanding record of achievement as to justify an abnormally high salary.

(1) Assignment of Coaches — Compliance will be assessed by examining, among other factors, the equivalence for men's and women's coaches of:

    (a) training, experience, and other professional qualifications;

    (b) professional standing.

(2) Assignment of Tutors — Compliance will be assessed by examining, among other factors, the equivalence for men's and women's tutors of:

    (a) tutor qualifications;

    (b) training, experience, and other qualifications.

(3) Compensation of Coaches — Compliance will be assessed by examining, among other factors, the equivalence for men's and women's coaches of:

    (a) rate of compensation (per sport, per season);

    (b) duration of contracts;

    (c) conditions relating to contract renewal;

    (d) experience;

    (e) nature of coaching duties performed;

    (f) working conditions; and

    (g) other terms and conditions of employment.

(4) Compensation of Tutors — Compliance will be assessed by examining, among other factors, the equivalence for men's and women's tutors of:

    (a) hourly rate of payment by nature of subjects tutored;

    (b) pupil loads per tutoring season;

    (c) tutor qualifications;

    (d) experience;

    (e) other terms and conditions of employment.

           f. *Provision of Locker Rooms, Practice and Competitive Facilities [Section 86.41(c)(7)]*

Compliance will be assessed by examining, among other factors, the equivalence for men and women of:

(1) quality and availability of the facilities provided for practice and competitive events;

(2) exclusivity of use of facilities provided for practice and competitive events;

(3) availability of locker rooms;

(4) quality of locker rooms;

(5) maintenance of practice and competitive facilities; and

(6) preparation of facilities for practice and competitive events.

           g. *Provision of Medical and Training Facilities and Services [Section 86.41(c)(8)]*

Compliance will be assessed by examining, among other factors, the equivalence for men and women of:

(1) availability of medical personnel and assistance;

(2) health, accident and injury insurance coverage;

(3) availability and quality of weight and training facilities;

(4) availability and quality of conditioning facilities; and

(5) availability and qualifications of athletic trainers.

h. *Provision of Housing and Dining Facilities and Services [Section 86.41(c)(9)]*

Compliance will be assessed by examining among other factors, the equivalence for men and women of:

(1) housing provided;

(2) special services as part of housing arrangements (e.g., laundry facilities, parking space, maid service).

i. *Publicity [Section 86.41(c)(10)]*

Compliance will be assessed by examining, among other factors, the equivalence for men and women of:

(1) availability and quality of sports information personnel;

(2) access to other publicity resources for men's and women's programs; and

(3) quantity and quality of publications and other promotional devices featuring men's and women's programs.

4. *Application of the Policy — Other Factors [Section 86.41(c)]*

a. *Recruitment of Student Athletes**

The athletic recruitment practices of institutions often affect the overall provision of opportunity to male

---

* Public undergraduate institutions are also subject to the general anti-discrimination provision at Section 86.23 of the regulation, which reads in part:

A recipient . . . shall not discriminate on the basis of sex in the recruitment and admission of students. A recipient may be required to undertake additional recruitment efforts for one sex as remedial action . . . and may choose to undertake such efforts as affirmative action . . .

Accordingly, institutions subject to Section 86.23 are required in all cases to maintain equivalently effective recruitment programs for both sexes and, under Section 86.41(c), to provide equivalent benefits, opportunities, and treatment to student athletes of both sexes.

and female athletes. Accordingly, where equal athletic opportunities are not present for male and female students, compliance will be assessed by examining the recruitment practices of the athletic programs for both sexes to determine whether the provision of equal opportunity will require modification of those practices.

Such examinations will review the following factors:

(1) whether coaches or other professional athletic personnel in the programs serving male and female athletes are provided with substantially equal opportunities to recruit;

(2) whether the financial and other resources made available for recruitment in male and female athletic programs are equivalently adequate to meet the needs of each program; and

(3) whether the differences in benefits, opportunities, and treatment afforded prospective student athletes of each sex have a disproportionately limiting effect upon the recruitment of students of either sex.

b. *Provision of Support Services*

The administrative and clerical support provided to an athletic program can affect the overall provision of opportunity to male and female athletes, particularly to the extent that the provided services enable coaches to perform better their coaching functions.

In the provision of support services, compliance will be assessed by examining, among other factors, the equivalence of:

(1) the amount of administrative assistance provided to men's and women's programs;

(2) the amount of secretarial and clerical assistance provided to men's and women's programs.

5. *Overall Determination of Compliance*

The Department will base its compliance determination under Section 86.41(c) of the regulation upon an examination of the following:

a. whether the policies of an institution are discriminatory in language or effect; or

b. whether disparities of a substantial and unjustified nature exist in the benefits, treatment, services, or opportunities afforded male and female athletes in the institution's program as a whole; or

c. whether disparities in benefits, treatment, services, or opportunities in individual segments of the program are substantial enough in and of themselves to deny equality of athletic opportunity.

C. *Effective Accommodation of Student Interests and Abilities*

1. *The Regulation*

The regulation requires institutions to effectively accommodate the interests and abilities of students to the extent necessary to provide equal opportunity in the selection of sports and levels of competition available to members of both sexes.

Specifically, the regulation, at Section 86.41(c)(1), requires the Director to consider, when determining whether equal opportunities are available,

> Whether the selection of sports and levels of competition effectively accommodate the interests and abilities of members of both sexes.

Section 86.41(c) also permits the Director of the Office for Civil Rights to consider other factors in the determination of equal opportunity. Accordingly, this section also addresses competitive opportunities in terms of the competitive team schedules available to athletes of both sexes.

2. *The Policy*

The Department will assess compliance with the interests and abilities section of the regulation by examining the following factors:

a. The determination of athletic interests and abilities of students;

b. The selection of sports offered; and

c. The levels of competition available including the opportunity for team competition.

3. *Application of the Policy — Determination of Athletic Interests and Abilities*

Institutions may determine the athletic interests and abilities of students by nondiscriminatory methods of their choosing provided:

a. the processes take into account the nationally increasing levels of women's interests and abilities;

b. the methods of determining interest and ability do not disadvantage the members of an underrepresented sex;

c. the methods of determining ability take into account team performance records; and

d. the methods are responsive to the expressed interests of students capable of intercollegiate competition who are members of an underrepresented sex.

4. *Application of the Policy — Selection of Sports*

In the selection of sports, the regulation does not require institutions to integrate their teams nor to provide exactly the same choice of sports to men and women. However, where an institution sponsors a team in a particular sport for members of one sex, it may be required either to permit the excluded sex to try out for the team or to sponsor a separate team for the previously excluded sex.

a. Contact Sports — Effective accommodation means that if an institution sponsors a team for members of one sex in a contact sport, it must do so for members of the other sex under the following circumstances:

(1) the opportunities for members of the excluded sex have historically been limited; and

(2) there is sufficient interest and ability among the members of the excluded sex to sustain a viable team and a reasonable expectation of intercollegiate competition for that team.

b. Non-Contact Sports — Effective accommodation means that if an institution sponsors a team for members of one sex in a non-contact sport, it must do so for members of the other sex under the following circumstances:

(1) the opportunities for members of the excluded sex have historically been limited;

(2) there is sufficient interest and ability among the members of the excluded sex to sustain a viable team and a reasonable expectation of intercollegiate competition for that team;

(3) members of the excluded sex do not possess sufficient skill to be selected for a single integrated team, or to actively compete on such a team if selected.

5. *Application of the Policy — Levels of Competition*

In effectively accommodating the interests and abilities of male and female athletes, institutions must provide both the opportunity for individuals of each sex to participate in intercollegiate competition, and for athletes of each sex to have competitive team schedules which equally reflect their abilities.

a. Compliance will be assessed in any one of the following ways:

(1) whether intercollegiate level participation opportunities for male and female students are provided in numbers substantially proportionate to their respective enrollments; or

(2) where the members of one sex have been and are underrepresented among intercollegiate athletes, whether the institution can show a history and continuing practice of program expansion which is demonstrably responsive to the developing interest and abilities of the members of that sex; or

(3) where the members of one sex are underrepresented among intercollegiate athletes, and the institution cannot show a continuing practice of program expansion such as that cited above, whether it can be demonstrated that the interests and abilities of the members of that sex have been fully and effectively accommodated by the present program.

b. Compliance with this provision of the regulation will also be assessed by examining the following:

(1) whether the competitive schedules for men's and women's teams, on a program-wide basis, afford proportionally similar numbers of male and female athletes equivalently advanced competitive opportunities; or

(2) whether the institution can demonstrate a history and continuing practice of upgrading the competitive opportunities available to the historically disadvantaged sex as warranted by developing abilities among the athletes of that sex.

c. Institutions are not required to upgrade teams to intercollegiate status or otherwise develop intercollegiate sports absent a reasonable expectation that intercollegiate competition in that sport will be available within the institution's normal competitive regions. Institutions may be required by the Title IX regulation to actively encourage the development of such competition, however, when overall athletic opportunities within that region have been historically limited for the members of one sex.

6. Overall Determination of Compliance

The Department will base its compliance determination under Section 86.41(c) of the regulation upon a determination of the following:

a. whether the policies of an institution are discriminatory in language or effect; or

b. whether disparities of a substantial and unjustified nature in the benefits, treatment, services, or opportunities afforded male and female athletes exist in the institution's program as a whole; or

c. whether disparities in individual segments of the program with respect to benefits, treatment, services, or opportunities are substantial enough in and of themselves to deny equality of athletic opportunity.

VIII. THE ENFORCEMENT PROCESS

The process of Title IX enforcement is set forth in Section 86.71 of the Title IX regulation, which incorporates by reference the enforcement procedures applicable to Title VI of the Civil Rights Act of 1964.[1] The enforcement process prescribed by the regulation is supplemented by an order of the Federal District Court, District of Columbia, which establishes time frames for each of the enforcement steps.[2]

---

1. Those procedures may be found at 45 CFR 80.6 — 80.11 and 45 CFR Part 8.

2. WEAL v. Harris, Civil Action No. 74-1720 (D. D.C., December 29, 1977).

According to the regulation, there are two ways in which enforcement is initiated:

• *Compliance Reviews* — Periodically the Department must select a number of recipients (in this case, colleges and universities which operate intercollegiate athletic programs) and conduct investigations to determine whether recipients are complying with Title IX. [45 CFR 80.7(a)]

• *Complaints* — The Department must investigate all valid (written and timely) complaints alleging discrimination on the basis of sex in a recipient's programs. [45 CFR 80.7(b)]

The Department must inform the recipient (and the complainant, if applicable) of the results of its investigation. If the investigation indicates that a recipient is in compliance, the Department states this, and the case is closed. If the investigation indicates noncompliance, the Department outlines the violations found.

The Department has 90 days to conduct an investigation and inform the recipient of its findings, and an additional 90 days to resolve violations by obtaining a voluntary compliance agreement from the recipient. This is done through negotiations between the Department and the recipient, the goal of which is agreement on steps the recipient will take to achieve compliance. Sometimes the violation is relatively minor and can be corrected immediately. At other times, however, the negotiations result in a plan that will correct the violations within a specified period of time. To be acceptable, a plan must describe the manner in which institutional resources will be used to correct the violation. It also must state acceptable time tables for reaching interim goals and full compliance. When agreement is reached, the Department notifies the institution that its plan is acceptable. The Department then is obligated to review periodically implementation of the plan.

An institution that is in violation of Title IX may already be implementing a corrective plan. In this case, prior to informing the recipient about the results of its investigation, the Department will determine whether the plan is adequate. If the plan is not adequate to correct the violations (or to correct them within a reasonable period of time) the recipient will be found in noncompliance and voluntary negotiations will begin. However, if the institutional plan is acceptable, the Department will inform the institution that although the institution has violations, it is found to be in compliance because it is implementing a corrective plan. The Department, in this instance also, would monitor the progress of the institutional plan. If the institution subsequently does not completely implement its plan, it will be found in noncompliance.

When a recipient is found in noncompliance and voluntary compliance attempts are unsuccessful, the formal process leading to termination of Federal assistance will be begun. These procedures, which include the opportunity for a hearing before an administrative law judge, are set forth at 45 CFR 80.8 — 80.11 and 45 CFR Part 81.

IX. *AUTHORITY*

Secs. 901, 902, Education Amendments of 1972 86 Stat. 373, 374, 20 USC 1681, 1682; Sec. 844, Education Amendments of 1974, Pub. L. 93-380, 88 Stat. 612; and 45 CFR Part 86.

GLOSSARY OF TERMS*

Abrogate — to annul or repeal a law or an order.

Appellant — the party who initiates the appeal to an appellate court.

Appellate Court — a court which reviews trials of lower courts for errors of law, to be distinguished from a trial court where the case is originally heard.

Appellee — the party against whom the appeal is taken; the party on the other side from the appellant.

Charitable Immunity — the freedom of a charitable institution, such as a hospital, from being held liable for certain actions rendered in pursuit of its charitable undertaking.

Defendant — the person defending against or denying a claim; the person against whom relief is sought; in a criminal case, the person against whom a criminal charge is brought.

Enjoin — a court's direction to a person or institution, usually to cease doing some particular act.

Governmental Immunity — usually called sovereign immunity; a limitation upon an individual or institution's right to sue the government for those functions which are held to be governmental in nature.

In Loco Parentis — in the place of a parent; someone who stands in the place of a parent and is charged with the same rights, duties, and responsibilities.

Injunction — an order of the court normally requiring a party or institution to cease taking certain actions

---

* With thanks to C. Thomas Ross — Attorney with the firm of Craige, Brawley, Liipfert and Ross, Winston-Salem, North Carolina.

which are alleged to be harmful or to take certain actions to alleviate harm.

Temporary Injunction — an injunction issued for a set period of time and which will expire upon the passage of time.

Permanent Injunction — An injunction issued which will stay in effect indefinitely from the date it is entered.

Judgment — in the legal sense, the official decision of a court of record.

Liability — in a legal sense, the responsibility for an action; in civil cases, most often expressed in terms of fault with an accompanying responsibility to pay money damages to an injured party.

Litigation — the filing and trial of a lawsuit between two or more parties for the purpose of enforcing an alleged right or recovering money damages for a breach of duty.

Moot — an undecided point not settled by courts but concerning some matter which has, as a practical matter, already been decided by the happening of an event prior to a court's determination.

Nuisance — anything which reasonably interferes with enjoyment of life or property to the detriment of another.

Plaintiff — a person who brings a civil action aganist another person or institution.

Prima Facie — Latin meaning at first sight; fact presumed to be true unless disproved by evidence to the contrary.

Remand — action by a higher court to send a matter back to the same court from which it came, with directions as to what must be done in the lower court.

Res Ipsa Loquitur — Latin meaning the thing speaks for itself; a theory of negligence arising when an injury happens, which ordinarily would not happen in the absence of negligence, and which requires the instrumentality which caused the injury to be under the exclusive control of the negligent party.

Respondeat Superior — Latin meaning let the master answer; a theory whereby a master is held liable for the wrongful acts of his servant or employee if the servant or employee is acting within the legitimate scope of his authority.

Summary Judgment — a judgment entered by a court without a trial because there is no genuine dispute about the facts; judgment is entered as a matter of law as applied to undisputed facts.

Tort — a theory of negligence involving a wrongful act or a violation of a duty; there must be a legal duty to the person harmed, there must be a breach of that duty, there must be damage to the person wronged as the usual (proximate) result of the breach.

TABLE OF CASES

391

Brigman v. New York State Public High School Athletic Ass'n, Civil Action No. 1973—347, 1978 (US District Court NDNY), ch. 8, n. 9.

Brown v. Board of Educ. of Morgan County School Dist., 560 P.2d 1129 (Utah 1977), ch. 7, n. 27.

Brown v. Board of Educ. of Topeka, 347 U.S. 483, 74 S. Ct. 686, 98 L.ed. 873 (1954), ch. 4, n. 32.

Bruce v. South Carolina High School League, 189 S.E.2d 817 (S.C. 1972), ch. 6, n. 32.

Byrns v. Riddell, Inc., 550 P.2d 1065 (Ariz. 1976), ch. 13, n. 14.

Cadieux v. Board of Educ. of City School Dist. of City of Schenectady, N.Y., 266 N.Y.S.2d 895 (N.Y. App. Div. 1966), ch. 9, nn. 18, 19.

Cape v. Tennessee Secondary School Athletic Ass'n, 563 F.2d 793 (6th Cir. 1977), ch. 4, nn. 34, 35.

Carabba v. Ancortes School Dist. No. 103, 435 P.2d 936 (Wash. 1968), ch. 8, n. 6.

Cardamone v. University of Pittsburgh, 384 A.2d 1228 (Pa. Super. 1978), ch. 13, n. 37.

Chabert v. Louisiana High School Athletic Ass'n, 312 So. 2d 343 (La. App. 1975), ch. 6, nn. 24, 29.

Chapman v. State, 492 P.2d 607 (Wash. App. 1972), ch. 13, n. 34.

Chiodo v. Board of Educ. of Special School Dist. No. 1, 215 N.W.2d 806 (Minn. 1974), ch. 7, n. 25.

Chuy v. Philadelphia Eagles Football Team and The National Football League, Nos. 77-1411, 77-1412, U.S. Court of Appeals (3rd Cir. 1977), ch. 10, nn. 51, 52.

Cincinnati Baseball Club v. Eno, 147 N.E. 86 (Ohio 1925), ch. 9, n. 11.

Clary v. Alexander County Bd. of Educ., 199 S.E.2d 738 (N.C. App. 1973), ch. 12, n. 36.

Colombo v. Sewanhaka Central High School, Dist., No. 2, 383 N.Y.S.2d 518 (N.Y. Sup. Ct. 1976), ch. 3, n. 29.

Craig v. Boren, 429 U.S. 190, 97 S. Ct. 451, 50 L.ed.2d 397 (1976), ch. 4, n. 30.

Cross v. Board of Educ. of Dollarway, Arkansas School Dist., 395 F. Supp. 531 (E.D. Ark. 1975), ch. 7, n. 2.

Curran v. Green Hills Country Club, 101 Cal. Rptr. 158 (Cal. App. 1972), ch. 12, n. 25.

Gilmore v. City of Montgomery, 473 F.2d 823 (5th Cir. 1973), ch. 12, n. 9.

Goss v. Lopez, 419 U.S. 565, 95 S. Ct. 729, 42. L.ed.2d 725 (1975), ch. 6, n. 10.

Gross v. Sweet, 407 N.Y.S.2d 254 (N.Y. App. Div. 1978), ch. 12, n. 46.

Haas v. South Bend Community School Corp., 289 N.E.2d 495 (Ind. 1972), ch. 4, nn. 24, 26.

Hackbart v. Cincinnati Bengals, Inc., 435 F. Supp. 352 (D.C. Colo. 1977), ch. 2, nn. 5, 6, 7.

Hanna v. State, 258 N.Y.S.2d 694 (N.Y. Ct. Cl. 1965), ch. 8, n. 8.

Hawayek v. Simmons, 91 So. 2d 49 (La. App. 1956), ch. 2, n. 24.

Hawksley v. New Hampshire Interscholastic Athletic Ass'n, 285 A.2d 797 (N.H. 1971), ch. 6, n. 38.

Hill v Nettleton, 455 F. Supp. 514 (D. Colo. 1978), ch. 7, nn. 7, 19.

Hinton v. Pateros School Dist. No. 122, No. 29847, Superior Court of Washington County of Chelan, 1976, ch. 8, n. 5.

Iervolino v. Pittsburgh Athletic Co., Inc., 243 A.2d 490 (Pa. Super. (1968), ch. 9, n. 9.

Jackson v. Armstrong School Dist., 430 F. Supp. 1050 (W.D. Pa. 1977), ch. 7, n. 4.

Jones v. Oklahoma Secondary School Activities Ass'n, 453 F. Supp. 150 (W.D. Okla. 1977), ch. 4, n. 36.

Jones v. Three Rivers Management Corp., 380 A.2d 387 (Pa. Super. 1977), ch. 9, n. 10.

Kampmeier v. Harris, 403 N.Y.S.2d 638 (N.Y. Sup. Ct. 1978), rev'd, 411 N.Y.S.2d 744 (N.Y. App. Div. 1978), ch. 3, nn. 20, 21, 22, 23, 24.

Kampmeier v. Harris, 411 N.Y.S.2d 744 (N.Y. App. Div. 1978), ch. 3, n. 25.

Kennedy v. Providence Hockey Club, Inc., 376 A.2d 329 (R.I. 1977), ch. 9, n. 20.

Kenneveg v. Hampton Township School Dist., 438 F. Supp. 575 (W.D. Pa. 1977), ch. 7, n. 5.

Kissick v. Garland Independent School Dist., 330 S.W.2d 708 (Tex. Civ. App. 1959), ch. 4, n. 18.

Kite v. Marshall, 454 F. Supp. 1347 (S.D. Texas 1978), ch. 6, nn. 40, 41.

Toone v. Adams, 137 S.E.2d 132 (N.C. 1964), ch. 8, n. 7.

Travernier v. Maes, 51 Cal. Rptr. 575 (Cal. App. 1966), ch. 2, n. 16.

Turner v. Caddo Parish School Bd., 204 So. 2d 294 (La. App. 1968), rev'd, 214 So. 2d 153 (La. 1968), ch. 9, n. 16.

Turner v. Caddo Parish School Bd., 214 So. 2d 153 (La. 1968), ch. 9, n. 17.

University of Denver v. Nemeth, 257 P.2d 423 (Colo. 1953), ch. 5, n. 6.

Vandenburg v. Newsweek, Inc., 507 F.2d 1024 (5th Cir. 1975), ch. 7, nn. 29, 33.

Van Horn v. Industrial Accident Comm'n, 33 Cal. Rptr. 109 (Cal. App. 1963), ch. 5, n. 8.

Watkins v. Louisiana High School Athletic Ass'n, 301 So. 2d 695 (La. App. 1974), ch. 9, n. 29.

Williams v. Day, 412 F. Supp. 336 (E.D. Ark. 1976), ch. 7, n. 15.

Wright v. Arkansas Activities Ass'n (AAA), 501 F.2d 25 (8th Cir. 1974), ch. 7, n. 13.

Wright v. Mt. Mansfield Lift, Inc., 96 F. Supp. 786 (D. Vt. 1951), ch. 12, n. 11.

Yellow Springs Exempted Village School Dist. Bd. of Educ. v. Ohio High School Athletic Ass'n, 443 F. Supp. 753, (S.D. Ohio 1978), ch. 4, nn. 27, 28.

Younts v. St. Francis Hosp. and School of Nursing, Inc., 469 P.2d 330 (Kan. 1970), ch. 10, n. 18.

Zeller v. Donegal School Dist. Bd. of Educ., 517 F.2d 600 (3rd Cir. 1975), ch. 4, nn. 2, 15, 16.

Index

FACILITIES—Cont'd
Religious groups.
Use of sports facilities, pp. 260, 261.
Ski slopes.
Assumption of risk.
Applicability of doctrine in North Carolina, p. 272.
Unsafe facilities.
Injuries attributed to, pp. 268 to 272.
Illustrative cases, pp. 268 to 274.
Stadiums and playing fields.
Artificial turf.
Injuries attributed to, pp. 285, 286.
Unsafe facilities.
Injuries attributed to, pp. 284 to 289.
Unsafe facilities.
Golf courses.
Injuries attributed to, pp. 274 to 280.
Illustrative cases, pp. 274 to 280.
Gymnasiums and adjacent areas.
Injuries attributed to, pp. 280 to 284.
Injuries attributed to, p. 268.
Ski slopes.
Injuries attributed to, pp. 268 to 272.
Illustrative cases, pp. 268 to 274.
Stadiums and playing fields.
Injuries attributed to, pp. 284 to 289.
Use of sports facilities.
Commercial groups, pp. 264, 265.
Generally, p. 259.
Non-partisan or non-denominational activities, p. 262.
Political groups, pp. 261 to 264.
Private groups, pp. 265 to 268.
Public facilities.
Various uses of public facilities distinguished, pp. 267, 268.
Religious groups, pp. 260, 261.

FENCING.
Equipment, pp. 307, 308.

FOOTBALL.
Artificial turf.
Injuries attributed to, pp. 285, 286.

INSURANCE.

Administrators.
  Medical services.
    Illustrative cases, pp. 123 to 127.
Litigation.
  Price of insurance becoming prohibitive, p. 4.
    Results, p. 5.
Manufacturers.
  Liability suits.
    Reported losses, p. 5.
Product liability.
  Reported losses, p. 5.

INVASION OF PRIVACY.

Joe Namath.
  Property rights distinguished, pp. 107, 108.
Sports Illustrated.
  Namath case, pp. 107, 108.

JOE NAMATH.

Invasion of privacy.
  Property rights distinguished, pp. 107, 108.

JUDICIAL CIRCUITS.

Map of eleven federal circuits, p. 92.

LITIGATION.

Administrators.
  Civil procedure.
    Charting the course of lawsuit, pp. 7 to 10.
  Involvement in lawsuit, pp. 6, 7.
  Lawsuit.
    Involvement in, pp. 6, 7.
    Prima facie case.
      Establishment of, p. 9.
  Prima facie case.
    Establishment of, p. 9.
  Trial.
    Several and distinct parts, p. 9.
    What to expect, pp. 7 to 10.